**Praise for *A House Divided*...**

*This book he and a counselee have co-authored is the engrossing chronicle of how that co-author, deeply troubled by scores of conflicting alters, achieves deliverance and unification.*

Dr. Vernon Grounds, Ph.D., Chancellor, Denver Seminary (deceased)

*A story that needs to be told...CJ tells about her incredible personal strength and journey. What a brilliant woman to have created all of those personalities as a way to survive her years of abuse and trauma—it boggles the mind and puts me in awe of her. This is a sensitive, beautifully recorded book.*

Mary Ann Carpenter, Ph.D., school psychologist

*A masterful job in demythologizing DID/MPD; a well-written and easily read book that the average person on the street will find difficult to put down.*

Rev. Less Avery, Diplomat in the College of Pastoral Supervisors and Psychotherapists

*Helps the reader to gain a clear understanding of the process one has to go through to deal with past abuse. The book is informative, straightforward and revealing."*

James Oraker, Ph.D., professor, therapist, consultant

*As a family physician, I was skeptical of even the existence of multiple personality disorder, much less the therapy for it.* ***A House Divided*** *has removed all my doubts and is an important tool for those of us in medical or counseling fields. The unique structure of the book—looking at each stage from the therapist's and the patient's perspectives—is very helpful. This is a must read for anyone in the field.*

Dr. Robert Williams MD

*This story as told by Catherine and Jerry will benefit not only counselors and therapists but any person interested in being a better friend.*

Rev. Joseph Beach

*The poetry written by Abby, one of Catherine's alters, is very creative, insightful and moving, helping the reader to identify with several of the personalities.*

David McDonald, counselor, consultant, former pastor

*A fascinating trek, Donaldson and his client take us on a frightening but ultimately inspirational journey from the netherworld of a fragmented human soul to the joyful light of health and wholeness. Sorting through the pieces of a personality shattered by trauma and abuse, therapist and client together describe the process of integration and healing with searing honesty and compassion. Similar to* **Irvin Yalom's** ***Every Day Gets a Little Closer: A Twice Told Therapy****, this book is a must-read for anyone interested in understanding the basics of emotional-spiritual healing and the profound importance of the therapeutic relationship in freeing oneself from the terror-filled memories of the past.*

Susan F. Anderson, M.A., L.P.C.

***A House Divided*** *will challenge the reader's perceptions of what counseling is about and ultimately will serve as an inspiring story of bravery that therapy requires. Not only is* ***A House Divided*** *a story of hope and triumph, but it will challenge the reader to examine his own life and deal with his own personal battles. A well-written and captivating book.*

Kevin Dyk, LPC, Owner and Director of
Family Life Counseling, Aurora, CO

*This is a harrowing story of the depths of inhumanity and brokenness matched only by the triumph of God's healing restoration. Compelling as it is challenging,* ***A House Divided*** *is a breathtaking invitation to celebrate what God can do through his grace and to trust him enough to face the truth of our own struggle.*

Christian Diffenderfer, D.W.S.

# A HOUSE DIVIDED

## Recovering from Sexual Abuse and Multiplicity

# A HOUSE DIVIDED

## Recovering from Sexual Abuse and Multiplicity

(Written by a Survivor and Her Therapist)

By Catherine Jean Johnson
& Jerry Donaldson

Philia Press
Doing the loving thing

Lakewood, Colorado USA

Philia Press
Lakewood, CO 80226 USA
www.ahousedividedbook.com

A House Divided: Recovering from Sexual Abuse and Multiplicity
ISBN: 978-0-9915240-1-3 (paperback)
978-0-9915240-2-0 (electronic)


jerryhousedivided@gmail.com
catherinehousedivided@gmail.com



Cover photo: Jerry Donaldson
Cover design: Sarah DeLong Godfrey
Editorial consultant: Phyllis Klein Ph.D.

Library of Congress Cataloging-in-Publication Data
Library of Congress Control Number 2014903174

This book is dedicated to
all those who have survived
innumerable types of trauma and have
worked diligently to become whole.

# Contents

# Forward

## Jerry Donaldson (JD)

Listening to another person's life story has always fascinated me. I believe that is why I enjoy counseling so much. People are usually more real in my office than in any other place. For their own reasons, they have decided to be open, honest and transparent with me, so I am privileged to know who the person actually is, rather than the projected persona most people see. Of course my clients are hesitant at first. They test whether I can be trusted with highly privileged, personal information, but they are usually already determined to get to the bottom of their perceived problems. Whether the struggle involves depression, anxiety, relationships, addiction, or any other unmanageable issue, people find cathartic help in talking out loud about what they are thinking and feeling.

What you are about to read is a ten-year therapeutic autobiography of two very average people. Catherine Jean Johnson (CJ) discovered her own multiple personality disorder (MPD) or what is now called DID, (dissociative identity disorder). I, Jerry Donaldson (JD), facilitated the healing conversation. We both want the reader, whether lay person or professional, to be inspired by our extraordinary encounter.

Our goal is to demythologize the DID (MPD) labels, to normalize for unfamiliar readers what "therapy" is all about, and to share the benefits of learning to relate to others. I cannot overstate the freedom my counselees give me to be transparent myself. Being who we are (warts and all) with each other enables healing, not only in the counselee but also within the counselor. I have learned more about life and myself through my clients than any of them have learned about themselves in my office.

CJ and I began writing about our ten years' experience independently, with very little collaboration. Chapters in this book alternate between the two of us as narrators. She tells her story chronologically, while I write more topically about what I was thinking, feeling and doing to facilitate therapy. Like CJ, I share personal experiences when I sense they might be helpful to the reader.

CJ's chapters invite you to empathize with her feelings and thoughts. Attempt to place yourself in her shoes as she progressively discovers her past.

As you read my chapters, imagine being a counselor—trying to make sense of what had happened to CJ, searching for a way to facilitate her healing and wholeness. You will also notice, even though CJ and I don't contradict each other, that our perspectives differ. After all, our temperaments, personalities, upbringing, and experiences are unique. However, we have found that when we connect on an emotional level, we can enter each other's stories.

I also hope our readers can apply the principles, strategies and attitudes expressed in the following chapters to their own lives, even though all do not experience DID (MPD). I am convinced that every human being is comprised of parts and pieces; like CJ, we experience ourselves as the sum of those parts. If we cannot free our parts to know and understand each other, we will suffer conflict within and live a divided, dualistic, incongruent way of life as well.

Reading CJ's story can help all of us as we struggle to know, understand, and accept ourselves. If we are willing, as she was, we can grow both intra-personally (relating to our different parts) and inter-personally (relating to others and their parts). If instead we choose to keep the parts of ourselves separated and even isolated, we will find it difficult, if not impossible, to integrate, to be consistent, to be real—in short, to be persons of integrity. When our parts conflict with one another, our emotional, physical, spiritual and relational capabilities are severely limited. Physical ailments, psychological impairments, relational conflicts and spiritual hypocrisy—all result from failure to know, understand and accept the parts of ourselves.

In some cases, individuals with DID may choose limited integration. Rather than integrate all of the parts (alters), they may reduce the number of alters through therapy, down to two to four, making the internal system more manageable. CJ made the brave choice to totally integrate more than one hundred and fifty parts. This is the story of how that happened. I see in her process a workable model for everyone, in the internal struggles we experience throughout life, and in our external difficulties in relating to others.

Several key themes recur in the telling of our two stories:

- Personal growth is possible only if we take personal responsibility for our feelings, perceptions and behavior. Blaming and fault-finding do not grow us.
- Interpersonal and intra-personal maturity is achieved by searching for the truth. This requires honesty and maintaining integrity (being who we really are).

- The only way we can experience health—psychologically, emotionally, physically and spiritually—is through self-knowledge, self-understanding, and self-acceptance.
- Relationships likewise flourish by means of knowledge, understanding and acceptance of each other. These three "awarenesses" enable us to love, which is demonstrated by grace and mercy.

Finally, trust and trustworthiness can be established only by incorporating these truths into our lives. Without trust, we will live with fear, self-protection and defensiveness, hiding our pain and causing more conflict.

Both CJ and I purposely have left out specific details about the abuse she experienced. However, we do disclose certain memories which had to be held by the alters, so readers can know and understand their feelings. The subject of sexual and Satanic ritualistic abuse is extremely dark and painful, and only a courageous empathizer can truly understand CJ's experience. She and I suspect that you will be conflicted, just as we were, but we hope the stories within the larger story will ultimately reach the caring, compassionate, loving side of each reader.

## Catherine Jean Johnson (CJ)

From the time I was diagnosed with MPD (Multiple Personality Disorder), now known as Dissociative Identity Disorder (DID), I have needed this book. While I was working through the therapy process, I searched high and low for resources addressing the issue of multiple personalities from the perspective of individuals who actually had been given that diagnosis. I found very little that was helpful or informative. That is my main reason for writing this book. Of course, writing my story has also been therapeutic for me, as I look back at the journey about to be completed in my life.

My intention is not to sensationalize DID, but rather to provide a greater understanding of this condition for individuals, their therapists and all others whose lives may be affected by this diagnosis. I approach my task from a Christian perspective. I worry that many members of the Christian community have little or no knowledge of the origins of multiple personalities and are afraid of individuals who have this condition. A uniquely valuable ministry is open to those who have the passion and perseverance to work with DID individuals through their healing process. I hope to shed some light for those who want to understand and form a bond with strugglers who journey toward recovery.

Every reader, and especially one who has been diagnosed with DID, must understand that each of us is God-created and unique. We are all different. In my opinion there is no set pattern for this condition or for the recovery process. Please be careful not to compare yourself with me or any other person with DID. Whether diagnosed with DID or not, individuals need to know themselves as they are, not as they compare themselves to someone else. Please also note that this book should not be construed as professional reference material, but rather as a human experiential perspective on being DID. If you will read this book with that goal in mind, my purpose will be accomplished.

I have chosen to remain anonymous in order to protect myself, my family and other individuals with whom I have been associated in therapy groups. The name I have chosen to identify myself (the host personality) is Catherine Jean (CJ) Johnson. Most other names have also been changed to protect identities.

# Introduction

> *...there can be something powerfully engaging about a fumbling therapist, a therapist willing to flounder with the patient until they, together, stumble upon an enabling discovery.*
>
> –Irvin Yalom, ***Love's Executioner***

I, Jerry Donaldson (JD), come to writing about dissociative identity disorder (DID*) with fear and trepidation, because I am by no means an expert in this area. In fact, much of what I did with Catherine Jean (CJ) during the years we met together was a trial-and-error process. I read all the professional information I could find, consulted with colleagues, and prayed constantly.

I played only a small part in the process of CJ's healing. Throughout the ten years of our work, CJ attended workshops and seminars, read relevant books and articles, was deeply involved in support groups, consulted friends, drew on the love and support of her husband and daughter, and without question was guided and upheld by her faith in God. Taking initiative throughout, she never became overly dependent on me or anyone else.

Reading CJ's story may raise questions about some of my strategies, techniques, and overall philosophy. Looking back and knowing what I know now, I see that I might initially have been more sensitive to CJ's aversion to touch. Now I might be more reserved about sharing my own experiences, perceptions and emotions. Perhaps I could have talked more about God. Probably some of my own issues sneaked into the mix during therapy (professionals refer to this as counter-transference). Plenty of "would-a, could-a,

---

* DSM-IV defines DID as:

- The presence of two or more distinct identities or personality states (each with its own relatively enduring pattern of perceiving, relating to, and thinking about the environment and self)
- At least two of these identities or personality states recurrently take control of the person's behavior
- Inability to recall important information—personal information that is too extensive to be explained by ordinary forgetfulness
- The disturbance is not due to the direct physiological effects of a substance (e.g. blackouts, chaotic behavior during alcohol intoxication) or general medical condition (e.g. complex partial seizures). Note: In children, the symptoms are not attributable to imaginary playmates or other fantasy play.

should-a" thoughts have come to my mind, especially after reading through CJ's and my notes.

Many times over these past years, I have wanted to abandon this co-authored book, thinking:

- What do I have to offer that hasn't already been said?
- What will other counselors think?
- What if I am incapable of expressing what happened during the time CJ and I worked together?
- What will people think about this multiple personality issue—will they believe the story?

I, too, struggle with questions about the truth or fiction of accounts of sexual abuse and satanic ritualistic abuse (SRA). Stories like CJ's fall outside of the realm of reality for most of us. Is it possible that parents, relatives, or any human being could be so cruel to innocent children? Until I began working with CJ and another client who was multiple, I hadn't even read a book about DID or satanic ritual abuse. I would have agreed that we are all capable of evil; we can be lustful, toy with pornography, and cherish appalling thoughts (and not just in the area of sex). Still it has been painful to realize that some of us humans do sexually molest the children in our lives, even forcibly rape the innocent.

However, I have now lived over seventy-five years, worked as a counselor for over thirty-seven of them and in youth correctional facilities for almost fourteen years before that. I have been forced to believe that people are capable of atrocities of all kinds. Since the beginning of human history, monstrous acts have been part of civilization: war, torture, ethnic cleansing, rape, murder. If our sinful hearts are determined to fulfill some perverted need, we will find a way.

Incest and satanic ritualistic abuse are among the most terrorizing and secretive of all acts of violence. Because both the perpetrators and their victims experience so much shame and guilt, both do everything possible to hide that abuse. Abusive cults in particular are very careful not to leave any incriminating evidence. Occasionally the truth about cultic and occult abuse is exposed, but because of the highly secretive mentality within these groups, the full extent of the abuse is seldom known or proven.

When abusers are exposed by their victims, those abusers will do everything possible to discredit the innocent party. Since abusers are virtually never caught in the act, their victims have to prove they were molested, but how does one prove something that happened 20, 30 or 40 years in the past? Furthermore, a victim cannot really desire total recall. When memories do begin to invade the present, those remembrances are vague, like a fog or a ghost, or like looking through distorted colored glass. The victim questions, "Am I remembering or creating the past?"

I had to settle my own questions about CJ's veracity. How did I know she had not "made up" her experiences of the abuse? Knowing CJ as I do after ten years of working together, I can see no other motive than bringing the truth to light. I ask my readers to consider: if she were fabricating, why would she create over 150 personalities?

...not because she needed attention (she would prefer the opposite)

...not because she wanted to get back at her parents for some reason (she is not vindictive)

...not because her life was boring (her daily life was and is full of activities and relationships)

...not because she had a break from reality (she is totally sane)

...not because she needed an excuse for being sexually unresponsive (she came to see me in the first place because she wanted to be more sexually involved with her husband)

...and certainly not because she wanted to spend thousands of dollars on individual and group therapy (she and her husband had to live frugally)

Why, then, at close to forty years of age, did CJ begin to remember her past? Perhaps because her daughter was going through puberty, or because her parental visits were becoming more and more difficult, feelings of dread, anxiety and fear surfaced. "Voices" of the past were interfering with her joy in the present and hope for the future. Perhaps, like most "mid-lifers," she was re-evaluating everything about her existence—her faith, her marriage, her values, her purpose for living. Once into counseling, we both found it significant that she had little or no memory of her childhood, especially about her feelings. CJ had many reasons for becoming more inquisitive about who she was and where she wanted to be in the future.

In this book, CJ and I write chronologically through our ten plus years of therapy together. I attempt to answer as many questions the reader might have with practicality and authenticity. We hope our stories challenge your thinking, help you face some of your own demons, improve your relationships, and make you more empathetic. We believe that understanding sexual abuse makes people better counselors and mentors. And we are all in some ways counselors and mentors. May our book encourage you to be a bold lover, of God, others, and yourself.

## Notes on My Approach to Counseling

Unlike many counselors, I am not a very good analyst, and in some ways, this helps me in my work. The real value of analysis lies in the client's ability to determine what they think is the problem. CJ was (and is) better at analysis than I am. However, some people, like me, prefer not to be analyzed, because they find analysts' assumptions to be suspect. For this reason I purposely avoid attempting to figure people out. I do not want to stereotype them. Presuming that I know in advance who my clients are prevents both of us from identifying the key issues together.

I have always been uncomfortable with assigning a diagnosis to a person. Of course, insurance companies need to have a "disorder" label, to justify payment to licensed therapists, psychologists and psychiatrists. And I admit that a diagnosis can be helpful in determining what direction to take in therapy. Just as medical doctors need to know what they are treating, so do counselors.

However, I see therapy more as a detective procedural: the counselor and the counselee investigate together to discover the core problem. Such a holistic approach, will consider a multitude of variables. Mental health includes the client's physical, mental, psychological, transitional, familial, environmental, regional, and spiritual experience and present situation. A one-size-fits-all methodology often fails because we are all so unique and complex.

When I first meet with a client, I want to learn whether they can balance how they think with how they feel. Most of us are aware of being stronger in one way or the other. Appropriately and typically, we accentuate our strengths. However, internal and external conflicts are exacerbated when we ignore our weaknesses. For example, in crisis and/or extreme stress, highly rational and cognitive people will become even more logical and reasonable, oblivious to their own and others' emotional needs. On the other hand, when highly emotional people become overwhelmed, they tend to ignore logic, become less reasonable, and over-react dramatically.

I myself have a bent toward the emotional end of the spectrum. I do admire those who can be calm and cool-headed in stressful situations. They appear to be self-confident and make logical sense in the way they communicate. I have wondered why such people come to me for counseling, since they seem to be able to focus, strategize and find solutions to their problems. However, in time we usually discover they are confused and frustrated by an inability to name and express their feelings. Their cool, calculated, matter-of-fact attitude can interfere not only in their relationships, but also with their internal well-being. Being unaware and unable to express anger, hurt, fear, and frustration takes a high physical and social toll.

From our first session, it was clear that CJ was more into the rational, reasonable thinking end of the spectrum. She had very little to say about her emotions. Because I believe that mental health requires balance between thinking and feeling, I began to zero in on how she felt about various situations and people.

I do not see my clients as mentally ill, but as fellow strugglers. We humans are all neurotic to one degree or another. We lack self-confidence and battle with low self-esteem in one or many areas. We become self-protective when we feel threatened. We can be selfish, egocentric, and indifferent to others' needs. When egocentricity becomes the norm, a person can lose any moral or ethical bearings and become sociopathic or psychopathic. Though I deplore labels, these terms admit that human beings can become totally indifferent to others, with no ability to empathize. I have met perhaps four or five such people in my thirty plus years of counseling. More about this topic can be found in Appendix B.

Of course I recognize the biological origins of some clients' problems. We know now that bipolar disorder is an inherited condition and can be treated with medication. It is much more common than schizophrenia, but again, this problem, which affects one's way of viewing the world, can be managed by medication. The movie "A Beautiful Mind" directed by Ron Howard, gives us opportunity for empathy and some degree of understanding of this ailment.

These "disorders" are real and limit one's ability to function in the world, but I still don't see these people as mentally ill. A person may be handicapped, limited and different, but still far more like the rest of humankind than different from them. All of us come into this life with limitations or handicaps, but when we label certain people as mentally ill, we limit our ability to relate to each other's humanity. In my view, diagnosis should be used only to understand others better, not to dehumanize them as "crazy." In this case, CJ fit no specific diagnosis, and it was clear from the beginning that she wasn't bipolar, schizophrenic, socio- or psychopathic, or any more neurotic than the rest of us.

A strong element of my identity as a counselor is my Christian faith. It comes into play in different ways. When I first met with CJ, she stated up front that she was a Christian and a pastor's wife. Though she had little recall of her childhood and was limited in expressing how she felt, her adult self was defined by her faith. When clients or others ask me whether I am a Christian counselor, I respond by saying I am a counselor who is a Christian. Too often I have found that the "Christian" label carries connotations that are not helpful to my clients. So, just as I avoid using psychobabble, I avoid churchy terminology that would locate me in the Christian sub-culture. At times a counselee is looking specifically for some kind of spiritual direction; if that is one of the desired goals, then we will discuss the spiritual dimension. I rarely pray out loud with my clients, for fear my prayers will become too leading, too preachy, and too rote. I do tell most of my clients that I pray regularly for them (i.e. just before they come in, while they are there, as they leave, and as they come to my mind).

My intent is to accept clients' spirituality as it is. All of us have parts, as CJ did, who are antagonistic toward God and who fear being judged, misunderstood, or even reprimanded. Also we have believing parts, like CJ's "Beth" who maintained a faith no matter what had happened and was always praying for the system. Maybe most of us have a "Beth" who prays without ceasing, a part that believes God always cares regardless of the circumstances. I've noticed that even an atheist will say, "Oh, my God!" when surprised, shocked, or astounded.

I usually shake hands or give my clients a hug when they enter my office. Hugs, an arm around the shoulder, or a warm handshake almost always put the client and me at ease. Such actions can be a bit risky if the client is not comfortable with any close bodily contact, if they are questioning my motives, or if they don't "feel" huggable. Contact like this may not seem professional, but I always want to communicate humanness more than professionalism. I have come to believe that the benefits of contact far outweigh the detriments. Almost all of my clients show immediate appreciation, and make it clear later on that the hugging validates their self-worth and facilitates a sense of safety.

It is also true that a very small percentage of people are uncomfortable with any kind of touching, and I sensed that CJ was one of them. However, I felt it was important for her to figure out why she was so averse to touch. That was a major reason why she had come to see me in the first place. I kept emphasizing that she was in control and that I would never harm her in any way. At one point I suggested holding her hand, which she at first refused to do. Eventually, with fear and trepidation, she agreed, and that first "touch" encounter finally drew an emotional response from her. CJ was no longer locked up "in her head" but had become aware of her body (the seat of all emotions). The exercise was traumatic for her, but the experience was the catalyst that began the unlocking of her suppressed emotions. Of course, at the time, neither of us realized that she had been sexually abused.

# PART I

# Building a Trusting Relationship in Therapy

CHAPTER

# 1

# Driven to Therapy (CJ)

*The basic premise of biblical trust is the conviction that God wants us to grow, to unfold, and to experience fullness of life. However, this kind of trust is acquired only gradually and most often through a series of crises and trials.*

–Brennan Manning, ***Ruthless Trust***

*...we must accept responsibility for a problem before we can solve it.*

–M. Scott Peck, ***The Road Less Traveled***

I needed help. I, Catherine Jean Johnson, couldn't fix this one by myself. We kept having sexual difficulties in our marriage, and I could see the major cause in my actions, or rather inaction. I had tried to solve the problem—praying, reading books and articles, attending seminars, talking to friends—but still I couldn't even imagine finding resolution. I was frustrated. I was a self-sufficient person and could generally deal quite logically and rationally with difficult situations in my life. But this one was beyond me.

## My Situation

My number one priority was figuring out how to be a better wife and a more satisfying sexual partner for my husband. I was nervous about seeing a therapist, and the nature of my problem made me even more reluctant and anxious. However, I was determined. When in 1987 Jerry Donaldson was recommended to me as a "good marriage counselor," I set up my first appointment. I hated going there, but I forced myself to do so. Jerry's office was small and made me feel slightly claustrophobic; even his open, easy-going manner made things only minutely more comfortable. I hated being there. I hated having to seek help from an outsider. I hated admitting failure. I squirmed in the chair as he asked me my reason for making the appointment. There was no other way but to get right to the point. I blurted out my dilemma.

"I want to be a better wife to my husband," I stammered.

Thus began a long, difficult journey for me. If I had known during that first visit just how long and painful the years ahead would be, I know I would have walked straight out and never looked back. Throughout that long and painful therapist/client relationship, I often wondered if Jerry wished he had referred me to another therapist, because I doubt he had a clue during that initial appointment what a troubled client I was. At times during the process I saw myself crumbling, right before my eyes. Everything I deemed important lay smashed at my feet in a pile of rubble, leaving nothing but blank space around me. That mental picture scared me to death. Frequently in my journaling, I vowed to make only one last appointment, or resolve that I was not going back to therapy ever again. In fact, however, I continued therapy sessions with Jerry off and on for over 10 years.

In the beginning, although I wasn't really aware of it, I basically trusted only one person—myself. Being the wife of a pastor, I naturally gave verbal assent to my trust in God. In fact, I had myself fairly well convinced that I trusted God completely. I also had a minimal kind of trust in my husband, developed over our fifteen years of marriage. But in truth, I did not depend on anyone. If I couldn't accomplish something myself, I wouldn't risk doing it. At the outset, I trusted Jerry to give me ten quick, easy ways to become the woman of my husband's dreams—but that was all. Even my journaling showed my distrust. I was careful to use shorthand when I wrote about thoughts and feelings that were intensely personal. I was nervous about someone picking up my journal, even though I kept it hidden. I felt a desperate need to disguise myself, protect myself. Despite my reluctance to trust, Jerry gradually drew me into the therapist/client relationship, because he was always genuine, empathetic and non-judgmental toward anything I talked about in our sessions.

I set up appointments with Jerry every three to four weeks during the first year. He was very good at building trust. He affirmed me by complimenting me on working so hard between sessions. He told me our sessions were vitalizing to him, not draining as I feared. Jerry's affirmations sounded really good to me, although I couldn't help wondering if his words were just therapist rhetoric. Could I really trust him to be honest and truthful with me?

For me, sessions with Jerry were traumatic and exhausting. I needed several days to prepare to meet with him and several days afterward to recover from the sessions. Before each meeting I would begin to feel very nervous. My stomach would hurt and I would have no appetite. These feelings would begin one to two days before the appointment and continue to intensify. On the day of the appointment I would usually suffer with diarrhea and anxiety. The anxiety would get so intense that often I would think I'd have to cancel. After the appointment my anxiety level would begin to dissipate, as I generally could come up with a "things-to-do-list" before meeting with Jerry again.

I would not have persevered in this gut-wrenching work if I hadn't been so determined to make myself and my marriage better. Jerry was always encouraging and came up with many books and articles for me to read. Being an avid reader, I found myself eager to follow his suggestions. One of the first books he recommended was about marriage. The book explained that sexual problems can occur when there are problems with a person's self-image. That was a new consideration for me! I always had bragged that I had an intact self-image. Suddenly, I wondered if I had been deluding myself. Did I have problems with sex because I was avoiding surrender, or was I simply undersexed? Why didn't I like being touched? Why did I almost always avoid touching other people?

I believed from the very beginning of therapy that I had to take responsibility for honestly looking at myself (especially my motives and behaviors) and for working on changes in me and my problems. I determined there would be work to do, and no one could do the work except me. Although I looked to Jerry for information, advice, and guidance, I was acutely aware he could not fix me (however much I would have preferred that!) I also knew I would need God's help to accomplish the miracle I felt I needed in my life. This task was not something I could do in my own strength and power. I knew I needed divine guidance and intervention to work through difficulties, but I was not daunted by my responsibilities. I have always been a responsible, hard worker, and in some ways, I saw therapy as a challenge—or perhaps even more as a puzzle containing thousands of pieces spread out in front of me. In fact, my analogy of a puzzle turned out to be a more accurate picture than I ever could have imagined.

When Jerry did not have specific assignments for me, I would devise my own list of things to accomplish before our next session. I was eager to fix my problems and ultimately very anxious to have an improved relationship with my husband. Here are some of the initial items on my "things to do lists:"

- Identify and acknowledge my emotions and the emotions of others
- Accept my weaknesses

- Continue to allow myself to be known by my husband and certain good friends
- Allow myself to make mistakes and errors without beating myself up
- Nurture myself
- Use more positive self-talk

Though I'm basically a positive person, and even though it seemed that my life was improving, I sometimes became very discouraged about my progress in therapy. I felt I was working really hard. Jerry agreed, yet I was making little or no progress in my marriage. I often asked myself, "Why aren't things changing? Why can't I love my husband? What is this stupid aversion I have to naked bodies?" Therapy was an exhausting and painful process, and often times I simply wanted to forget the counseling and just be content to be miserable for the rest of my life. Jerry continued to encourage me to keep on. He gave me hope when I had none for myself or for my marriage. He encouraged me to read books about dealing with pain. In one of them, I read that pain is a teacher, helping us to bring about change in our lives. I personally discovered this to be correct: pain is the driving force in change. Pain drove me to discover myself.

## Realization of Need

Not long into the therapeutic process, both Jerry and I became aware I was good at hiding in my mind and consequently steering clear of my emotions. He talked with me often about acknowledging my feelings. Frequently he would ask me how I felt about a situation or person, and usually I was at a loss to come up with even one feeling word. Through our discussions, I became acutely aware of how often I ignored, denied, or covered up my feelings. This had seemed perfectly normal to me.

"After all," I mused, "aren't most feelings un-Christian, unbecoming for a woman of God, a pastor's wife, for heaven's sake!"

Jerry encouraged me to identify my feelings and attempt to honestly share those feelings with others, especially my husband. He told me a person who didn't express passion couldn't really give of herself in a sexual relationship, because there would be no submission but rather a continual fight for control. Jerry spoke about acknowledging emotions so often that the word "feelings" began to seem like a dirty word to me. I dreaded to hear it! For the life of me, I couldn't understand why he put so much emphasis on it. I was positive that working through issues and situations cognitively was a much more valuable tool. I figured his obsession with feelings just came from his own touchy, feely type personality. I had gotten along very well by thinking things through. Feelings were not a viable commodity to me, and certainly not a solution to life's problems.

Later in my therapy I experienced a great deal of remorse, as I realized how my coldness and lack of emotion had affected the people I love, especially my husband Martin and daughter Janelle. I had only grudgingly dispensed very little physical affection to them in our everyday life. Although I considered myself to be a loving wife and mother, I realized that much of my relationship with Martin and Janelle consisted of "doing" things for them—cleaning the house, making meals, doing the laundry, taking Janelle places—all with little emotional connection. We had a "good" family arrangement, but there were important components missing. I am a fix-it person and it took Janelle to help me see and understand that most times she didn't just want me to fix her problems; she wanted me to listen and hear her heart as she talked about her difficult situations. It was not unusual for Janelle to say in exasperation, "Mom, I don't want you to fix this for me; I just want you to listen to me, to hear me!"

As I asked God to forgive me, I wondered how many past incidents I would have to revisit before I was healed of my emotionless state. After the first few years of therapy, a day did come when I realized I was "waking up" emotionally, but as if from a drugged sleep. I felt slow and groggy, unsure whether I really wanted to take this path. Still, even as I realized how dead I was emotionally, I also recognized there was a small part of me that yearned to be alive. Sometimes I was not satisfied to be non-feeling, even though I felt more comfortable in that state. Sometimes my feelings reminded me of going to the dentist. Like the Novocain wearing off, there was a slow awakening of my emotions.

I hated those times, all too frequent in the therapy process, when I became emotional. Weepy was weak to me, and I hated feeling weak and powerless. Being strong was being silent and unemotional. I hated to talk about my feelings. That seemed too self-absorbed, as though I wanted to be in the spotlight. It seemed much better to stuff my feelings and simply grin and bear whatever was happening.

I didn't understand the emotional side of myself. Sometimes I felt distinctly separate inside. There seemed to be two very different parts of me that I could not bring together. There was the analytical (rational) side of me, looking at my dilemma with utter amazement and disgust. Then there was the screwed-up irrational side, that couldn't see black from white and used only emotion to deal with life. This irrational side was self-destructive and wouldn't listen to reason. I saw the analytical, rational side as good and the emotional, irrational part as bad. The analytical side seemed strong and calm, while the emotional side was out of control, angry, frustrated, full of panic, guilt-ridden, weepy—in short, a wimp. Now the responsible, analytical part of me was slipping, staying in control only by sheer force of will. My emotional part, responding to this weakness, was gaining strength, eating away and destroying my safe foundation of intellect.

I knew I had always loved being in control. I enjoy order and organization. Right out of high school, I began working as a secretary and then moved to a legal secretary position. This led to work in a computer software environment. All these positions required accuracy and good organization skills, so I excelled in my career by my highly structured and perfectionist ways. When I knew what to expect and there were few surprises, I felt good, safe, and calm. Yes, I had realized that controlling things made me disconnected, not easily upset or bothered. But I reasoned that it was helpful to be able to remove myself from situations and analyze them. I had always felt God wanted me to be in control of myself and my life. In retrospect, I now believe I had taken control of my life away from God—not intentionally, but for self-preservation. When I wasn't in control, I found life annoying, disconcerting, or sometimes even intensely frightening.

In my marriage, part of me wanted to be open and expressive, but I didn't know how to begin, while my reasoning part rebelled against losing control. Doing things correctly was my highest value; if I didn't know how to do something correctly, I avoided doing it at all. In counseling with Jerry, I began to wonder why I tried so hard to impress others by my self-sufficiency. Did I depend on approval and acknowledgement from other people, and get it by doing things right? Deep down, did I actually doubt myself?

As I faced my desire for control in my life, I was surprised to discover how often I still allowed my husband and others to rule or run certain aspects of it. For instance, when something in a conversation rubbed me the wrong way, I would generally ignore my feelings. I realized I didn't like conflict, and that is why I often just gave in to a situation. I was assertive in some contexts, but commonly in conflict, I would back off and become handicapped and powerless emotionally. Could I be okay with allowing someone else's opinion to prevail, and not feel powerless in the process?

### Recognition of Distrust

These journal entries come from the early days of my therapy with Jerry:

June 4, 1987 and July 2, 1987

*Today in our session Jerry said he wanted to give me a hug. He always wants to give me a hug as I leave his office, but I always shy away from it—due to body space issues. It felt like Jerry more or less forced a hug on me today. He told me I needed to feel. As an experiment, he said he wanted to give me a hug and then talk about it afterward. He told me to think about it, that it was my choice. Some choice! I guess I know the importance of what he is talking about—those stupid feelings again. Anyway, I let him hug me. At first it was comforting, then I felt guilty, and then angry with him because he caused me to have all those disturbing feelings. I hated the hug and wished I had never agreed to it.*

*Jerry said that for some reason I'm afraid of physical contact. He said it could be due to something that had happened in the past. I denied the fear, but he said empathically, "You are too afraid. I can see the fear written all over you, in your eyes, your expression and your gestures." I denied it, but he's right, I am afraid. I'm very apprehensive of physical touch, actually scared of it, and I don't know why. Jerry suggested at the next session I consider pursuing this topic of physical touch. He gave me control and said all I would have to say at the next session was "I want a hug" and then we would again talk about the experience.*

July 4, 1987

*I'm so afraid of Jerry hugging me and yet I don't know why. I think of my next appointment with him and I just shudder and shake, yet I don't know why! This is on my mind a lot. I do wonder if, as a child, something traumatic happened to me that I spaced out. I don't really want to know if it did. Anyway, what would it matter at this point? I still have to work through all this stuff.*

July 8, 1987

*I didn't realize until after I had talked with my friend, Michelle, that if someone refuses to touch her she feels rejected, that they don't like her! I hadn't ever thought about that side of it at all—only the side of how repulsive touch is to me!*

July 9, 1987

*At our session today, Jerry asked me if I had decided to try his hug/touch suggestion. I reluctantly said yes and he asked me how I wanted to accomplish it. I was mortified. I couldn't answer the question. Finally he suggested we hold hands. I agreed mostly because it seemed the least violating thing to do. I hated the thought of him holding my hand or touching me at all and it took me a while until I allowed it. As he held my hand, Jerry asked me how I was feeling. I was angry and scared. I finally asked him to let go. I was a wreck! Later in the session, Jerry took me by surprise. He asked me to stand up and he hugged me—but I couldn't hug him back. The hug upset me a lot; it took me a while to recover. Afterwards I felt emotionally bruised from the session. My stomach hurt badly. At this point, I don't know if I'll ever go back. Also, I feel guilty about holding another man's hand. I feel like I have betrayed my husband.*

July 10, 1987

*My reaction to the last appointment with Jerry—I still shudder when I think about handholding. But surprisingly I do have warmer feelings toward him, because he is trying so hard to help me. I feel he really did his homework and was well prepared for our last appointment. But I am NOT attracted to him sexually.*

July 16, 1987

Question: *Why don't I like to be touched by Jerry?*

Answer: *It scares me.*

Question: *Why?*

Answer: *I'm afraid he will hurt me?*

Question: *Why?*

Answer: *I don't know.*

Question: *How will he hurt me?*

Answer: *Physically!*

Question: *I have the power to say no at any time, right?*

Answer: *I think so—maybe—*

Question: *Why do I think Jerry would hurt me?*

Answer: *Because he is a man.*

July 12, 1987

*I've been more consciously aware of the need to hug others, not so much for my sake as for their sake (my husband and daughter). I really don't care for any kind of touch for myself. I feel badly that I've not recognized this need in others and that I have been apathetic about their need for touch.*

I was in the beginning stages of waking up emotionally and beginning to explore myself internally, but I could not see the long, arduous journey ahead.

CHAPTER

2

# Beginning Encounters (JD)

*The everyday habits of life's best survivors include curiosity, playfulness, empathy, needing to have things work well, feeling completely responsible for their lives working well, and learning how to influence events to result in good outcomes.*
–Al Siebert, ***The Survivor Personality***

I am always a bit nervous when I first meet with a client, and meeting with CJ was no exception. It takes considerable courage for a person to walk into a counselor's office and, perhaps for the first time, admit being stuck with an unresolved problem. That person has determined to look for a solution only because the pain has reached an unbearable level. It's painful for me to see another person hurting, but it is a counselor's privilege to go through the pain with them. Even though I am nervous, I attempt to set aside my feelings and listen with a non-critical ear. I am responsible to put them at ease, to relate to their situation, to demonstrate that I can partially understand their plight, and to make my time with them as safe as possible.

Sometimes people who come to see me who take a victim stance are quick to blame others for their pain. Often such people only want me to take their side, or do not really want to change. Not CJ. She immediately blurted out her problem (as she saw it); she wanted to improve her marriage, and she was not being the sexual partner her husband wanted.

## Initial Impressions

During that first session CJ impressed me as being a very intelligent, loyal, faithful, responsible, and insightful person. Though she admitted being very nervous, she was determined to be a better wife and mother. She was a counselor's delight. From the very beginning, she had what it takes to make therapy successful.

- She didn't expect me to "fix her"—she saw that as her responsibility.
- She was open to do whatever was necessary to become unstuck and grow.

- She prepared herself for each session by following through on "homework."
- She was asking God's help in her attempt to relinquish control.
- She started out determined to trust me and continued to build that trust.
- She was honest and real—whatever she disclosed to me could be trusted to be true and non-manipulative.
- She was willing to work to make the necessary discoveries.
- She was faithful to make her scheduled appointments.
- She had been victimized, but she refused to be a victim.
- She would not blame others, and she was willing to learn how not to blame herself.
- She made me aware when I was suggesting or doing something counter-productive.
- She would look for activities outside the office that would reinforce what we had discussed during our sessions.
- She was very considerate of my private life and only phoned when desperate. She promised me she would call when life became unbearable (which I needed her to do so that I wouldn't worry).
- She would keep confidences, which freed me to be myself.

Neither she nor I had a clue what would develop over the next ten years. As a rule, I generally don't do long-term therapy. I see myself as more of a crisis counselor; the sooner I can get my clients through the therapy process, the more successful they and I feel. But in this case, I saw that building trust would take time. CJ's eyes, body language, tone, and facial expression all revealed much anxiety. During those first nine months my goal was to establish the beginnings of a trust relationship. There were times when she would connect with me on that trust level, but usually it was a mind-to-mind connection. I admired her thinking and courage, and likewise she seemed to respect me. The unrevealed parts of who she was would have to wait until more trust was gained.

That first year, on several occasions, I asked CJ to share memories about her childhood. Remarkably, she could not remember any specific incidents, either positive or negative. She could only generalize that her father had a temper and was over-reactive, her mother was unexpressive and showed little emotion, and the family was not affectionate but loved each other. When I asked her how she knew that she had been loved, she had no clear response. I suspected that her childhood had not been pleasant and that she had disconnected from her past, choosing to ignore the pain and minimizing its effect on her present life. Although I challenged her to come up with memories, she was resistant. At that point, it seemed more appropriate to address the issues she wanted to work on, rather than on what I thought was important. However, I would occasionally encourage her to write down any memories she had—houses she'd lived in, rooms that stood out, seating arrangements around the dinner table, accidents, vacations and so on.

## The Kid Within

My questions about CJ's childhood were not idle curiosity. Our early life experiences shape the way we experience and respond to our world as adults. As I explained to CJ, when our emotions are out of control, when we are not thinking clearly, and when our behavior is erratic, the child within has taken over the expression of our feelings, thoughts and actions. For example, I told her, when I was very young, I perceived that my father thought I was stupid. He often said, in a very condescending, parental tone, "Why don't you use your head for something besides a hat rack," or "You haven't got the brains that God gave a goose," or "That was a stupid thing to do," or "What's the matter with you?"

My perception as a child was that I could do twenty things correctly, and my father would point out only the one thing I did wrong. The harder I tried to gain my father's approval, to do things right (the way he wanted them done), the more quickly he pointed out flaws. He could always do it better, he emphasized; only if I'd been as smart as he was, could I have done it equally well. Now, as an adult, I affirm in my head that my Dad loved me and thought I was reasonably intelligent, but my emotions and intuition still don't agree. To this day I am very sensitive to perceived criticism. I attempt to please others, especially people I respect and from whom I want approval, so that they won't think I'm stupid. This super-sensitive, self-conscious attitude comes from the child within.

The inner child isn't essentially logical or reasonable. He/she behaves in a very "childish" manner when feeling out of control emotionally. Even in my 70's, I find this little kid sometimes has more power than my adult side has. However, there is another delightful side of my kid within, the child-LIKE. He's creative, spontaneous and fun loving. The childlike me is in the moment, enjoying every second: when I'm playing with my grandson; when I'm painting, fishing, drawing, building furniture; or when I'm enjoying an intimate time with my wife. But when fear and hurt enter the picture, I can become very child-ISH once again. I have been known to sulk when my wife comments on my driving, to throw my golf clubs, or to hate myself when I think I've blown it with a client.

This factor in human development underlay my approach with CJ. She had very little awareness of her childhood, nor did she seem to be having much child-like fun in the present. As children, we feel more than we think; therefore I wondered if something had happened, as it had with me, which was preventing her childlike part from participating in her life as an adult. Because CJ did not or could not emote as an adult, I surmised that the inner child was holding those emotions for her. So I kept encouraging her to remember her past, even if it was painful for her.

CJ was unable to respond in a childlike manner with her husband, particularly in the sexual arena. Both science and experience confirm that intimate sexual encounters are only possible when partners are both being childlike. We are no longer being childlike when we "perform" sexually; we are concerned about "doing it right" and meeting each other's expectations. Most sex therapists agree that performing, self-consciousness, and "doing it right" are causes of sexual dysfunction. The best atmosphere for healthy, enjoyable sexual encounters is created when partners are being childlike.

I believe that all of us are sexually dysfunctional to some degree, just as I believe that everyone is somewhat neurotic. It's just a matter of degree. Peer pressure, hormones, inappropriate sex education, bad experiences, parental interactions and other variables spoil sex for us. Our perceptions concerning sex are distorted, and many of those perceptions are held by the "kid within." As adults we can and do have different perceptions; however, when we are being affected by the emotions and experiences of our inner child, sex and other areas of our lives are affected illogically. CJ's reasoning powers were and are very astute, but when her emotions took over, when she felt sexually pressured, and when she feared disapproval, logic went right out the window. She was seeing me to find a solution to this dilemma. (More on this topic in Appendix A.)

All messages are interpreted through this mental and emotional grid of the inner child's feelings and perceptions. So we easily blame ourselves and believe that if we had "done things right" we would not have been punished. When we become adults, however, with greater cognitive skills and reasoned responses, we can calm the inner child as a loving parent would do with his child.

Throughout that first nine months I kept directing CJ to feel and express her emotions. I repeatedly clarified that her feelings were neither good nor bad in themselves. CJ consistently judged herself for having feelings and habitually avoided them. As she began to open up with me, I encouraged her to be honest with her husband as well. She found it very difficult to express what she felt, rather than what she thought to him.

At this juncture, my wife and I took a sabbatical from our fairly routine life to spend a year working with missionary kids and their families in the Philippines. CJ seemed to be in a stable place and was ready for a break. In fact, she stopped seeing me six months before my wife and I left on our trip.

---

## For Further Information

Siebert, Al, ***The Survivor Personality***, Why some people are stronger, smarter, and more skillful at handling life's difficulties and how you can be too, A Perigee Book, 1996.

Missildine, W. Hugh, ***Your Inner Child of the Past***, Simon and Schuster, 1963.

CHAPTER

3

# Deeper Disquiet (CJ)

*One of the most arduous spiritual tasks is that of giving up control and allowing the Spirit of God to lead our lives.*
–Henri Nouwen, ***Here and Now***

Jerry and his wife decided God was leading them to go on a mission trip to the Philippines, so he would be away from his practice for approximately a year. I was feeling abandoned, although I tried desperately to logically think things through. I wrote Jerry a "goodbye" letter—in effect, I terminated my therapy with him before he could leave the country and terminate me. I had a feeling Jerry was somewhat discouraged with the progress I was making, and blaming himself. I felt bad about that too. I always want to do my best in every circumstance, so in a weird way I blamed myself for not working hard enough.

## Two Years' Personal Work

Still, I reflected I had learned quite a bit about myself during my time with Jerry. I had come to realize that I felt very uneasy about my own body and also intensely uncomfortable with other people's bodies. The discomfort I felt didn't make any sense to me. Once Jerry had asked me to describe myself. He said, "Finish this sentence: CJ is physically.....?" I couldn't think of any answer to his question. In fact, the question itself deeply upset me. I became frustrated and anxious. I didn't want to think of myself in a physical way. I didn't want to think about ANY body, male or female. In fact, the thought of physical bodies repulsed me, and I had no idea why.

Following that session, Jerry gave me an assignment. He wanted me to stand in front of a mirror at home, completely naked, and assess myself physically. I never accomplished that assignment. I could not even tolerate the thought of being naked, let alone observe myself in that state.

Those sessions motivated me to write a list of what I was coming to see as "misbeliefs" about myself and my concerns. Jerry had originally pointed out a few of these erroneous ideas, but for the most part I was able to assess my own self after some directed introspection. These misconceptions were affecting the way I thought about God and myself. I tried very hard to see through my self-talk. Here are the misconceptions I identified, and my responses to them.

*Misconception 1*—I sin when I turn my husband down and don't have sex. Response: I guess I don't necessarily sin; I just keep us from enjoying what God gave us.

*Misconception 2*—Sex is a waste of time. Response: Not true. It is a time of closeness and release, enjoyment and exhilaration.

*Misconception 3*—I must make others happy no matter how I feel. Response: It is good to make others happy, to give in, but not at the expense of my own happy, fulfilled life.

*Misconception 4*—I'm a boring person. Response: I am a calm person, well organized, easy to please. I have varied interests. But I still do think other people find me boring. I wonder if God finds me boring?

*Misconception 5*—We must have an exciting, very active sex life in order to have a perfect marriage. Response: If we had to live the rest of our lives without sex, it would not destroy our marriage.

*Misconception 6*—I'm sexually and physically unattractive. I had no rebuttal to misconception 6 because I believed it was true.

Despite these misconceptions and feelings of failure in my life, I remained positive about the value of therapy. I truly believed things would get better. I knew I wasn't a terrible person. I believed I had deep feelings and hoped I would learn how to express those feelings on a more regular basis. I believed after therapy I would be a stronger, more complete and well-rounded child of God. Still, Jerry's leaving the country took the wind out of my sails. I felt alone again, unable to deal with events in my own strength and power. So I handled his departure the way I handled most things in my life—I made the choice to forget about him and therapy. I had no plans to resume therapy if or when he returned to the States. For the most part, that choice worked for me. I knew I had learned a lot about myself and could build on that knowledge. I continued writing in my journal:

> *I am a perfectionist and I know it. My life is a carefully regimented performance. My expectations of myself are extremely high, and those expectations spill over into my relationships with others though I believe to a lesser degree. I always have an extremely detailed 'things to do' list.*

*Actually I have multiple lists. I have a list for home, many lists for work, and a list for personal tasks that need to be accomplished. I'm a poor communicator when it comes to what I'm feeling. I'd rather have peace than my own way—most times. Stuff it, stuff it, stuff it is the name of the game when it comes to emotions. I have a desperate need to control my space, my own world, and myself. I am an overachiever. I detach myself emotionally from uncomfortable situations or conflicts. I don't think I can admit that it's impossible for me to do everything perfectly. In my mind, I believe it's possible to do a complete and perfect job of all that I undertake. Yet when I play the piano at church, I make mistakes. I hate it when I make mistakes, but I have come to the point where I can give myself permission to make mistakes when playing the piano. No matter how hard I practice and try—I cannot play perfectly.*

During the time Jerry was absent, I believe God took the information I had learned about myself and continually showed me what needed work. During that year God placed other people in my life, who took time to draw me out, who allowed me to talk about attitudes and desires that lay deep within me. Also God began to deepen His work within me, reminding me He loved me, even though I was a poor communicator and couldn't play a song without mistakes. I had always felt the need to be "right" and "good" in order to be accepted, because I believed neither God nor people would respect me if I were imperfect or made wrong decisions. Now I was realizing that I was totally unable to live up to my own expectations. This was the beginning of God's instilling deep within my heart the concept that I was valuable to him. Through my simple experience of making mistakes while playing the piano, I learned God still loved me even when I could not perform perfectly. He continues to love me unconditionally.

During this period when Jerry was gone, I also experienced great stress at work. I had been transferred into a challenging new position that required more time and energy. Probably I wouldn't have had the extra energy to work at therapy during this time. Again, I believe God provided this respite period, so I could solidify myself in this new position without the outside distractions of therapy. I noticed in my career that I began to be more assertive and confident, a direct result of my early days of therapy and my application of those therapeutic principles. Over and over I was taken by surprise on the job, when my suggestions and ideas were eagerly accepted and put into practice!

My personal life did not improve. Near the end of Jerry's absence, my husband Martin left our home on an eight-week sabbatical. He took time to delve into his own life, reviewing and evaluating his career, family life, personal life and spiritual life. While he was gone, I determined to spend extra time with our daughter, Janelle, and to do some evaluation and analysis myself. The U.S. went to war with Iraq (Operation Desert Storm) during this time, and the televised news reports seemed to intensify my gloom. Then our daughter went on a three-day youth retreat, leaving me by myself at home, with extra time to think about my marriage. I was plagued by our ongoing sexual difficulties. Although we had always been absolutely committed to each other and our marriage, Martin and I continued to struggle. As in the beginning, I still had difficulty connecting with him on a sexual level. We talked about the problem on a fairly regular basis, but there was still no resolution. I tried to keep the problem at the back of my mind, but I worried continually that I was not fulfilling my wifely responsibilities. My lack of progress added discouragement to the despair I was feeling.

When I learned that Jerry was back from the Philippines, I sought him out. I longed to find a real solution to my sexual dysfunctions. As I re-entered therapy, I had a sense deep within myself that danger of some kind loomed ahead of me, but again I had found no other way to resolve my problems. Too often I felt torn up inside myself. I hurt physically from the inside turmoil I felt about our marriage. Sometimes the pain became so great I forced myself to put everything out of my mind so I could rest. Compartmentalizing offered relief, but no change.

## Resuming Therapy

Jerry's first assignment in our second round of therapy was that I perform at least six spontaneous acts, for others and myself, before our next appointment. This was a difficult assignment for me, but I was determined to follow through. Before my husband returned from his sabbatical, I pulled out all of our photographs, from the beginning of our dating relationship. My spontaneous act was to look through them. Even with my strict resolve to accomplish this task, I found myself "feeling" many different emotions. Something hurt really badly deep inside of me. That hurting place felt empty and lonely. I stared at pictures of our dating time and wedding. I noticed the tender way we had looked at each other. I remembered how we both had wept when we had to leave each other. I wondered what had happened. To us? To me? I felt guilty. My inability to respond sexually had caused our original softness and love to harden.

I believed that I had squelched our spontaneous love for each other. I was far too serious about life, too driven to accomplish tasks and goals, too determined to do everything perfectly. I realized we would never be able to recover those precious early days, and I believed my attitudes loomed over our marriage like a black cloud of doom. I so much wanted us to be best friends again, but I doubted we could recover our first love with our present level of maturity. I prayed for God to forgive me and free me from my guilt and shame. Sometimes I had the feeling that in attempting to change myself, I was turning myself inside out. Often I had a huge ache deep down inside me that I could not connect with any single event. I reasoned that I truly must still love my husband a great deal, since I was going through this stupid therapy regimen.

For my next spontaneous assignment, I stopped one day on the way home from work and bought myself some flowers. I was almost embarrassed to do what seemed like such a simple and frivolous act. But after that, I couldn't think up any other spontaneous activities, and I was supposed to do four more! This seemingly insignificant assignment jarred me emotionally. I remarked in my journal that "all this digging at emotions and being spontaneous is very wearing." I felt drained at the end of each day. Was I doing the right thing, pushing to change myself? What if I was trying to change something within myself that didn't need to be changed, that shouldn't be messed around with at all?

I kept working on the assignment. Spontaneous act number three was writing a friend a special note thanking her for her friendship. For spontaneous act number four, I called my mom and told her how much I loved her, appreciated her and valued her friendship. I registered that my comments to her were not totally truthful. As a family, we rarely expressed our love or affection for each other through words or touch. I didn't really have much of a relationship with my mom or dad, so the word "friendship" was a bit of a stretch, but at least I was accomplishing my assignment!

As the next therapy appointment came closer, I started to feel fear and dread. I could not determine exactly what was concerning me. I wondered why certain situations made me feel fearful. I knew I felt a deep fear and dread of making mistakes and errors. I feared my errors would hurt not only myself but others. I was terribly afraid of being out of control. I feared any type of uncertainty or change. It felt like an accumulation of many fears. But the dreaded appointment turned out to be uneventful. Jerry just encouraged me to continue to journal and to keep attempting to act spontaneously.

Although the appointment was relatively easy, I now began to feel a huge hole opening up deep with me. I had no idea why. I reasoned it was because I was missing my husband, but there seemed to be something else going on. Something unknown. I was so afraid of the unknown that I was physically weak, emotionally and spiritually drained. I hated the feeling! And when I acknowledged the fear and tried to figure out the cause, I felt worse. I felt so empty inside and so afraid, that I actually cried. And I rarely cried about anything.

Now emotional pain completely surrounded me. I struggled to find something, anything, that would make me feel better. I carefully listed the blessings in my life, but mental acknowledgment of these good things had no effect on my distress. I fought to find some reason for my emotional turmoil. I couldn't remember ever feeling this intensely shaken in my whole life. It was possible these intense emotions had accumulated after the past few weeks of acknowledging my feelings, but I wasn't sure what to do with my feelings after I acknowledged them. Once again, I was terrified of not knowing how to deal with the situation. I felt as though I had opened up Pandora's box and might never be able to close it. What else would I find in the box? Could I cope with those discoveries? In an increasing panic, I called my husband, and admitted my fearfulness to him. He is a feeling person and tried to understand. He encouraged me to proceed slowly and be in a spirit of prayer. Although this was good advice, our conversation did little to calm my anxiety.

## Looking Further, Needing Help

None of my analysis or problem-solving eased my emotional terror. Physically sick, unable to concentrate, I finally broke down and called Jerry. I did not want to call him. I did not want to bother him outside of office hours. I did not want to admit that I was helpless. I did not want to depend on him. But I was at the end of my rope. When I got him on the phone, to my surprise he said he was glad this was happening to me, that this was progress! To me, it felt like destruction, not progress. He described what was happening as a "small leak" and encouraged me to keep journaling and to move along with the pain and fear. He warned me to avoid stuffing my feelings. He told me he knew this process was painful, but over and over he assured me that I was really okay, I was not losing my mind, and I would not totally lose control.

I did sense some relief after our phone conversation. I felt a little safer. I was calm enough to realize that this was not a logical problem. No amount of analysis could fix my emotional state. But even though Jerry assured me I was in control, I felt as if I had absolutely NO control. I felt taken over by fear. As I opened my journal, I decided I might not want to change after all. Perhaps I was afraid of myself. The only thing I knew for certain was I wanted to stop the hurt inside me. I felt like I was standing on the edge of a cliff with my toes hanging over. My body was teetering back and forth. I could fall over the cliff, and nothing could save me.

The next day I woke up in a state of overwhelming rage. I've never been an angry person, so this was a new experience. I was furious over losing control of my emotions. I was angry because I hurt so badly and angry because I was being forced to change my life. I was even angrier that I had to deal with all this therapy and emotional crap. I felt burning anger about everything in my life. I started journaling furiously about my anger, listing all the causes. As I began another statement with, "I'm angry because…" I stopped myself mid-sentence, appalled at what I had almost written. I had started to say "I am angry because… my Dad hit me with a belt and an aluminum pan." I didn't want to finish the sentence. I didn't want to admit what had happened, let alone think about it.

Utterly miserable, I ended up seeing Jerry that same day. Me, Miss Always-So-Even-Tempered and Calm, Logical and Sane was an absolute basket case! Now I felt ashamed and helpless as well as out-of-control angry. Jerry offered me encouragement. He said that the difficulty, anger and pain I was experiencing would later be replaced with tenderness, passion and compassion. I did not reply directly, but on the inside I was disputing every word he was speaking. In spite of the trust we had established in our relationship, I could not accept his encouraging words about the hell I was experiencing.

Jerry went on. He said my growing-up experiences with my family might very well have affected my present relationship with my husband. He even brought up my resistance to touching. I wanted to scratch his eyes out for reminding me of that. And he went further, considering that I probably had shut off my emotions as a child and had kept them well under control for all those years. So now those blasted "feelings" wanted out, and I must let them come out. Since I now recognized my lack of trust with others, he said, I must continue to be aware of my feelings, try to understand why I was feeling the way I did, and risk trusting others in the future. These are the assurances Jerry gave me during our session:

I was not crazy.

I was not falling apart.

I was a strong person and could handle what was going on in my life.

Finally, Jerry suggested that I allow myself only certain set times to deal with these difficulties. I still needed to carry out my responsibilities at home, work and church. I was deeply weary when I left his office, but I did feel better—not so panicked or out of control. Jerry's calm and understanding manner and his clear words placed me back on solid ground. He tapped into the part of me that desired change and would do the work to accomplish it. I had to trust God would deliver me, not just in the future, but starting today.

Shaken and tired, I pleaded with God to give me a resting period. It turned out that my work was often a diversion for me and gave me some resting time. At work, I could focus on something other than myself. My work was challenging enough to demand my attention, creating a good respite for all the turmoil going on inside me. I have had several friends who were unemployed while working through recovery, and I've often wondered how they managed to stay sane. During my ten years of therapy, I worked at the same company, but in several different jobs, including coordinating direct mail and telemarketing, pricing and marketing, and eventually software testing engineering. The latter job, testing our company's software packages to find problems before they were released to our customers, was the most demanding and challenging of all my positions..

The week of awakening emotions was the beginning of uncovering a past that had been so traumatic that I had hidden it deep in the recesses of my mind for many years. If I had retained a conscious awareness of my early environment, I could not have survived. My mind had established a way to protect me from destruction. I believe God used this way to preserve my mind, body and spirit.

CHAPTER

# 4

# Deepening Awareness (JD)

*Accepting someone's help is as good as giving some help.*
–Matthew 10: 41 (***The Message***)

When my wife and I returned from the Philippines and I re-established my counseling practice, CJ initiated therapy again. We were able to pick up where we had left off. Her relationship with her husband had not changed circumstantially, but CJ was beginning to identify how she felt. Now she could say she had felt somewhat abandoned by my absence. Although I had attempted six to eight months in advance to prepare her and other clients for my leaving. I could still empathize, I'd have felt abandoned if I'd been in their shoes.

## Lack of Growth/Change

CJ was more aware of her emotions, but this was making it more difficult for her to be sexually responsive. She and her husband were trying to cope, but they were still unable to fulfill each other's expectations. She was attempting to be more honest and open with her husband, but when she attempted to change the family system, as typically happens, resistance mounted. They were in a cycle of opening up, then shutting down. One of them would express thoughts or feelings which created conflict; a few apologies would be made; the subject would be dropped; they would ignore each other for a few days; everything would "return to normal."

It appeared to me that CJ's past was powerfully affecting the present, so again I challenged her to recall childhood memories. She could still remember very few incidents, and what she could recall was mostly negative. When she had recently recalled the past, the incidents she remembered were usually about her father. She recalled only bits and pieces—awareness of nudity, hating genitals, and other sexual thoughts.

After several months we began to meet weekly to address these important issues more intentionally. Meeting every three weeks or so, it seemed as if we were starting over each time, which was too painful and counterproductive. CJ made it clear that she wanted guidance. She had never trusted others, but now, she said, "I can't even trust myself." Her goal was to move forward, and she was depending on me to lead the way. This was uncomfortable for me at first. I wanted the timing of discussing issues to be under her control, I didn't want to lose the trust I had gained, and I didn't want to ASSUME there had been trauma in her background. Usually my approach is more intuitive than directive; however, once CJ gave her permission, being more directive was more comfortable for me.

## Facilitating Memories

Our priority was learning more about CJ's childhood. I suggested that she start by journaling her memories as a child in five-year increments. Most of what she wrote concerned her father—her wanting his approval, her sense that she could not get it, her father's angry temper and his "strange" way of expressing affection. Gradually additional generalized memories surfaced, about nudity and sexual feelings, with some incidents verging on abuse. She observed, "I learned to detach from my father. It was too uncomfortable otherwise." CJ had a difficult time journaling about the memories because they "seemed to ring true," and that made her "pretty miserable, more aware of me," more aware of how she was feeling about things, more empathetic and less detached. It was hard for her see herself as less self-sufficient. Once, she exclaimed, "The little girl in me—she's not me." She admitted being "afraid of what was there." She resisted talking with her husband, because the memories then became "more real" and thus more painful.

It became steadily clearer to me that I had to help CJ connect her past with her present. Dissociation was damaging her internally and externally. She needed to move from her head and into her heart. What a dilemma—she couldn't help being her own worst enemy as she tried to relate to her husband sexually. Before she could enjoy life, I saw, she was going to have to deal with the past and feel the emotions connected to past events. Pain needed to come before she could move toward joy, peace of mind and contentment.

What would it take for CJ to unblock her memories, write down and verbalize what was going on inside, feel her real feelings, and face the conflict sure to emerge? She would have to learn to empathize with the little girl inside, and to listen to the parts and pieces within herself, without judging, fixing or ignoring them. And she would have to reveal what she was discovering, to me and to others. All this was terrifying, as anyone who has gone through the process will testify. CJ's inappropriate dissociation had protected her: now, giving up that defense mechanism would feel like dying. (Note:

There is such a thing as appropriate dissociation. More will be said about this later.)

### The Dam Is Breaking

Two weeks prior to a visit from her parents, CJ reported that she was exhausted with all the planning and preparing, trying to make everyone happy. When her family actually arrived, their presence overwhelmed CJ. "I am remembering something…I'm falling apart," she told me. "I have suicidal thoughts. THE DAM IS BREAKING." Though she reported that she had learned a lot, and that "God showed Himself," she didn't or couldn't explain what she meant.

Now her loneliness intensified as never before. She felt she had nowhere to go except to me and she despised being that dependent on anybody. Furthermore, the escalating stress took its toll on the marriage. Both partners, seemingly, had lacked intimacy in growing up, and both resisted it now. Apparently neither wanted to depend on his/her partner, or to fully trust the other. Both partners were dissociating. CJ reported information, trying to ignore her emotions, while her husband, Martin, became extremely emotional but would not confront their problem.

A major issue between them was that Martin had always been very quick to express his feelings. CJ would complain, "It always comes back to his feelings. Mine aren't heard nor reflected." I let CJ know this obstacle was not unique to them. In fact I myself could certainly relate. Whenever my wife and I argue, we don't listen well. I want to "fix it" and make me—and her—feel better (in that order). It is hard, even at times impossible, to put our own feelings and thoughts on "Hold" giving our attention to the other person who is saying painful things. From my perspective, however, CJ and Martin were not at a dead end. After three and a half years of challenging both of them to be open, honest and intimate with each other, I noticed that occasionally they were beginning to talk, trust, and feel with less dissociation and more connection. The freedom they were just beginning to experience was uncomfortable and unfamiliar, but still a hopeful sign, I thought.

The more CJ remembered, the more she saw the little girl inside, and the more she thought about ways she "should have done something [to keep something from happening] in the past." The "little girl" had memories. Not good ones. And she felt out of control, weak, forced to give in, powerless. It was easier for CJ not to empathize with that little girl, but to attempt to shape her up.

CJ noted and reported the thoughts going through her mind:

*I feel responsible for my husband's negative feelings.*
*I think God turns His head when I enter the room.*
*I don't feel good enough.*
*I always disappoint myself.*
*The more I think these thoughts the more I want to die.*

She took part in a support group, and summed up her reactions:

*Self-pity turns me off.*
*I can identify; therefore, I feel saner.*
*I don't learn a lot but it does provoke my thinking.*
*I can be honest but I can't ask for help. I don't want or need anybody.*
*I am very successful at hiding (especially memories) and not drawing attention to myself, which bothers me.*

Later she observed:

*I don't get angry, it won't do any good.*
*If I can explain feelings it takes the feeling away.*

That was an incredible observation. It's a paradox. Sometimes when we **name** a feeling, we feel relief, so we are free to **feel** that emotion. However when we explain why we feel the way we do, we reduce the emotion to a thought. Emotions come from our bodies. We don't feel with our heads, we think with our heads and feel through our physical beings. Naming emotions (not explaining them) helps us find a feeling word that fits with what our bodies are experiencing. A number of years ago, in a men's group gathering, I found myself sobbing uncontrollably. I wanted to explain rationally why I was crying, but intuitively I knew that I was receiving the "gift of tears," which I rarely experience; the emotions from my body needed to be accepted, not explained..

As an adult, CJ had always known what she was thinking, but she was out of touch with her body, detached from her physical being. Now she was beginning to learn to read her body. Something she noticed was her lack of relationships. At work and at church she felt like a guest, while at home she had little interaction. There she felt lethargic and ambivalent. She hated weekends, when she became totally unmotivated. She summarized by exclaiming, "In relationships either I'm a guest or it's too intense."

As our sessions continued, CJ gradually began to accept her memories as reality. What she was remembering had actually happened. She could not share very many of her memories with her husband, because she felt he couldn't hear her, and speaking about them out loud was too painful. Sometimes when she was writing down the memories, "they just flowed," but they also made her feel alone and dirty. She wished her past had been a dream. It was hard for her to accept that the memories had been hidden in her mind for years and years. She wondered if "sex without strings" was possible. Would she ever trust? Each time CJ and her husband were intimate physically, she felt like a "piece of her was taken."

She didn't want to go to church, but believed that as a pastor's wife, she had to attend. Since she saw everything in life as good or bad, right or wrong, she was constantly grading herself. Shades of gray caused great consternation. She was unable to have childlike experiences or participate in childlike activities, but she now was beginning to let her inner child out when she was alone, acknowledging and trusting her a bit. Sometimes she could "remember things," but not feel them. If feelings came with the memories, they were too painful for her to acknowledge. CJ swung between advancement and regression in her work toward association. But this brave lady willed to keep moving forward, because she wanted to live her life with joy.

CJ and Martin came in together to debrief with me about changes during the previous year and to set some goals for their future. I sensed that they both understood each other better. They had stopped performing and were feeling better about themselves and each other. At times they could even approach intimate subjects without arguing and shutting down. Sexually they had a long way to go, but they were putting less pressure on themselves and each other. CJ continued to feel guilty and Martin continued to get angry, but they wanted to stop being victims of one another. CJ was working on becoming more spontaneous, and Martin tried to be less hurried and preoccupied.

## Journaling

Though CJ had found journaling to be helpful all along, now she began journaling in earnest. Often she could not stop writing. She told me she was very frightened because "the handwriting wasn't mine and I lost track of time." For the first time I began to surmise that CJ was MPD—a person with what is now called DID (Dissociative Identity Disorder). Then she reported that there were "voices"—a *"predominate voice that was very angry and a second voice that was mellow and childlike." "Someone had written some thoughts and feelings, strong angry strokes, a page was almost ripped and there were irrational memories about the father."*

Later I will say more about Post Traumatic Stress Disorder (PTSD), but CJ's situation had many parallels to the experience of returning military veterans. The mind suppresses awful events to help the soldier survive, but afterward the body, the whole person, remembers and reacts. When people begin to confront the past, memories begin to surface more frequently. For CJ, memories felt like blind-sided attacks. They showed themselves "in the shadows" of her mind, out of the corner of her eye, vague and un-detailed. Early in this process, all her memories were about her father, but now she was experiencing memories of her paternal grandparents as well. The circle of childhood abuse was widening. CJ had glimpses of nudity, a sense of being hovered over, and powerful feelings of powerlessness, fear and confusion. She repeated to me some remembered words from her father; for example, "Why do you make me hurt you?" In a detached voice she recalled, "I was comforting him [in the midst of the abuse or shortly thereafter]...strange." Later, I asked her how she felt toward that child of four or five. *"I felt more apathetic toward the child inside than angry."*

Typically, perpetrators blame their victims for "tempting" them. This gives the abuser a rationale for "punishing" the victim. Persons who suffer abuse are "trained" to take on the responsibility for "making" their abuser hurt them. Perpetrators do not take responsibility for their own feelings, perceptions and behavior. Instead they allow themselves to be held hostage to addiction, anger and/or physically abusive behavior, so they also become victims, having no control. They say and think things like "YOU make me feel…," "YOU are too sexy and sensual for me to resist," "If YOU didn't nag me, I wouldn't…," "If YOU would stop provoking me, I wouldn't… ."

When we human beings blame others for our destructive behavior, we believe we are off the hook. If we regard ourselves as victims, we think we have no choice but to give in. In cases of physical or sexual abuse and /or sexual addiction, we see ourselves as both perpetrator and victim. Such a person feels caught in an inescapable web. One moment we feel shame and guilt; the next frustration, anger and helplessness; then compulsion to flee the bad feelings by repeating the behavior. Please understand that a child or an abused spouse IS indeed the victim at the time of the abuse. Children, having no power over an older person, are unable to change their situation. They are taught by their perpetrators how to comply and take the blame. But even at the age of 4 or 5 they sense that there is something they can do to avoid the pain—they just haven't figured out what that is.

As children, most of us received negative messages about ourselves from our caretakers, or, at the very least, we have interpreted these messages negatively. Incorporated into our psyches, these messages become our truth, even after we become cognitive adults. We meet others who attempt to reason with us, to point out what is really true (or at least what they believe is true). Often in good faith, others will argue with us, push us, or manipulate us, trying to change our perspective, but we usually just become more entrenched in our version of truth. We see this happening regularly between various faiths—Mormon versus Baptist or Muslim versus Christian. Arguing, explaining, or debating rarely changes another person's mind. As a rule, each side just becomes stronger about his or her beliefs.

Therapy involves becoming more aware of possibilities beyond our habitual ways of thinking. The purpose of a therapeutic relationship is to provide a safe place where truth can be discovered, not to achieve a counselor's goal of convincing the counselee that he is right and she is wrong. Instead, both become more open to truth, willing to learn, change, and grow. No matter how painful the process might be, it is worthwhile because lies enslave us and truth frees us.

It is frightening to open ourselves to new truths about who we are, how we relate to others, and what has happened in the past. Instead we often go to great lengths to build faulty infrastructures: *"I'm doing fine—I have no need to rock the boat—my way of coping has worked for years—ignorance is bliss,"* and so on. But in crisis, deep down inside, we find that "our truth" is being shaken, doubts are overwhelming our faith, and we don't have energy to get through the day. The pressure of constant anxiety and/or depression challenges us to change.

Truthfulness and healing demand that we understand how past trauma affects the present. We must discover our own shut-down memories and attend to dreams that can reveal what our subconscious is battling. It is necessary to recognize the way guilt and shame arrest motivation and how multiplicity keeps us fractured. As our awareness increases, we can begin to develop healthier relationships and hope for a more meaningful and contented future

## For Further Information

Goleman, Daniel, ***Emotional Intelligence, Why It Can Matter More Than I.Q.***, A Bantam Book, 1995.

Powell, John, ***Why Am I Afraid to Tell You Who I Am?***, Argus Communications, 1969.

PART II

# Invading Memories

CHAPTER

# 5

# Invaded by Memory (CJ)

*God will help you deal with whatever hard things come up when the time comes.*

–Matt. 6:34 (***The Message***)

Whenever I was asked about my growing-up years, I would shrug and say, "I had a normal childhood." In fact, though, I couldn't remember much about my past, and I assumed that was true for everyone. Yes, I could remember the various houses we had lived in, the different schools I had attended, the names of my relatives, and a few major events. But I could not recall any specific Christmas holidays, birthdays or conversations with friends and relatives. I believed that was normal, until I married Martin. When he would (frequently) relate many childhood experiences, I just shook my head in amazement—what a phenomenal memory he had! I reassured myself that my life had been so perfect and normal that no high points or catastrophes made specific events memorable. Looking back now, I realized that many of my life experiences, which I had assumed were routine, were actually terribly abnormal. My images of the perfect life disintegrated on this therapeutic journey.

## Recalling Basic Memories

I began to understand the way my family had shaped me. My mother had been raised in a small Midwest country town with two sisters. Their father had died when she was seven years old. My father grew up on a farm in the Midwest with one younger sister. I was born in the fall of 1952 into my family which already had a five-year old daughter. My father worked on farms and in factories, wherever work could be found. My mother worked on and off throughout my time at home, mostly in retail jobs. Both my parents were very religious; we went to church every Sunday morning and evening and Wednesdays for prayer meetings. Occasionally, my parents would involve the family in long, laborious family devotions. We were forced to watch the Billy Graham Crusades when they were broadcast on TV. My parents were moderately active in whatever church we were attending at the time. We moved often, usually when my father was laid off from the factory that employed him, living alternately in small country towns and mid-sized cities.

My parents were not very affectionate. I always told everyone that kissing and hugging were not really necessary because we "knew" we were loved. Growing up, my dad had received little or no love and approval from his parents. Even in his adult life, he still did everything he could to gain their approval. His parents were very demanding and cold. I remember my father saying he never had heard his father say "I love you." My father himself was a domineering man, a sort of Archie Bunker type. His word was law simply because of the position he held. My sister and I were not to have differing opinions, let alone express them. He never explained his rationale for any decision; our job was to simply accept and obey without question. My father became very angry when he perceived he was being opposed, even in the slightest way. Once set off, he would yell, curse, flail his arms, spank, and kick the dog or whatever was in his path. His tirade would end with him in tears, emotionally spent and often apologizing for his outburst. Still, as a child, I remember always wanting to be with him, no matter what he was doing. I always hoped he would be gentle and affectionate with me. Even when I became an adult, during my parents' visits, I would work hard to get my dad's attention, with a perfectly clean house and good meals.

My mother was quieter. She seemed unsure of herself, although she was competent in tackling work or outside demands. My father's words and behavior often reduced her to tears. If she tried to reason with him, he would have one of his fits of anger. I remember only one time when my mother actually left my father. After an angry bout, she promptly packed her suitcase, walked out of the house and stood waiting for the city bus. I watched her from the kitchen window, terrified my sister and I would be left alone to deal with our father. However, before the bus came, she returned to the house and unpacked the suitcase. Sometimes my mother, my sister and I would discuss my father and his unreasonableness, but we never got close to any solution for the problem. Life just went on. I believe we all came to accept my father and his outbursts as normal, and we learned to live within those boundaries. I have my mom's personality. Like her, I am able to live in the moment, not think about the past, and push hurt and pain down inside myself. Even though we are alike, however, we never knew each other below the surface in an emotional way. My mom provided for my physical needs, but that was all.

My sister and I were rarely allowed to participate in school activities. Our father often worked the night shift, and my mother never learned to drive a car. Although she tried to learn several times, my father thwarted each attempt. We were able to go to church youth group activities when my father was available and had an inclination to transport us. Even after I got my own driver's license, he severely restricted where I could and could not go. We never invited friends to our house. I don't remember anyone telling us not to, but we all knew some unwritten rule which couldn't be broken. My parents rarely entertained, and we were always uncomfortable and uneasy when they did. Gatherings never felt fun or natural. They felt dangerous somehow.

## My Real Childhood

Early in 1991, when I was 39 years old and about four years into therapy, I began to recall some experiences from my childhood. One of the first was being punished. It was not uncommon for my dad to pull down my pants and whip me on bare skin. I didn't like that memory much, and tried to remember other times my dad had touched me. To this day I have only a few recollections of any nurturing father/daughter encounters. Many times he would tickle both my sister and me so hard it hurt and I hated it. As I started to remember childhood events, days would go by while I refused to write in my journal. My memories of my father began to include ones with physical and emotional abuse. I did not want to make any new discoveries. Nevertheless I tried very hard to follow Jerry's instructions to not stuff my emotions or block out memories. I felt like I was standing close to a fire; as long as I kept my distance from the fire (my memories and emotions) I was okay. If I got a little too close, I got singed, and if I somehow got into the middle of the fire, pain would destroy me. I balanced on the edge, yet at the same time I longed for truth and emotional growth. I would work very hard internally for a while, and then I would have to take a break. For days or weeks at a time, I would not think or feel at all, just try to maintain my life.

Even my normal life situations were now triggering emotional responses. Often strong feeling preceded a new memory. I had memory flashbacks at the most awkward times. In close intimate sexual situations with my husband, appalling new memories would surface. I kept asking myself, "Why am I making up this stuff?" When I asked Jerry, he assured me over and over again that I could not be inventing all these memories.

One day Martin and I took our daughter to the zoo. There I witnessed a man punishing a boy, probably his son. In the middle of the zoo, the man pulled down his son's shorts and underwear and publicly spanked him. I disapproved, but not until later in the day did I recognize how I was reacting. When we got home, I became very angry with my husband and daughter, scolding them over insignificant things like not picking up after themselves. My anger intensified throughout the day and evening, and I ended up lashing out at my husband. I said mean things about his actions and character. The scene was ugly and vicious. I watched myself in horror and yet seemed unable to stem the flow of angry words. Finally I went to bed, trying to stop the anger. As I lay in bed and calmed down, I realized I wasn't angry with either my husband or daughter. I was furious at the scene I'd witnessed earlier at the zoo. If I'd still been there, I would have slugged the guy. I wanted to pound on him for what he had been doing to his son. Then I realized I was angry with my own father for his inappropriate parental behaviors. He was the one I wanted to hit.

I got out of bed and went to ask my husband for forgiveness. I tried to explain what was behind my rage. I was ashamed and scared. Jerry had told me I wouldn't lose control; but I had, and in the process I had hurt someone I loved. I was totally sick in my heart and soul. Again, I wanted to escape the pain. It was difficult for me to pray, because I felt too guilty, but so very easy for me to cry, because I felt so weak. I wasn't feeling sorry for myself as much as I was needing release. After a couple of days my husband seemed to recover from my outburst. He understood a bit of my reaction and forgave my meanness toward him.

At our next therapy session, Jerry showed his excitement about what was happening. I shook my head in disgust. How could he be happy about my failure and misery? In resentment I decided to deal with my own life without a therapist. After all, I knew the basics now. I decided to slow things down and work through everything in my own way. I would keep journaling, read books about emoting, and pray for God's help. I did not share my new plan with Jerry, but my resolve to handle things on my own lasted only a few weeks.

I was reading a book on marriage. The author asked the reader to visualize the first childhood home they could remember and also visualize the people in the house. I didn't want to do that exercise! But I went on. At first I was afraid I would be the only one in the house, all by myself. As I went through the exercise, my fears came true. In my mind, I went from room to room looking for my mom, my dad or my sister, but no one was there. I moved on to visualize our next home. There I found my mom and sister, but they had no faces and couldn't talk. This was a very disturbing exercise. Shortly after, I wrote in my journal: "Sometimes I'm a little fearful I was molested by someone as a child—but I just can't see how that was ever possible. Life scares me a lot more than anyone realizes. I'm not an "all together" person. Sometimes I lie on the floor in pieces." That was the first time I had even allowed myself to believe the possibility there might have been abuse in my past. Looking back, I realize this was a huge step toward my recovery. And it was my insight, not Jerry's direction. He never urged me toward any specific memory; he allowed them to come up naturally, without planting suggestions in my mind. I saw the integrity of that approach. After I acknowledged the possibility I'd been abused, I was very careful not to read any first-person articles or books on abuse. I did not want to take on someone else's memories as my own. I wanted to be certain my memories were truly mine.

## Connecting Emotions with Memories

Another book I was reading stressed the importance of writing down memories, but as these dark memories began to return, I couldn't do that. If I recorded the memory in my journal, the memory became too real for me. I was praying that God would unlock my memory and emotions, especially when I began to sense there was more inside me that needed to emerge, but I felt helpless to facilitate the process. My awareness of bodily sensations sharpened. I noticed more and more how touch from another person caused me discomfort. Sexual touching seemed to trigger more memories than anything else. I became consciously aware of my intense dislike of the male sex organs. I wondered why my mind wouldn't stop working while my husband and I made love. I was constantly thinking about what would happen next, rarely able to enjoy the moment. I asked myself, *"Why do I avoid sex? When did my aversion to sex begin?"* My mind became immediately aware of my dad's merciless tickling me, his large body looming over mine as he tickled me hard. I felt suffocated just recalling those times. I would cry out, "Stop, stop!" but he would not, until he was ready.

According to Jerry, once you can verbalize something that is going on inside, the intensity of the feelings eases. The feelings build until they are released, and then other thoughts can enter the mind. That did not comfort me. I felt that everything within me had gotten out of control, and I wanted my control back! Thoughts and memories came to me, which I rejected and discarded, telling myself it was my overactive imagination. I could not believe what I was remembering was the truth. Yes, a grain of truth was possible, but I decided that most of what was in my mind was lies. I was terrified it might be true. I theorized that as a child I had been carried away with my imagination. I felt so much safer when I believed what was in my mind was fantasy. But then I had to ask myself—why would I make up these thoughts? I could not find a reason. I used my journal to list the evidences of abuse in my life, and all the possible reasons I might have had for inventing those evidences. It really frightened me that I could not come up with many reasons.

I did not want to believe my memories were true because: 1) I couldn't trust myself; 2) the memories were too bizarre, even incredible, not at all rational; 3) I didn't want to remember events that made me hurt and feel bad; 4) I didn't want to acknowledge my father was an abusive person; 5) I didn't want to do the work necessary to become a whole, healed person; 6) I didn't want to be vulnerable; 7) I was worried I would fail in the process.

Now my thoughts, memories, and the anxiety that came with them threatened to consume me. I fought for control. I felt guilty about focusing so much attention on myself. It couldn't be godly to think about myself so much! I prayed God would give me just one day of peace. I hid my anxiety from my husband and daughter and prided myself on being a good actress. I hated seeing so much weakness in me. I cursed the day I had prayed for God to unlock my memory and emotions. I was afraid to face the "me" that would be left after all this purging. Would I like what remained? Could I still respect myself after I had completed the process? Yet deep in my heart I sensed that God was answering, in the very pain of the process.

Jerry's calm interactions helped keep me stable. He identified me as strong, even though I felt very weak. Jerry said what I saw as weakness was really a new kind of strength. He pointed out that now he felt closer to me than he had four years ago when we had first met, because I had bravely opened up and shared myself with him. He talked to me in rational terms, affirming my memories, and reassuring me that I was now looking through adult eyes, so the memories could be revisited from a different perspective. The new pattern was for me to talk to myself as though I was a child, to attempt to see the memories through the eyes of that child, and then allow my adult to interpret those memories. He also urged me to take action to change my perception of the male genitals, to remind myself about the miraculous results of sex, such as the creation of our daughter. At times when my anxiety was the most intense, I hung onto every word that came out of

Jerry's mouth. I desperately needed to hear rational, cognitive truth. I needed to escape from the craziness inside.

Journal entry—March 30, 1991

*I'm really a mess. I've barely eaten in 24 hours. I'm easily distracted, I can't concentrate and I'm not at all motivated. I'm terribly tired, but when I lie down I can't rest. I can't be still for any length of time. It's difficult for me to get beyond denying everything. My stomach feels like chopped liver. I've cried so much my eyes sting. This journal tells very little of the anguish going on in my heart and mind. I've been exercising a lot which I think helps me. When I think of eating, I want to throw up.*

*I know I can't make any progress until I accept the truth—but what is the truth? I'm so afraid I'm fabricating this whole story. I'm afraid my "imagination" will slander someone I truly care for and love. I can't trust myself anymore. I'm so tired and I just want to sleep. I feel like I'm fighting this "thing" whatever it is, all by myself. It's so lonely.*

*I made a discovery today. I realized for once in my life, I couldn't trust either my emotions or my mind. I realize I've never really trusted anyone except me. Now I'm floundering because I can't be self-sufficient anymore—I can't trust myself anymore. I can't trust anyone—God included. I'm so lost. I believe I've lost control of myself in every way except eating. I must force myself to eat, yet I don't want to relinquish the only control I believe I have (not eating).*

*All that keeps coming to my mind is the bedroom in our old house when I was four years old. The bedroom, my bedroom. I know someone is in the room with me and I don't want to know who it is.*

I began to understand that I could not make any progress in my recovery if I kept denying my memories. I often felt like a yo-yo. At times during the memory recovery process, I would wearily accept my memories as truth. At other times, I would deny them in one breath and in the next breath confirm them. I was at a turning point. Incredible as it seemed and as difficult as it was for me to accept, I finally admitted to myself I had been sexually abused as a child.

When we met, Jerry encouraged me to be open to my memories, to be curious about them. Curious, what a strange word to use! I resolved to be diligent in dealing with both the memories and emotions; I reasoned that if God had chosen this time for me to deal with my memories, then God had confidence in my ability to work through all the "stuff." And if God trusted me in the process, who was I to doubt? I prayed God would not allow my mental state to hurt any of my friends or family members. I pleaded with God to protect my mind—to not allow me to go completely crazy. I prayed that God would protect me from Satan, so I would not be influenced by his evil intentions. I asked God to control my thoughts.

Jerry told me I needed to trust my inner child. (I asked myself, "What the heck is my inner child?") He showed me that all my life I had trusted only my intellect, and for good reason, but it was time to trust God, other people, and MYSELF. In one session with Jerry, he showed me something very important. When I used only my mind to explain events, I didn't have to face my feelings about those events. If I could come up with explanations about why I had been abused, I could avoid feeling the pain of the abuse. I could in some sense excuse it. But now, if I didn't excuse (explain away) the abuse, then I would have to deal with the reality of it, and feel the emotions that surrounded that abuse.

After remembering a particularly difficult memory, I wrote in my journal;

> *I'm not dirty, am I? I feel dirty and I always feel alone in my mind. I feel like my whole being is stuffed into my mind. Safely tucked away. So far away, no one can touch me or hurt me. But I'm all alone. My body moves automatically. It knows what to do by itself because my mind is too busy hiding. I'm hiding in my mind. My mind will protect me, won't it? I don't want to come out of my mind. If I do, I have to deal with the hands, the fingers, the snakes, the sticky, the faces and the words. I feel alone and dirty. I hurt on the edge of my mind. Something has gotten into my mind and is making me see the truth. I want to hide again, but the place where I was hiding has grown smaller and I can't fit myself in there anymore.*

Waves of memories began to surface quickly, with little time for me to rest and recuperate between them. When I tried to ignore the memories, they built up to a huge crescendo inside, threatening to burst out of me. At first I could not distinguish the face of my abuser; I fought NOT to see the face. But eventually a familiar face appeared on the body—the face of my father. In the initial shock of the memory, I felt tremendous shame, embarrassment and guilt. Remembering was totally disgusting and abhorrent. I felt dirty and ugly. When I pictured myself as that little girl, I found I hated her. I hated her weakness, her lack of control, her vulnerability, her neediness, her need for approval and love. I hated her! I didn't want to be a part of her. She disgusted me. I couldn't think of her in a loving way. She was stupid. I did not like one single thing about her.

At times when I went through a memory in a session with Jerry, it seemed to me as though I had fabricated the whole scene, because I felt so far removed from it. Jerry explained that I was reviewing the memory as an adult, not as a child, so I felt removed; therefore, the memory seemed unreal. He explained that memory retrieval involves having the child re-experience the trauma, not simply having the adult remember it.

I really did not want to hear that. My life had been a whole lot simpler before I started working on all this stuff. I sometimes wondered if I had made the right decision to pursue therapy. I just wanted to snap my fingers and have everything worked through and finished. I had once been able to live more simply, with hardly a bump in the road. Now life was unruly and unmanageable. Therapy seemed to have taken on a life of its own, racing onward, seemingly out of control. I was so tired of FEELING. I was sick of my emotions, and I wished I could simply vomit them out of my life.

No wonder I wanted to vomit. I now remembered how I was often abused in the morning when I was a small child. For that reason, I wanted to be up and dressed quickly, rather than lying defenseless in bed. When I was still in bed, I would hear my perpetrator moving around. I would do one of two things. I would lie very quietly and clench my legs together as tightly as I could, or I would pretend I was asleep. Neither of these maneuvers saved me. In my journal I recorded this memory from when I was 4 years old:

> *He calls out my name, but I don't answer. He calls again and again as he comes through the door. Maybe he'll leave me alone and go away. He keeps calling my name, 'CJ, CJ, wake up.' I roll myself up in a tighter, smaller ball, but he still comes. I feel fear and dread. My breathing is faster. I feel both hot and cold. He's at my bed now. He leans over me calling my name again and again, I don't answer—I pretend I am asleep. I remain very still. God, please make him go away. He turns me over and lifts me out of bed into his lap. He holds me there saying my name. My eyes remain clenched shut. I hold myself tightly closed in all ways. Maybe if I don't let my legs open he'll go away. Mama, please help me. Come home, Mama. He rubs my shoulder with his hands. He holds me closer to him. I like to be held tight—close to him, because then he can't get inside of me. Hold me tighter, Daddy. Tighter. Maybe it will be okay now. I snuggle closer to him. He takes off my shirt. I feel his chest hairs and the hair on his arms. His face sticks me. I want to go back to bed—no, I*

*want to go outside and play. Mama, Mama, please come home. He takes off my panties. I have no clothes on. He has no clothes on. He holds me tight on his lap. It's warm and sticky. He is still and hard against me. His snake is hard and warm and sticky and it jumps sometimes. The sticky gets all over me. I want to wipe it away. The sticky is on my face and in my mouth. Mama, come home. The snake is in my face and it scares me. I can't swallow. Mama, Mama! I lie back in bed. I'm all sticky and dirty and alone. Mama, come home. I'm dirty and alone.*

After recovering this memory of my father abusing me, I said to myself, "He may have had my body, but he didn't have my mind or my emotions." I realized that throughout the abuse I must have separated myself somehow, because I always seemed to be viewing the memory from way up in the corner of the room. Somehow that distancing made me feel good, giving me at least some kind of control, separating myself from the abuse as it was occurring. At the same awful moment, I bewilderedly asked myself, "Can that really happen? Can a grown man penetrate a four-year-old child?" I couldn't bring myself to think about the horrible possibilities! I just wanted to escape into the safety of distance, as I had growing up.

As I began to work through my memories, I felt horror and shame, but none of the emotions I felt brought any tears for me. In fact throughout my life, I had rarely ever cried. I didn't think that strange; I simply thought I was a strong individual, able to keep emotions in check. I didn't cry at funerals, not my grandparents' or other people's. Sometimes I realized I felt cold and hard. I joked with friends that if someone told me my house was burning down, I would simply acknowledge that fact and go on with my life. Now I wrote in my journal that I wished I could sob and wail. Yet I needed to stay in control. I was afraid to allow tears to even form in my eyes, afraid that if I started crying, I'd never be able to stop. Eventually, my emotions seemed to loosen a little. Very rarely now, and only if I were alone, I might cry for hours without stopping, cry for the little girl and for the mixed-up adult, both packaged up inside me. But after such an episode of crying I would get angry with myself and tell myself to *"grow up and move on."*

As the memories began flooding back, I had times when I didn't want to live. At first these were not serous suicidal thoughts but purely desire to escape the pain and torment I was experiencing. I alternately wanted to run away or simply lie down and die. Intensifying my pain was the hideous and heavy shame I felt. I kept telling myself I should have told someone about the abuse. I should have had someone stop the abuse. Why hadn't I told someone? Had I in actuality enjoyed it? No! Of course I hadn't. Then why hadn't I told someone? Why?

I was wretchedly confused about the physical response of pleasure I had felt during the abuse—remembering that made me hate myself even more than I already did. I was disappointed in myself, my actions; I was absolutely ashamed of myself. I felt dirty and sinful—evil. I remembered one incident where my father and sister were together in a sexual way. Now I cringed to admit I had been feeling jealous of her. I felt more like the sinner than the victim. I was weak, weak, weak, and I hated weakness! A part of me really felt I had brought the abuse on myself because of my stupid weakness. In my journal I wrote about myself:

> *I hate you CJ. I can't stand what you did, how you felt or what you allowed. You're disgusting. I could just throw up when I look at myself. I'm unclean—a whore-child. I just hate myself. I'm sorry God, but I'd be lying if I said anything different.*

I wanted to beat my breasts black and blue, and yet at the same time to fold my arms around myself for comfort.

It was not unusual for a bout of depression to precede a new memory, and depression became my frequent companion. I was unmotivated and not interested in anything. I worked because I had to. I went to church because I had to. I performed my motherly and wifely duties because I had to. Once I understood that such depression was normal under my circumstances, I tried to embrace it and simply go with it, but that wasn't always easy.

CHAPTER

6

# Perspective on the Past (JD)

*Security is mostly a superstition. It does not exist in nature, nor do the children of men as a whole experience it. Avoiding danger is no safer in the long run than outright exposure. Life is either a daring adventure or nothing.*

–Helen Keller

## Post Traumatic Stress Disorder (PTSD)

PTSD is a form of psychological shock. Most of us know something about physical shock, which seems to cover up pain for a short period after a serious accident. The adrenaline is flowing, our focus is on the damage, and the body rushes to deal with the injury. Years ago, I experienced physical shock when I was in a serious bicycle accident. Tumbling over the handlebars at about 30 miles an hour, I was badly hurt, but I felt almost invincible. I felt no serious pain, and I was thinking clearly. When a motorist stopped to help, I picked up my bike, put it in his SUV, and told him I was fine and would just appreciate a lift to a phone so I could call my family. Bless him for taking me to the local hospital instead! Then it hit me. The shock had worn off, I was covered in blood, with a bad case of road rash and severe pain in my shoulder. I almost passed out. I had broken my collarbone, and later I needed over 100 fine stitches on my forehead and nose. Physical shock is amazing, but also dangerous.

Likewise, PTSD, psychological shock, is amazing but dangerous. In order to get through a traumatic, stressful situation, we can put our feelings on "hold" and do whatever is necessary to survive. Under horrible circumstances, we are forced to detach from our feelings in order to think about how we can make it through the trauma. PTSD does protect for the moment, but the longer we avoid remembering and dealing with the traumatic experience, the longer it will take to recall and feel again. In CJ's case it was impossible for her to complain or resist at the time of the abuse. She was not allowed to talk about the "secrets" and was ordered to "keep quiet forever or else!" Her enormous pain had to be hidden rather than felt, so she detached herself from her emotions and did as she was told.

The silence lasted for many years. She could function in a limited way but as long as the stress and trauma were kept inside, she could not be happy or relate deeply to her husband. My job was to help her remember the trauma and its associated feelings, so that there could be a cathartic release. As the memories came, I challenged CJ to verbalize those memories and to give as many details as possible. This is a wrenching, conflicted place to be. Remembering would make her feel, in the present, the feelings she had blocked out in the past, and if those took over, she feared she would never be able to put herself back together again. However, if she continued to avoid remembering and experiencing those devastating feelings, she would stay stuck, unable to connect on a deep level with family or friends.

As a counselor, I too had mixed emotions; I wanted to facilitate those memories and emotions, but then again, I didn't. I hated to see CJ going through that painful, devastating process, but I knew if she didn't, she wouldn't experience peace, joy and contentment, nor love more deeply and allow herself to be loved. Around this time, her husband was out of town, and CJ had some time alone to remember and to feel the emotions connected to some of those memories. When her husband returned, she tried to share a few of her discoveries. She even allowed Martin to read excerpts from her journal, but was hurt when "He didn't know what to do." CJ told him that she didn't want him to DO anything—just listen and try to understand.

But how could he, how can we, understand? Martin was overwhelmed by the ugly truth that parents who are supposed to protect and love, could act so horribly. He could not make sense of it. In fact, we humans cannot make sense of disasters and tragedies. We too may feel overwhelmed, but it is imperative that we listen empathetically to another's story. This in itself is healing. Martin was not yet able to listen this way. CJ didn't know what to DO, so again she asked me to take the initiative. At this point my leadership involved probing, facilitating a deeper awareness, validating her feelings, empathizing, continuing to build her trust, and assisting her to set goals—immediate, intermediate and long-term—which would bring healing.

## Dreams Can Reveal and Heal

C.J began to have vivid dreams, through which she became aware of more sexual memories. I encouraged her to pay close attention and write about them. Dreams can be powerfully therapeutic, because they are one way the subconscious can reveal to us what's going on deep inside. When we sleep our guard is down, and whatever is on our minds will spin its way to the surface. Even dreams which seem somewhat bizarre point to foundational realities.

For CJ, dreams allowed fragmentary parts of herself to communicate their feelings and perceptions. All of us have parts and pieces inside, and dreams permit these various perspectives to communicate to us. Of course, some dreams are caused by eating pizza or by seeing a violent movie! But recurring dreams, intensely emotionally packed dreams like CJ was having, can reveal unresolved issues. These disturbing dreams can be amazingly enlightening as well.

In her dreams, CJ was often very young, with little or no power or choice. The subject matter of her dreams was usually sexual and abusive in nature. Her dominant dream feelings were guilt and shame. She would wake up feeling intensely angry, but she didn't understand why. When her dreams and memories became so intense that she felt herself losing control, she would withdraw, dissociate, and if possible, literally leave the place, retreating and disconnecting, physically and emotionally. She kept trying to think her way out of her emotions.

Our sessions were usually cyclical. CJ would come in feeling "up" and excited about her progress. Her relationship with her husband would be better. They'd be talking and sharing. There would be understanding and compassion. Inside she would feel more settled and safe. Then at the next session the bottom had fallen out, and she felt defeat and discouragement. Her situation felt hopeless, she was exhausted and at times suicidal, she had been hurting and/or crying for hours and giving in to sleep. But even the sleep had been disrupted by the nightmarish dreams.

There would follow times of numbness, flatness, and a regrouping. Dissociation was the only way she could gain relief or energy. The cycle was mirrored in the experience of most of my other clients: one session would be intense and painful, the next would bring incredible insight and awareness, and the third would be bland/mediocre. Life in general seems to go like that, with periods of growth and delight, periods of crises and trouble, and then periods of mundane dailiness.

CJ finally told herself, "It's time!" She had been resisting knowing that her father and others had abused her, but now she could no longer deny the memories. This did not mean that she never again had doubts, but she faced the fact that she had been horribly sexually abused. Although she could not rage or retaliate, she now knew it had happened.

## Memories: True or False?

We have heard or read of debates about the veracity of recovered memories. From my vantage point, all human memories are false in some ways. No one of us has a perfect 20/20 memory. When our emotions become involved, our memories can "feel" right, but they may be inaccurate. My wife and I often disagree over details of our past. She will comment that we'd had an argument in the kitchen, and I will retort that it was in the bedroom. Both of us "know what we know"—it's my/her truth. We are not lying or attempting to deceive; we are stating the truth as we remember it. Strong emotions tend to exaggerate experience. By intense focus, we are "making a point" or emphasizing "This is how things felt." It is hard to discern what actually happened. When we make "always" or "never" statements, the other person can point out an exception, and then we argue about the exception—rather than truly "hear" how something felt to our partner.

False (or, more accurately, *distorted*) memories arise because a child sees things differently than an adult does. When we visit a house where we lived as a child, we are surprised at how much smaller the house looks to us now. Each room has a different look and feel. If for example we were usually punished in the basement, then that room will feel uncomfortable. For us, it holds "bad memories." Or if we had many happy meals or gatherings in the kitchen nook, the space will still feel warm and friendly. A stranger or a prospective buyer will experience these rooms quite differently.

Our emotionally laden memories will cause a particular experience to feel "good" or "bad." In this process, we are assigning a value to that experience; in fact, we are making a judgment based upon our emotions. Memories can only be "as we remember" the past. So as I listened to CJ's perception of the past, I had to bear in mind that she was telling me the truth as she knew it, but it could be involuntarily distorted

The defensive mechanism of dissociation will also distort memories. At this point in CJ's therapy, she and I began to realize that there was more than one part within her recalling the past. (We would eventually become aware that the parts had names and that they were personalized.) The more fragmented the memories, the more parts/ego states/personalities involved, the more complicated the recovery process becomes. Each part holds experiences, and feelings and perceptions of those experiences. Looking back at CJ's father, one part might see him as a loving father, another as a pervert. Another part may totally fear him, while another feels pity, or yet another is angry. Rarely do their views of the past coincide. Consider further that each part has a distinct self-concept or self-image and a particular way of self-protecting and handling the abuse. Each part wants to be heard and understood. Each has needs and must get the other parts to cooperate for these needs to be met. Seeking truth and wholeness in such a situation is extremely complicated.

We human beings all want to be healthy, feel okay, and have a happy life, but each person contains unique parts, variables, perspectives on the past, strengths and weaknesses, distorted memories, fears, hurts—a very knotted ball of yarn. Since there are so many unique combinations of our humanity, there can be no set formula that will help us reach our goals. The hard work of therapy is to find the way to wholeness. I would often have to assure CJ that in her exploration of the past, she was "not making all this up." She found it difficult to trust herself once she discovered that she had "many selves." Which self was accurate, right, being truthful? All of it felt crazy. Who was she to believe?

As her guide, my responsibility was not to determine the literal factuality of her memories, to judge or validate every past experience. Instead, my responsibility was to listen, to reflect what I heard being said, to build a trusting relationship, and to facilitate her awareness and discovery. I avoided "suggesting" possible scenarios/memories. I refrained from asking "don't you think" questions. I refused to be a rescuer or caretaker, because CJ was no longer a victim, but a decider. Together we put the pieces of the puzzle in place. The memories were only valuable if they helped her know, understand and eventually accept the parts within. Then eventually she could see the big picture.

If CJ had been looking for someone to blame for the situation she was in, or if she had needed excuses for irresponsible behavior, no doubt she could have created stories in an attempt to get me on "her side." But this was not the case. She wasn't being the victim and I wasn't rescuing. "Victims" don't take responsibility. And "rescuers" don't empower others—instead they take on the hero role in order to "feel good." In the process such a "rescuer" lets the "victim" off the hook of becoming a whole person.

CJ was beginning to believe that the abuse hadn't been her fault and that she hadn't instigated it, but she still felt that she could have "done something different." She had always attempted to be a responsible person. From my vantage point, the upside of responsibility is taking initiative in life's situations, not letting others control our responses. Here CJ ran into the downside—taking on responsibility for all circumstances and for others' feelings, perceptions and behaviors. We cannot be responsible for the uncontrollable, yet somehow CJ felt that she had been. I kept returning to the fact that she could not have changed things. No matter how she had dealt with the abuse (gone along with it, or fought it) the end result would have been the same. She would have been abused. Facing truth is especially difficult if we have denied or ignored the truth for years.

At this point, my own experience helped me to understand. As I mentioned earlier, I have all my life believed that I'm unintelligent and inadequate. It's a message I heard constantly for eighteen years. In spite of being a college graduate and having hours of advanced graduate courses under my belt, I don't FEEL intelligent. I have struggled all of my adult life to sense that I AM adequate, okay, capable, and even wise. But that little kid inside still holds those old messages.

No wonder CJ had difficulty in facing the truth about her abuse. The messages from her father had sunk in: "You deserve this, your truth is not reality, you are choosing to tempt me, and I wouldn't be doing this if you were acting differently." Always remember that children only know the truth they have been told. As adults, we begin to distinguish truth from lies, but if the little kid inside is still emotionally in control (or being controlled) the lying messages prevail. Truth cannot stick.

When we continue thinking and feeling like children even though we are now adults and responsible, we can't separating the here-and-now from the past. What is happening now is overly related to the past. Making sound decisions in the present is complicated by the ever-present past. If the situation is confusing to you (and I have to admit that I'm struggling as I write to explain the unexplainable), can you imagine how CJ felt?

## Managing Dreams

Paying attention to CJ's dreams was an on-going part of the counseling process. At first she experienced such overwhelming fear that her dreaming was counter-productive. Then I suggested that CJ could learn to manage her own dreaming, to keep from feeling so out of control when she was dreaming. Though the idea may seem strange, I suggested that she could stay somewhat detached in a dream. In fact, most dreams start out with a degree of detachment. We usually begin "above," looking down upon what is happening to us. As the dream progresses, we tend to get more enmeshed in the events and can no longer separate the dream from reality. Each part, person and picture in the dream is a piece of how we perceive ourselves, or at the very least, how we have experienced life. Analyzing our dreams can give us great insight. When we stop analyzing, we become overly attached to the emotions in our dreamy state. At this point, our dream "doesn't make sense" because it's highly emotionally laden.

Our dream feelings can be both constructive and informative, but once we become totally overwhelmed by the emotions, the dream begins to control us, as opposed to us "controlling" it. Nightmares are not pleasant for most people (I say most people, because one client of mine couldn't wait to go to bed so he could have exciting nightmares. He was fascinated with his dream stories and emotions, using prescription and non-prescription drugs to heighten their intensity. He had learned to be somewhat detached and, to a degree, dissociated in the dream.)

In light of dreams' value, CJ and I talked together about her present dreams—about what they seemed to mean, about what kind of opportunities for discovery the sub-conscious was inviting, and about ways to keep her dreaming from being counter-productive. My sense was that she could wake herself up when she sensed that the dream was becoming too overwhelming, if she stayed appropriately detached during the dream. She could tell herself when a dream became a nightmarish dream, *"Okay, that's enough this is too weird; it must be a dream, so I'm going to wake up now."*

Prayer could also help CJ during this process. Before sleep, she could ask God to reveal what He wanted her to understand. When the negative part of her subconscious began to take over, she could ask God for the wisdom and strength to stop the dream and to let His spirit take over. For myself, I can't say that I like all of MY dreams, but I've learned that through dreaming I can work through many unsettled issues. Once I wake up, I can consciously work on what I need to address. In CJ's case, hundreds of fragmentary memories were holding her hostage, and dreaming was one way to bring them to the surface so that problems between the parts and pieces could be resolved. We could say that the dreams were the windows to the souls of the alters. (Note: there are many good books on dream analysis.)

All this sounded as strange to CJ as it probably does to our readers. But she was, and is, such a trooper! Rather than dismissing my suggestions, for two weeks she attempted to "manage" her dreams. She was willing to stick with the dream until it became destructive, and then she would wake herself up. She couldn't believe it. "It worked!" she told me at our next session. Discovering that dreams were not all bad and that they could be teachers, CJ was able to look forward to sleeping, rather than dreading nighttime. Waking up feeling rested gave her more energy. She was also paying attention, honoring the parts inside who wanted and needed to be heard. While fighting our dreams takes a heavy toll, trusting and flowing with them can be life-giving.

PTSD, post-traumatic stress disorder, limits personal and relational growth by putting off the feelings of traumatic events. Feeling those memories in the present helped CJ clear out blockage to further understanding of her past. Once she realized that the PTSD was preventing her growth, CJ pushed on to remember as much as she could. Consequently, her dreams became so intense that she needed to learn how to manage them. She also had to determine whether she could believe her memories.

As her trust developed, her memories and feelings began to flow; she was learning more fully what a functional relationship was all about. CJ hoped the memories would now be quickly discovered and resolved. However, neither of us understood how far she had to go.

---

### For Further Information

Viscott, David, ***Risking***, Pocket Books, 1977.

Putnam, Frank W., ***Diagnosis and Treatment of Multiple Personality Disorder***, Guilford Press, 1989. (A technical, clinical explanation and treatment of DID.)

CHAPTER
7

# Family Fall-out (CJ)

> *It's quite simple. Do what is fair and just to your neighbor, be compassionate and loyal in your love, and don't take yourself too seriously, take God seriously.*
>
> –Micah 6:7 (***The Message***)

Even in the early stages of therapy, I realized I would probably never again be satisfied with surface relationships with my family and close friends. I wanted more from relationships than I had received in the past, and I also wanted to give more. I didn't really understand how to have more intimate relationships, but I wanted to try. Now, at times when I wasn't feeling completely overwhelmed by my memories and emotions, I pushed myself to keep feeling my feelings and to express them on a daily basis. It would be all too easy to fall back into my comfortable old way of handling things, detach myself and stuff my emotions.

## Effects on Immediate Family

Although I had always loved and cared for others, especially Martin and Janelle, I saw I had kept myself disconnected and detached. Looking back on my mothering skills, I realized how little I had touched, hugged and or caressed Janelle, especially when she was a toddler. Because I had never known loving touching, it had not crossed my mind to touch her in a healthy way. I did, and do, dearly love Janelle, but during her childhood and early adolescence, I touched her only when necessary. When I began to see myself as physically disconnected from my family, I experienced deep regret. Slowly I began to try making physical touch a priority with them. At first my actions were mechanical, but over time, I have grown to enjoy receiving hugs and caresses, even from individuals outside our family. I also sincerely love to hug others, as I had never done until I processed my memories and dealt with the different parts of myself.

Although I worked as hard as I could on these new skills, I found myself isolating more and more from my husband. New tensions seemed to interrupt the easy flow we had going in our relationship. Listening to and hearing each other became more difficult. I gradually but steadily withdrew from him, unable to share the deep turmoil within me. Now I see that we both had great needs, yet we were unable to fulfill each other's expectations. We resorted to many different protective maneuvers; each of us tried to protect our own feelings, without regard for what the other was feeling. Resentment and aggression were boiling just below the surface of our marriage and threatened to overflow at any moment. When I suggested that we see Jerry together, my husband refused.

I think we were both struggling against the changes taking place, especially within me. We were making attempts to bend our relationship to establish a new norm. Jerry told me when one person within a marriage begins to change, the entire system is shaken, and we proved him right. Martin truly wanted me to "get fixed," and could accept my going to see a therapist, even though he disliked my sharing intimate details of our lives with someone else. We had both hoped that my therapy would give us a quick fix. It certainly did not. That fact discouraged Martin even more than me. While we both needed to work through specific issues in our individual lives and marriage, my own problems were most obvious. Martin, on occasion, would ask me in frustration, "Didn't that counseling do you any good?!" Although I too was frustrated with the seeming lack of progress and slow pace of the therapy, I knew how hard I was working and how difficult the process was.

I now believe that Martin could not always sense my pain, because his own hurt was so tremendous. He told me that our sex life was boring, that he was starving from lack of touch and affection. I had to admit he was right, and I felt paralyzed. Often during our "love-making," past traumatic sexual events flooded my mind. Trying to perform better, I felt I was physically and sexually unattractive. I wondered how Martin could be interested in me at all. I was afraid once I had finished therapy and was on the other side, I wouldn't feel any differently about sex. Then what would I do? If that happened, would the process have been worthless?

Each of us had experienced so much pain and hurt in this area of our marriage that I often felt we should simply ignore the subject. But of course that wasn't working. Still, not everything was negative. As therapy progressed, Martin and I were sometimes able to discuss sex more openly, though the conversations were generally tense. Also on the positive side, we were both committed to our spiritual relationship with God as well as to our marriage. At our wedding, we had decided that, whether we would be happily married or miserably married, divorce was not an option. I believe our strong commitment to God and to our marriage gave us the staying power to weather this extremely difficult time.

I carried a great weight of guilt about the state of our marriage. I wasn't able to satisfy Martin's emotional and sexual needs, and my emotional and sexual needs were not being met either, though I didn't know much about that. I felt I was constantly wounding Martin by my inability to love him completely, in all ways. Often he said, "I don't interest you anymore," and I could honestly see how my behavior would make him think so.

Because the problems in our marriage were extremely emotional and highly charged, our discussions often became heated and angry. In anger, we made hurtful accusations to each other, things we would not even have thought, let alone said out loud, under ordinary circumstances. I couldn't tell whether my actions or my words were more wounding to Martin, and I tried very hard to keep a tight rein on what came out of my mouth. Especially during those heated discussions, I carefully chose my words so I had less to feel guilty about later. Sometimes, much as I tried to keep up a protective barrier against being hurt myself, Martin's words would pierce my heart. Once he told me he "preferred to spend time with our daughter rather than with me because the time was more enjoyable." This hurt me deeply, but I could also understand and empathize with him.

Sometimes I felt Martin expected me to do all the work. He would tell me that our problems were my fault, and I needed to straighten up and act like a proper wife. Several times during my therapy with Jerry, Martin asserted that I should be discussing my problems with him, not a "shrink." For my part, I told him little about the therapy sessions. Going through my memories was a brutal experience, and retelling them was intolerable. When I did tell Martin my experience of Jerry's holding my hand in one session, he reacted angrily. I offered to set up a time for him to talk with Jerry about his methods, but Martin was so angry, he said he'd never go to see him.

In some ways, I wanted Martin to be involved in therapy. Several times Jerry asked him to join one of our sessions. Martin refused, saying this was "my problem and my responsibility to fix it." I suspect he was really afraid, afraid to know what my problem was, and afraid he might have to look at himself. He was not at all ready to do that. Just once he agreed to see Jerry with me, on condition that the session didn't turn personal for him.

### Bringing Them into Conversation

A long time passed before I mustered up the courage to tell Martin I believed that I'd been sexually abused as a child. I didn't give him specifics, just a general announcement. When I told him I had shared this information both with Jerry and a girlfriend, Martin was very upset. He thought I'd made a bad choice of confidante. I assured him that no one would actually be hurt even if she did betray my confiding, and he protested, "But it's embarrassing." Then I asked Martin for his support, concern and compassion—what I needed from him. He replied that he had none to give. Despondent and disappointed at his reaction, I simply detached before the pain felt too bad. I tried to remember he was fighting his own demons.

One awful memory was a flashback to being forced to perform oral sex. When I got up courage to tell Martin about the memory, he asked some questions, but I didn't feel he believed me. Actually, I don't think he wanted to believe this had happened to me. He didn't understand at all what was going on with me internally, or if he did, he didn't have any idea about how to respond to me. He argued that even if the memory was true, I was an adult now and should be able to get on with my life.

After I had disclosed the sexual abuse to Martin, I asked him to attend a session with me. Although I wanted to tell my husband what I was remembering, I felt it would be safer if Jerry were present. I also hoped Jerry could explain some things I was too uncomfortable with to talk about in detail. But Martin refused to go with me. At first I was devastated. I sobbed. I felt rejected. I felt terribly alone in dealing with the whole process. But I was also amazed—at the depth of my own emotions. In the past I would simply have disconnected from the situation and the hurt. This time, the pain was really bad for several hours, and then my mind kicked in:

*I now understand loneliness and people who experience it.*

*I understand how it feels to be rejected*

*Since I have made a conscious choice that my relationship with Martin is worth fighting for, I realize I am going to get hurt again and might have to give more than I receive at times. In spite of the pain, I am making a conscious decision to rise above my pain and think about a friend who is facing a difficult situation herself.*

## Re-Visioning Reality

For the first time, I could have some sort of balance with feelings and thinking in my life. I now had a glimmer of hope. In fact, I sort of liked the new me! I did, however, make a decision I have since regretted. I kept silent with Martin about my struggle, because his reaction made me feel unimportant to him. Looking back now, I can see that Martin was dealing with his own issues and had no idea how to enter into my struggle. I sometimes wonder how different my recovery period would have been, if I had chosen to keep him involved.

Despite Martin's vow not to talk to Jerry, he did join me on several occasions. Jerry kept telling me the problems were "ours" and not just "mine." After one such session, Jerry told me he thought Martin and I had a good marriage! He observed that we trusted each other, but neither of us trusted anyone outside of our relationship. He encouraged both Martin and me to cultivate good friendships outside our marriage, where we could be vulnerable. I gave Martin my formal permission to talk about our problems with a person of his choice.

Both my husband and our daughter, Janelle, reacted against the changes that were occurring in me, upsetting our normal life at home. They were shaken by my being more real. I was not as stoic and unemotional as I had been. I appeared to be confused and frustrated during this time, often depressed, despondent, and entirely disconnected from our family. They wanted the old me back. It made sense, so I tried to remain loving and understanding of their points of view.

That wasn't the whole story. Sometimes during my recovery, Martin truly tried to be more helpful and patient, a better listener and a more understanding spouse. At such times, he encouraged my therapy with Jerry and gave me good solid advice. One evening he pointed out that I must quit denying, or I would never get any healing. He was right, of course, but it was easier said than done. Still, his expression of belief in me gave me courage to keep working through the process. I know I did not make it easy for Martin to take an active role in my therapy. When I wanted to share something deeply personal with him, it often took me several days to prepare myself, and when I did talk to him, the process was painfully slow and the details were sparse. If I sensed he was at all bored or not interested, I would immediately stop talking and retreat back into my shell.

Marriage is hard work even under normal conditions. My particular problems and Martin's issues made our marriage even more difficult. Two things carried us through: (1) our individual commitment to God and (2) our commitment to each other. We certainly had some miserable years, but I can now attest that the good years have far outweighed the difficult ones.

# PART III

# The Overwhelming Struggle Within and Making Sense of It All

CHAPTER

# 8

# Making Sense of Struggle (JD)

*You're blessed when you get your inside world—your mind and heart—put right. Then you can see God in the outside world.*

–Matthew 5:8 (***The Message***)

Progress in going deeper enables a person to develop relationships with others, as CJ was beginning to do. In the past, she had kept herself somewhat isolated. As a pastor's wife, she guarded against "favoring" people in the congregation, and her trust level was very low. However, as she sensed the freedom that comes from being open, she started growing closer to a friend named Maggie. CJ learned she could find considerable relief by sharing what was inside. Then Maggie announced that she was moving to another state. CJ told me tearfully how scared and devastated she felt. Then she admitted to her husband how discouraged she was.

## Impact on Family and Daily Life

Martin had been hurt, disappointed and jealous during the first five or six years of CJ's therapy. The process was difficult for him. Like any of us, he suffered because his wife was unable to be affectionate and sexually responsive. His pain showed itself in frustration, and then anger, causing CJ to pull back and give even less affection and fewer sexual encounters. Martin was also disappointed that he could not help fix CJ's problem. As she began to disclose her feelings and the sexual abuse in her background, he had trouble relating and setting his own feelings aside. When her closest friend left town, he empathized a bit with her sadness, but he wanted to blurt out "Now maybe you'll talk to ME more."

I recognized the marital dynamics here. Over the years, I have sometimes been jealous of my wife's friends and relationships, especially when we are not doing well in our marriage. Of course I have wanted her to seek my counsel; after all, I am a professional counselor. However, often when I attempt to fix her situation or advise her, my input isn't well received. Allegra wants me to listen and reflect back her feelings and thoughts. She wants an empathetic ear, not advice. Furthermore, she doesn't need me to bring up my own feelings. She wants me to remain somewhat detached from my own stuff and listen like a good friend. This is why CJ could more easily open up to her friend, who didn't feel inadequate if she didn't have an answer or couldn't fix the problem.

You can see that the spouses of sexually abused partners are in a very difficult and helpless position. It's likely that they will not get their sexual and affection needs met for a long time, maybe never. Marriages do fall apart in these circumstances, but Martin and CJ kept struggling forward, hoping through trial and error, for improvement. As my wife and I have learned to do in our marriage, I urged them to be as honest as possible and to intentionally communicate their feelings and perceptions. CJ and Martin truly loved each other, so their physical and emotional intimacy did increase over time. Honesty and communication are essential to intimacy, regardless of specific issues in a marriage (see Appendix A).

Life goes on normally while a person is in counseling, except that everyday events are magnified. CJ's parents came to stay for a two-week vacation. Her work was intensely demanding. The marriage continued to suffer. Saturday nights were the worst: a pastor is preoccupied, preparing for Sunday morning services. For CJ in the moment, "Everything was happening at once." At this same time, CJ's memories of childhood continued to reveal horrible and more extensive sexual abuse; her dreams or dreamlike thoughts pointed to her father as a main perpetrator..

CJ tried to keep the lid on the pressure cooker, but the stress made her feel that everything could explode at any minute. Martin noticed she was changing, telling her, *"You're not as closed…and you share your feelings more."* His affirmation felt good, but CJ still staggered under the stress. *"I don't trust myself, I am still dissociating, I'm mad at God, men can't be trusted and God is a man,"* she wrote. Her feelings about herself and men intensified as she continued to "duke it out" with Martin, God and me.

When her parents returned to their home, CJ admitted that she was totally exhausted, physically and emotionally. I suggested that she see a medical doctor who could prescribe an anti-depressant. She was very resistant. (Later on I discovered that she had been drugged through much of the satanic ritualistic abuse she had experienced.) In my clinical experience, medications can be great allies. They can assist clients to sleep better, take the edge off intensely depleting emotions, and restore sufficient energy for a person to continue counseling. Anyone who is tired, depleted, overwhelmed, and seriously depressed cannot think clearly. Overtaxed emotions can cause "crazy thinking" so that suicide may become an option for someone who has never considered taking her life. Combining medication with therapy can mean survival.

I was fearful about CJ's emotional state, but she continued to refuse medication. She firmly said, "I don't want to take it and Martin doesn't want me to take it." While I was attempting to convince her to use prescribed medication, her husband was pressuring her to avoid it. He had probably been hurt when his wife relied on my advice, and now he insisted, "We'll find out who you respect more, me or Jerry." When CJ finally saw a doctor, who prescribed 20 mg. of Prozac, I was relieved and grateful.

Another factor in CJ's therapy was participation in a new group for abuse survivors. All of them were encouraged to tell their story, but CJ resisted. "I don't want to," she insisted. These were her reasons:

- I don't want to expose myself that much.
- I don't want to feel the emotions.
- When I tell my story, it becomes more real.
- I don't want to hear anybody else's story, because it makes me relate.
- I become embarrassed about blanking out—therefore I can't maintain control.

But because CJ was determined "not to let me down" and wanted to "get past this," she did follow the protocol and faithfully attended the group meetings.

As the group facilitated her expression of feelings, CJ's time in therapy and her at-home journaling surfaced her "worst memory yet." Although the memory was incomplete, just glimpsing the appalling encounter caused CJ to cry uncontrollably. Somehow there had been a knife, three males, and sexual abuse. She said that being stuck in the chaos was probably worse than remembering fully. I suggested that she tell me about the incident in the first person, present tense. This would help her to remember details and the connected emotions. Very bravely, she did as I suggested. Please note that I was suggesting, asking, encouraging, challenging, facilitating—but never insisting. For her recovery and autonomy, CJ needed to choose for herself, not be forced or coerced a second time.

So she remembered, speaking in the first person and in the present tense. Details and emotions came pouring out. I realized she was having an abreaction—she was experiencing the memory in the here and now. She was feeling massive emotion, fear, and shame. Afterwards, CJ confessed that she had been physically hurting herself, mostly by cutting and scratching. When psychological pain is too intense, the pain feels stuck inside, and a person often resorts to physical self-injury. It gives some relief to the inner pain, or may work as self- punishment, like doing penance. Even though her newly self-inflicted wounds were superficial, her behavior still frightened CJ and me, as I realized how much pain she was in. Only in re-living the memory could she gain relief and begin to assign it to the past where it belonged.

CJ shared this memory with her husband and reported that he had believed her. She felt closer to him, and he reminded her that her past unwillingness to share had caused him to feel shut out and added to his own feelings of rejection. This was another step toward increased intimacy between them. CJ was aware of the support she was getting from the group, her husband, and me, and she was grateful. However, her overriding feeling was intense shame. She was not yet angry with her perpetrators. My hope was that she would soon put the anger where it belonged rather than taking it out on herself. Anger is very motivating. Shame is not.

## Dealing with Shame

When we feel shame, we sense that we don't measure up; our gut says we are unacceptable, never deserving, unworthy, incomplete. Rarely is shame based on reality. Instead it usually comes from moralizing, comparing and seeking approval. We discount our positives, magnify our flaws, judge ourselves by unidentified ideals, and attack our character rather than the problem. CJ was immobilized by her shame.

We are taught to shame ourselves. Often we hear from our teachers, parents, pastors and others that we "should be ashamed." If our peers tease us, our faces will get red, and we feel embarrassed and then ashamed. Let's recognize that shame has some value. "Good" shame can warn us of danger and help us keep our standards, stay in touch with who we really are, manage our passions, and be more discerning. Such awareness is generally objective and reasonable. When shame becomes destructive, however, it imprisons us. We feel less than human, perverted, and in every way unworthy. One of the greatest challenges for people who have been abused, and "kept in their place," is to get beyond their disappointment in themselves.

## Acceptance: The Cure for Shame

Although CJ was beginning to see the self-defeating power of her shame, she could not independently escape it. She needed to sense that she was acceptable, complete, and whole (even though imperfect)—but she had been used, and blamed for her abuse, in effect condemned and rejected by her parents and grandparents. Lewis Smedes suggests that the underlying dynamic of shame is fear of rejection. The fear of non-acceptance and rejection is perhaps the most terrifying of all fears. In our therapeutic relationship, CJ gradually came to believe that I accepted her. Even though she still felt unacceptable, she saw that her friends, her husband and I cared for her. Now as she shared intimate, "shameful" experiences with us, she understood that we would not despise her. The cure for shame is acceptance. Rejection increases it. Not all behavior is acceptable, but all people need and deserve acceptance. After all, we are made in the image of God. And CJ was beginning to understand how much God loved and accepted her, after all.

We know how shame sticks when we have been rejected, blamed, or abused by our parents. I've been a grown man for a long time, and I know that my wife, my friends, my children and my God all accept me—but to this day, I still hear my Dad's criticism and rejection of me as a child. The way I "parent" myself continues the way my father parented me. I tried to help CJ recognize the way she constantly parented herself via shame. She could not accept herself as she was, and neither could the fragmented memories/personalities she was remembering. There was war within her, preventing self-acceptance and peace, Continual shaming between parts of herself blocked her growth.

The memories kept coming: ten more concerning her father, three involving grandparents, and some with her sister. Recalling these events would make CJ emotionally sick which would bring on physical sickness. To CJ's knowledge her sister has no recall of the abuse, but had been "emotionally unstable most of her life." It seemed that the sister had responded to the abuse by marrying a controlling, quietly dominating man much like her father. CJ believed her sister was also much like their father—very emotional, over-reactive and unreasonable.

After several years of marriage, the sister divorced, became less responsible, and took on a victim role, virtually opposite to CJ. Her dissociative style was to deny, ignore, and make others responsible for her unhappy life. CJ has maintained contact with her sister, helped her out repeatedly, and offered opportunities to talk about the past. However, her sister has been unappreciative. She contacts CJ only when she wants something and is unwilling even to acknowledge their past.

CJ continued her lonely journey into the past. She did not always give me details of the abuse, but when she did, it was extremely painful for me to listen. She recalled sacrifices of animals, blood, rapes, difficulty breathing, physical torture along with emotional and sexual battering, from her very early childhood and continuing through her teen years. Only when she married and left the house did the abuse stop.

Three fourths of the way through this year in therapy, CJ said, "The pressure is too great." She had begun "shutting down big time" and purposely forgetting dreams because "everything has been too much too fast." Memories often surfaced in my office because she couldn't let herself deal with the past while she was at work. Of course she needed to concentrate on her job, but she also needed the workplace to escape from her inner conflict, to have a normal life. For a while, then, CJ gave more attention to her job and less to her past. A person in therapy can only work so hard for so long. When energy runs out, there must be periods of easing up, stepping back, regrouping.

It was during a late summer session that CJ said, *"I want to be free, live my life, not be bogged down, trust myself, God and others, I want a healthy wholesome relationship with my husband."* I saw that now she was clarifying what she did want rather than what she didn't. This was permission for me to push forward again. She still seemed to be bottling up too much inside, so I asked her to stop "editing" what needed to come out of her. She dragged her feet, afraid that I would be disgusted and reject her. If I rejected her, who would she turn to? But I reminded CJ that my track record should speak for itself. In our times together, I had often shared personal experiences that were embarrassing; I, too, had fears of rejection. However, we agreed that we'd set a pattern: if I trusted her, she would in turn trust me more. To go forward now, she'd have to risk a deeper trust in me.

Out came a very detailed memory—her grandfather in a robe, over her, hurting her, rag in her mouth, feelings of not being able to breathe. A cat, her cat…It is not appropriate for me to share further details, nor would it be of help to the reader. The memories were appalling. I have to admit that human inhumanity is beyond description and logic. Awful as this process was, CJ began to see that until she released her memories in the present, she would still be hooked to the past. She mourned that she "felt fragmented," and she wanted to "feel whole."

Now CJ wondered out loud, "Where was God in all this?" As a Christian she was deeply disturbed to reflect, "The sacrifice of His Son and His blood was not any different from all the ritual killings." Such questions, such reactions are healthy natural outcomes of facing mistreatment which has been denied. Another client of mine was unable to participate in Christian communion, because the imagery of "the body and blood of Jesus" was too close to her experience with satanic ritualistic abuse. CJ could now be very angry with God: "I'm tired of performing, I haven't had devotions and I don't feel guilty about it either, I can only pray for others, not myself, right now I'm apathetic toward God." In fact at times she wanted Him out of her life. From my point of view, what she was thinking and saying about God was healthy. What DOES a good God have to do with evil? I reminded CJ that most of the saints in the Bible had the same thoughts, feelings and questions. It was progress that at last she was getting angry with *someone*. I promised her that God could handle her anger.

CJ canceled her yearly gynecology exam. With all the sexual memories she was having, we both thought it advisable for her to wait. I was glad that she was not pressuring herself, and suggested that she hold off for several months. I also knew that she would eventually go, to care for her own health, because she is responsible, loyal and a person of her word.

I continued to encourage her to share the discoveries she was making with her husband. With fear and trepidation she did, and was rewarded by his empathetic ear and some disclosures of his own. Even though their game continued—"Tell me, don't tell me" and "I want to tell you but I don't"—they were finding that the rewards of transparency far outweighed the liabilities. CJ's desire for a closer relationship with her husband was slowly being realized. It was also going to be harshly tested.

That Halloween season evoked many horrible experiences for CJ. Memories of her past included real bonfires, sacrifices, the smell of burnt flesh, cutting, full moon rituals, and hooded people. Halloween costumes and decorations didn't just remind her, they re-created sensations and brought out even more memories. CJ was nearly overcome. She described her reaction, "*I had a hard time coming back* [into the counseling session] *because it felt like it was happening right now.*" She was experiencing flashbacks. As I wrote earlier, these are a kind of arrested emotional memory. The memory is retained, and might even have been reported, but the accompanying emotions have not been felt. The longer the delay in experiencing feelings, the more difficult it is to recall them, and the more intense they are. Experiencing the memory in the "here and now" is called an abreaction. The event CJ was remembering had happened 25 years ago, but the feelings were happening in the present. She was reduced emotionally to the age she had been when the abuse happened.

CJ saw life as disheveled and out of control. It "feels like towels that are thrown into the closet but not folded," she complained, and Martin added,

"It feels like a fire I can't stop." He too emotionally sensed that everything was unmanageable. However, in spite of all the confusion and struggle, they felt closer to each other and were doing better as a couple. Neither of them took what was happening personally. They were not finding fault or blaming; instead, they were beginning to differentiate their "personal" stuff from "their marital" stuff.

The Christmas season arrived, making pastors' lives even busier. Children's programs, music, cantatas, sermon preparation, parties, presents and all the other holiday activities added to stress levels for both CJ and Martin, but also brought some diversion.

Nevertheless, CJ's horrible memories kept coming, now one concerning a "baby sacrifice." This became a turning point. It was too hard for her to tell me in person.

CJ wrote and mailed me this letter approximately four years into her therapy.

> *Jerry, Thank you for being so willing to help me. I think I do trust you, but sometimes I'm not totally convinced. You've never given me reason not to trust you—it's just me. I want to be whole. I would like to recapture myself. But I'm afraid. I know I must make responsible decisions in order to work toward being whole. I know I must be very strong and bold even when I feel very wimpy. I must try hard to accept myself—all of the parts of me, whether I like or trust them or not. I know I must acknowledge them and the safest place to acknowledge them is with you—of that I have no doubt. You said your intent was not to hurt any of us, just to understand us and reason with us. So I shouldn't be afraid to name them. Yet I feel that I'm surrendering somehow. Even though I don't trust and/or like some of them, I feel the need to protect the whole. It's like, if one of them is exposed, then we all crumble. When probably the exact opposite is true, if exposed, we all live or in a healthier way. When you've asked for names, I've always cringed and felt like I'm shrinking/shriveling up. Yet I know there is a need/desire in a couple of them to talk to you. Some I think want to tell you off, but others want you (need you) to be their ally, like you've been to me. I don't actually know them all that well, yet for whatever reason, I seem to be able to distinguish them from each other, though not always. I'm going to try and name some of them in this letter, because it seems easier to do it that way, I think. But I hold you to your word about not telling anyone else. I would also like you to destroy*

*this letter after you read it, please (obviously I did not comply with her request). I don't have any idea where their names come from. I don't remember thinking about their names, they just were and I knew who they were. I only know of four of them, yet for some reason there seems like there's at least one more that I can't identify now. I hate it sometimes when they talk—yet on the other hand it's a relief to me. There's one of them that takes care of me when I can't do it anymore. In fact, she tries to take care of everyone. She's good. She never trusts anyone. And she's smart and wise. She talks all of us through things. She's like a good, faithful mother. She's always calm and doesn't get her feathers ruffled very often, unless we get hurt and then she tries to protect us. She seems neither young nor old. But she is an adult, I know. She wants to talk with you. She's interested but on guard. She thinks you could be trusted, but she needs to check it out. However, she is upset at you because you probed too much in your office. That wasn't her in your office yesterday, but she heard what went on. Her name is Anita. Strange name—I don't know anyone else by that name, but it fits her. Even though I told you she wants to talk to you, she may not, I don't know. But I want her to talk with you. I think it will be okay. She's rational. She's a thinker. She's safe to be with. She's a helper. She almost always knows how to deal with a situation. I trust her. I wanted to give you more names, but I don't think I can. It's not safe yet. They don't want to talk, I know. They don't like you. You're a threat. One of them hates me too. I know. She's told me she wants me to die She wants to get rid of me. She thinks I'm stupid and I mess things up. She does okay with Anita though. Anita is the glue for all of us, I think. The hateful one is often irrational. She doesn't listen to reason and truth. She feels more than she thinks. I hate her as much as she hates me—but more than that, I'm afraid of her. She's unpredictable, not to be trusted. Yet she can be very persuasive. I try not to listen to her. She's talked to me before though—several times in my journal. She just took over my pen and of course she wrote highly emotional, irrational things. She's loud and I go far away when she does come out. I can't tell you her name now. Will you please go carefully with the information I've given you? I must think you will, or I wouldn't have told you. I hope I can be strong enough to mail this letter. I want to be ME, Jerry. Will you help me? CJ*

A part of CJ had shown herself but wouldn't talk. It was an "alter," verifying what I had been suspecting. Now CJ and I both realized that she was a MPD/DID.

## Human Awareness Is Fragmented

Each one of us is a conglomeration of parts and pieces. When these parts of us are in conflict and unwilling to cooperate, we will feel split, be torn by divided loyalties, and wonder which part to believe. We often view different aspects of ourselves as either good or bad. For example, one part of me loves to eat (often unhealthy food) and another part wishes to stay slim and trim. It's easy to label the part that loves eating junk food "bad" and the one who exercises "good." Such moral labeling, whether applied to our inner selves, a political party, a religion, our partner, or an opponent, is always unproductive and in some cases, dangerous. When we identify something simply as "good" and its opposite as "bad," we narrow ourselves. We polarize, limit understanding, defend, and argue, losing the opportunity for these parts to dialogue. If we can't dialogue, we can't cooperate. If we can't dialogue and cooperate within, the "enemy" will be in our own household. Jesus said, "A house divided against itself can't stand." We are in danger of falling apart if we don't listen and empathize with the various parts of ourselves..

Notice, we don't have to agree with every vantage point. We need to empathize, not analyze. When we analyze, we dissect, look for a logical explanation, and tell ourselves how things "should" be. When we empathize, on the other hand, we listen to all of the parts' perspectives, avoid judging, and reflect back to each part what we understand them to be saying. Our motto should be, "We don't debate; we relate." Sometimes I experience my own inner forum as one big argument. Part of me tries to convince myself (or a particular part of myself) that I'm wrong, bad, screwed up, or stupid. I try to parent a child part in me, without hearing what the child part has to say, or what the parent needs.

A part of CJ resisted and fought valiantly against taking medication, because that part had been drugged many times unknowingly. Since that's when much of the SRA (Satanic Ritualistic Abuse) took place, this part of CJ was arguing, "If I don't take drugs, then I won't be abused." The part of her that needed medication was overwhelmed, tired and suicidal. For this part of CJ, drugs might be the only way to get rest and stay alive. CJ had to get these two parts to listen to and dialogue with each other. It was matter of life or death.

For those who are deeply divided within, peace and contentment are impossible. We cannot be congruent when parts of ourselves are not in agreement with each other or with reality. A person in this situation is a house divided. To lay the groundwork for cooperation, one must acknowledge the various parts, and understand their roles, feelings and perceptions. We have to trust that each part of ourselves is well intentioned, acts out of the need for survival, and wants to be understood. To achieve congruence within and without, CJ would now need to identify the parts of herself, seek to understand their perspectives, and build a spirit of cooperation among them.

## For Further Information

Smedes, Lewis, ***Shame and Grace: Healing the Shame We Don't Deserve***, Harper Collins, 1993.

Gottman, John, ***Why Marriages Succeed or Fail…and How You Can Make Yours Last***, Simon and Schuster, 1994.

Allender, Dan, ***The Wounded Heart***, NAV Press, 1990.

CHAPTER

# 9

# Worse Yet (CJ)

*The collapse of illusions always results in depression.*
–Alexander Lowen, ***Bioenergetics***

## Hopelessness and Suicidal Thinking

After my first disturbing memory, when I began to believe myself, the memories started coming fast and furiously. Sickening, terrifying, overwhelming. My energy was sapped. I could barely keep going in my challenging full-time job, or in my duties as a pastor's wife and a mother. Some days I used all of my energy just to drag myself out of bed. Eventually this regimen wore down my body, mind and spirit. My pain was so great, I seriously considered ending my life. Never had I even imagined feeling terrible enough to kill myself. But now I felt hopeless. The harder I had worked, the worse my life had become. I could not pull myself out of this pit, not with continued therapy, not with prayer, not even with help from friends and my family.

I kept journaling, trying to express my despair.

July 20

*The last few days have been very difficult. Yesterday I wanted to do myself in. I got out some over-the-counter pain-killers and counted them twice, then put them back into the bottle. I wasn't sure there were enough to work. I called Jerry and he asked me to come in for a session. I didn't want to, but I went anyway. I'm not exactly sure what's happening to me—except I know I'm in a self-destruct mode. I hate myself and blame myself for what happened. After I talked to Jerry, I decided pills are not the answer. It's not a sure thing. For some reason I'm obsessed with destroying myself. I've thought of a couple ways to take care of things—but I've not fully thought them through. I want to devise a plan and have it ready. Even as I sit here writing, I'm amazed at how calm and calculated I can be about the whole matter of ending my life. I'm not sure I want to do this. I just feel more in control if I have a plan in place. I feel angry when people tell me what to do—no that's not exactly right. I feel rebellious whenever I feel like someone is controlling me. I feel a rebellious spirit rise up inside me. It feels good to resist. I hate myself. I'm dirty and ugly and bad. I would like to hurt myself. It feels good to make myself feel hungry and not allow myself to eat, or to hurt myself in other ways. It feels real good. I find I'm also doing other things like walking outside later at night than normal, and thinking about turning out in front of an oncoming car. This should be freaking me out, but I have very little concern about it. I'm not sure if that's because I'm numb or because I know I'll never do anything like that, or if I just don't care. Sometimes I need to call Jerry but I don't want to bother him, especially at home. I hate doing that. I feel I'm infringing on his limited free time. I wish I could just talk to him for 15 minutes. I need a sanity check.*

July 23

*I want to quit. Where is my eternal optimism? I'm down and depressed, and I don't want any more memories. I just want to heal—now. I don't want to feel like a victim. I don't want to feel anger. I don't want to love my inner child. I just want to quit yet I feel forced to go on because I'm a responsible person (or try to be). I want to do the right thing—all the time. I want to always finish what I start. I always do what I should do. Oh, shut up! I don't want to hear myself any more.*

July 25

*I JUST WANT TO GO TO BED FOREVER. Jerry called yesterday and made me promise to call if things got bad. I promised and lied, all in one breath. I only promised to make him feel better. I could care less about myself.*

August 4

*I'm really having trouble today. I want to hurt myself badly.*

August 10

*Weekends are not always good for me—too much time on my hands. When I go to the store I look at the sleep aids on the shelves and wonder how many would be enough. I have a morbid interest in that particular aisle in the store. I'm certain Satan is hard at work and I feel so weak. I feel so empty emotionally.*

August 12

*I wonder if I should give myself an ultimatum to either get rid of myself once and for all or to grab the bull by the horns and put all suicidal thoughts behind me? Maybe I want to hang on to those thoughts so I can get pity and attention? Or maybe it makes me feel powerful and in control to have that option available to me. I don't know, but I know those thoughts are morbid. They say the more you allow those thoughts to play in your mind, the easier it is to act on them. I don't know about that.*

August 25

*I know I shouldn't say it, but I do hate myself. I hate myself for taking the abuse without a word. I hate myself for covering it up for all these years. I hate myself for hurting Martin all these years. I hate myself a lot today. I know I shouldn't be saying such negative things, but it's what I feel. I would like to just starve myself to death. In fact, that's what I planned to do last night. I don't know if it will work. I thought about other methods. But this way gives me the option to change my mind if I decide to. The other ways don't give much choice once I act on them. I just want to be alone. I like being alone. Sometimes (much of the time) I don't do anything—I just sit in a chair and am sort of dead. No feeling—no thinking—just numb.*

August 28

*I feel so depressed and in despair yet cannot find a reason for it. Sometimes my entire body is like a huge pain and I writhe in agony without knowing why. What is my disease? The results of the sin and pain of incest? The lasting scars of incest?*

August 29

*I called Jerry to find out if he could tell me what is wrong with me. He wanted me to come in. He also wants me to consider going to the doctor for medication. I refused the latter, but did meet with him.*

September 1

*I've been sleeping a lot, partly because I've been taking some sleep aids. It's tempting to get drawn into using them more often to dull the pain, but so far I'm in control.*

September 2

*I had deep urges to take pills the last few days, but I only took the correct amount and refrained from taking any at all last night.*

September 3

*If I can't straighten things out pretty quickly, I will have to get a doctor's help. I really don't want to do that because of my pride and because I don't want any medical record of my craziness.*

September 4

*I want out of life. I don't care if that's weak and wimpy—I want out. Life is not joyful or peaceful. Life is turmoil and agony. I hate it. I don't want to be thankful. I don't want to live.*

September 5

*I'm very confused about everything. I'm on the verge of being very upset. I would like to take some pills. Yes, that sounds very comforting to me right now. I would like to just take one pill, just to feel better.*

September 12

*My session with Jerry was hard today. It was very negative. I didn't realize how depressed and hopeless I was. I hardly ate anything yesterday and I'm not hungry today. I don't want to eat anything anymore. I would like to die. I know it's selfish, but I want relief. There's a dark cloud that has completely enveloped me. I can't find my way out of it and I don't care if I do. Jerry said perhaps I need a new therapist. That hurt. Does that mean he's tired of dealing with me or that I'm an utterly hopeless case? He suggested a woman counselor. Am I hopeless? I don't know. Is he trying to get rid of me? That hurts, if he is.*

September 24

*Last night I started to feel anger for my abuser, but I quickly suppressed it. It scared me badly. I then started to turn my anger inward. I got all the pills I could find in the house and wanted to take them. The only thing that stopped me was the fact I was so weary and tired, I didn't know if I had enough pills to do it. I wanted to take the pills with me to work today.*

October 29

*All I think about is self-destruction—my only escape from life. I guess it sounds stupid, but I still feel drawn toward the idea. I'm tired of struggling with my marriage and this stupid incest and getting nowhere. I can hardly stand the thought that I was raped and by whom. I still feel I may have fabricated the past. I know suicide is a coward's way out, but who cares? I'm tired of living and struggling. I'm numb this morning. I think I scared Martin last night. He thought for a while I had taken pills or was going to. No, that wasn't my plan last night. I hate myself. I'm sorry, Lord, but I do. I just want to crawl into a hole and lie there until I die. I'd like to go to sleep forever. Yes, I know it's selfish, but I'm tired. Martin wanted me to promise I'd never do anything. No way would I promise that! I promised Martin for last night and today—no more. I want at least that much control over my life. Or is that giving control to Satan? Who knows? I'm too tired to think. I don't care what anyone thinks about me anymore.*

Through the next six months I teetered on the edge of self-destruction. At that time I was not aware how critical my situation was, but Jerry could tell. He began to talk with me about visiting my doctor and the possibility of taking antidepressants.

May 31

*I saw Jerry and we talked about antidepressants. He said I could very easily be chemically imbalanced and depressed and might need medication. He said medication could calm things down so we could really get to work on some of the core issues. I also talked with a friend who recently had started taking antidepressants. She said taking them had really helped her. I want to make responsible decisions for my family and myself. I don't want to have a negative effect on the lives of Martin, Janelle and my friends. I keep thinking I can control the depression myself (which I can't). Then I think I'm a failure as a Christian because I don't let God handle things for me. I guess I don't want to be labeled a crazy person. I have this gut feeling that if I don't get some help I'm going to crack. I'm also afraid that Martin will look down on me if I take medication, that he will think I'm weak.*

June 6

*I went to the library today and researched various antidepressants. The drugs both intrigue and scare me. I also checked out a book on depression. Some of the material encouraged antidepressant use but also emphasized diet and exercise. I attended a workshop at our health clinic. The speaker explained that with Post Traumatic Stress Disorder when someone experiences the original trauma, instead of the brain sending out appropriate chemicals in the brain, the signals were stopped and the experience was buried. With the onset of memories, the trauma is reopened and the chemicals are released as intensely as they would have at the time of the original trauma. Part of me says I'm at the end of my rope and need help. Another part says I should just start a rigidly healthy diet and rigorous exercise program. Yet that seems like an insurmountable feat for me right now. The health professional from the clinic said it was fairly normal for incest victims to use an antidepressant temporarily. What should I do?*

June 7

*I called my doctor a few days ago and she prescribed Prozac. I haven't started using it yet because I've felt pretty good, that is, until today. I'm nervous about using it. I need to be in control and I'm afraid the medication will take some of my control away.*

For several days I kept the Prozac in my possession without using it. As my depression worsened, I began taking the drug. I was so frightened of being drugged that (I now believe) my anxiety produced some phantom sensations. My husband and I went to a movie as we'd planned, and I felt weird throughout the show. My face felt swollen, and I kept checking my mirror to reassure myself that my head and face were not distorted with swelling. Several times during that day, I became very jittery and extremely anxious. I had to cognitively calm myself down, and decided I would take no more of the pills. Not until two years later, when my depression reached a greater intensity, did I use medication. The reality is that I went on and off antidepressants several times throughout my years of therapy. I would take the anti-depressants, feel better, then stop taking them. The cycle recurred several times.

In 1991, after approximately four years of working with Jerry, I became impatient with the slowness and cost of therapy. One of my girlfriends, to whom I had confided my abuse, invited me to join a women's group with her.

This would be a 12-week group, for women with sexual abuse in their past. Initially, I was not very open to attending. I was already feeling a little shaky about trusting my friend with my memories. Had I had been foolish to trust her? In a group with her, I'd have to further expose myself.

I took a big risk and signed up for a group, but I chose one where my friend was not a participant. I was nervous about going, but even more nervous about explaining my decision to Martin. Although he assented, he seemed to see the group as one more hopeless endeavor.

At that same time, my parents planned visit to us. I was really afraid to attend the group while they were at our home. Early on in my therapy, when the memories had begun to unfold, I'd decided that I would not confront my father about the abuse. At first, of course, I did not feel sure of myself. Heck, depending on the day, I might or might not believe myself! I did not want to make waves or threaten my entire family. Furthermore, I didn't think my father would admit to the abuse. It seemed that confrontation could help me only if my father admitted what he had done, and deep within, I knew he never would. Now I just wanted to keep myself under control and act "normal," so my parents wouldn't notice or worry about me during their visit.

That first night at the women's support group, I wanted to scream out, "I don't belong here!" What an awful reason to gather. But down deep in my heart, I knew I did belong. Underlining that truth, on the same day I started group, my parents arrived for their visit. It took everything I had to stay in control for the two weeks they were with us. Anxiety about attending the group kept me on the verge of panic, and it was exhausting to keep all of my memories and emotions stuffed down. I felt as though I was living between two worlds, trying to keep everything normal, stretched to near breaking.

While my parents were with us, I probed my mother for details of my early childhood. What she told me confirmed my own memories. Dad had worked nights much of the time my sister and I were growing up. Mom agreed that when my Dad became upset and emotional, he often didn't remember events very clearly. As for me, she had noticed that from 2-5 years old I was unhappy, very shy and not confident. She said I changed when I started school, becoming more confident and independent, but still staying mainly in my own little world. My mom had also learned that my sister remembered very little of her childhood. Dad had treated me differently than he had my sister, Mom told me. He had paid more attention to me and treated me better.

Several times during my parents' visit, I felt as though I was falling apart, into pieces, a broken person. In my distress, I met with Jerry, and told him I was completely out of sync. That wasn't true, he assured me: I was just being my real self, softer and more vulnerable. I couldn't see that as positive in any way. I felt runny inside, like jelly all melted and spilled out over the floor. All I could feel was dying, one part at a time. Jerry told me I was moving through the process of hurting, hating and finally healing. I was sick of the pain and longed to jump right to the healing. When my parents' visit finally ended, they seemed not to have noticed the turmoil going on in my life.

## Admitting the Truth

The women's group for sexually abused women wasn't as bad as I'd feared either. In fact, it actually opened the door for me to tell my daughter about my abuse. Janelle was about 15 years old at the time. I had carefully explained to her that it was a religious women's group. That statement wasn't really a lie, but it certainly did not explain the true focus of the group. However, she had overheard a conversation Martin had with Jerry and put two and two together. My daughter came to me, very upset because she felt I had deceived her. I spent over an hour talking, explaining and finally praying with her until she calmed down. Of course, she wanted to know the identity of my abuser, but I sidestepped her question by admitting only that the abuse involved a family member. Facing my husband and daughter was tense and difficult, but I felt a strange sense of relief. I didn't have to hide the truth from them any longer. I would have preferred a more nurturing reaction from Martin and Janelle, but I understood they needed time to work through this new information too. In fact, at my next session with Jerry, he told me I looked at peace and that he could actually see emotions spilling across my face.

Nevertheless, I really dreaded attending the women's group. If any of the members were absent, the session became more demanding because I had to participate more. I frequently attempted to hide my distress from the other group members, though sometimes I couldn't help showing it. I didn't want anyone to know the depth of my pain. I wanted to appear strong, not weak. I was obsessed with "looking" strong, or maybe I was just hoping to deny my memories. Often I felt stone cold, numb, the entire time. However, the conversations that transpired during group chinked away at my armor. At one meeting we were asked to describe our abusers. Although it hurt to listen to the others, it was even harder for me to verbalize my own story. Our facilitators told us to follow our inner person, our gut, but I didn't trust my gut. Heck, I didn't even know what my gut was! During one group, Cindy (named changed) shared about her uncle having oral sex with her. I didn't want to hear her talk; I wanted to cover my ears and hum. I was appalled at her story, because I could completely understand her memory and identify with it.

The group setting helped me to admit my abuse to the others. I could no longer keep denying the truth. I wrote in my journal on August 14, 1991:

> *I am an adult survivor of childhood sexual abuse. I WAS abused. When I was a child, I WAS sexually abused by different individuals. There, now I said it. I feel numb as I say it. I made a conscious decision to be honest. I'm telling myself—admitting to myself—that I was sexually abused. My innocence was stolen from me. My childhood, as God planned it, was taken from me. My perpetrators cheated me. I was sexually molested many times. I was not loved in an appropriate way. I was helpless and defenseless against my perpetrators. I chose to deny the truth for 35 years. I've lived a lie for 35 years. I want to live the truth now. I want the real me to be. I want to live life with all its flavor. I choose to accept the hurt and pain, grief and loss, joy and happiness, peace and passion, as it comes into my life. I will not use any armor to deflect life. I will acknowledge my feelings. I will use my intelligence to understand my feelings. I will seek God for guidance and strength in my life. I had a rotten childhood, but I'm here today to live a fulfilled life. I'm choosing this course of action for myself—I am not being forced into it. The sexual abuse is finished—I will now conquer its effects. I will work the process so that the sexual abuse will not continue to control my life and make me feel dead inside. I know I will feel depressed and feel hurt and pain, but I refuse to sit in my own crap and wallow in it. I will survive this. I will begin a new relationship with God, one based on truth, honesty, and integrity.*

The first women's group I attended lasted 12 weeks. In the eleventh week we were asked to say how the group had affected us and to point out any differences we saw in ourselves since beginning the group. At that meeting, I admitted I was a pastor's wife, something I had intentionally hidden from the others. I also honestly admitted where I struggled the most—with denial. I acknowledged my feelings more in that meeting than I had ever done in a public setting. I actually admitted I felt weak, which was a huge disclosure for me. Afterwards, I was affirmed and validated by the other group members. This meeting helped me feel okay about where I was in my process. I also was helped by hearing about other women and their growth and healing. Because I believed I had made real progress, I promptly signed up for another 12 weeks.

To my surprise, I was sad during the last week of group. I realized I would miss the women who were not returning for the next session. Now I had to grieve the loss, another new experience for me. I went on to attend several more 12-week sessions of the sexual abuse survivor group. They were never easy. At the end of one session, the facilitators asked us to prepare to tell our stories at the next meeting. We could choose simply to give the facts, but it would be necessary to be *present* when we were talking (or in other words, to dissociate as little as possible.) I freaked out. After group, I approached one of the facilitators, crying, pleading that I was too afraid. She responded that I could just try. Later I took my dilemma to Jerry. The experience would be good for me, he said. It would help me to associate instead of dissociate. I was dreading not only sharing my own story, but listening to the painful stories of the other group members as well. In fact, it was difficult. Yet I found it liberating to speak, and I felt great affirmation and support from the other members of the group.

At another group session, the facilitators introduced us to working with our inner child. My task was to envision my little girl (the child I had been before the abuse) by a quiet stream. My present grownup self was to go to her, hold her hand, and tell her something. Then I had to picture the same little girl after the abuse and say something to her. After that I was supposed to jump into the stream and play in the water with her. At first, I found that I couldn't look at the little girl at all; she ended up walking behind me. I told her I didn't know who she was. I couldn't look at the older girl either. She also walked a short distance behind me. I could not say anything to her. Finally we stood on the side of the stream, but we didn't jump in.

After that particular group exercise, I worked on my inner child on my own. I envisioned her standing outside a door, not saying a word, just looking extremely sad. Then Jesus was standing beside her. He took her hand, and held it out to me to hold. I saw that I needed to continue to face my child within, but I was very apathetic toward her. I didn't love her. Most times I didn't hate her; I just didn't care about her.

Another group session required us to bring pictures of ourselves when we were children. I had no such pictures, so I called my Mom. Strangely enough, she seemed reluctant to send any. When I insisted, she sent one picture of me, at age five, with my older sister. I looked older than my years, unsmiling and holding my sister's hand. Both our faces had serious expressions. Our group assignment was to show the pictures to the others and tell what the little girl wanted to say. For my turn, I said I didn't know what she wanted to say, because I didn't know her, but if I had to guess, I thought she'd say she was confused and didn't understand.

## Depression and Recovery

Later I wrote the following story about my inner child:

> *There once was a little girl. She was happy and innocent until she was snared in a trap. She was pushed into danger. She was too young and too innocent to see the danger. She didn't even know what she needed to protect herself from. She was small and ugly; however she did have pretty eyes that hid the depth of her knowledge and pain. Her hands had been placed in areas they shouldn't have been for many, many years. Her innocence was ripped away from her by cruel, uncaring adults. She was lied to, physically hurt, violated, abused, taken advantage of, and many more horrendous things. She was used, and used and used again and again by sick adults. But her mind kept its sanity. I'm sorry the little girl was hurt so much, that no one protected her. She is still ugly and dirty to me. She took part (I guess willingly) in some terrible, sinful things. People say it's not her fault, but she seems sinful and beyond the redemptive power of God. I think she cavorted with the devil and his people. Can she ever be forgiven? Some say she doesn't need to be forgiven because what happened wasn't her fault, her sin. But she feels guilty and like a doomed sinner. I believe God sits in judgment of my sins and me. I'm that little, ugly girl. She's fat and has pimples and only her cat loves her. Only her cat doesn't take from her.*

My increasing awareness took great effort and lots of help. When Jerry would leave town on business or vacation, things would get tough. I would feel alone and fly out of control, so I attempted to plan for the times when he would be gone. This is one of the plans I made:

> *I've decided that in order to feel safe while Jerry is away, I need to formulate a written plan of action in case things get bad.I need a 1-2-3 list of things to do and people whom I can call just to talk to me if I need them to. I will keep that list with me at all times and probably never have to use it or at least I hope I won't.*
>
> *Plan of Action*
>
> 1. *Journal*
> 2. *Take a nap/go to bed early/take a walk*

3. *Call Linda, or*
4. *Call Cindy, or*
5. *Call June or*
6. *Talk to Martin or*
7. *Call one of the group facilitators or*
8. *Go shopping, buy a cake and eat the whole thing! (I like this one. I think I should move it up in the list!)*
9. *Phone the on-call therapist Jerry recommends*

*Hopefully this plan of action will take away some of my anxiousness. It's okay if things get out of control for a while—it wouldn't be the end of the world. I could handle it. I've handled it before and I can handle it again. I might fall apart in the next few weeks. But falling apart doesn't mean I can't handle things, it just means that things seem unmanageable. Time usually defuses the situation. I will try to keep communications open within myself so that I can be alert to potential problem situations/memories, etc. I will also try to keep outside activities to a minimum so I won't feel so overwhelmed and stressed out. One thing I will try hard NOT to do is ignore my memories. I will try to face things head on and deal with them. The tough things can always be broken down into small pieces that are tolerable to deal with. I can break them into as many small pieces as I need to in order to feel safe.*

My peers in the groups I attended provided constant reality checks for me, and the facilitators guided us all on our passage through acknowledging and living with our past abuse. The support groups I attended throughout my journey were extremely important; especially the groups I participated in after I began to actually acknowledge the many different voices within me.

CHAPTER

# 10

# Maintaining a Cool Head and Warm Heart (JD)

*....sometimes our humble hearts can help us with our proud minds.*

–I Corinthians 8:1 (***The Message***)

(Early in this chapter I refer to CJ's "alters" or parts within before CJ writes about them in chapter 11, but I include these references here to explain my need to figure out a way to maintain "a cool head and a warm heart.")

During these past months, I have been re-reading CJ's case file, recalling our time in counseling, and processing what really happened during those ten years. As I attempt to write truthfully, in a non-clinical manner, I am flooded by my own feelings: insecurity, wonder, fear, and inadequacy. In some ways, this is like going through a form of PTSD myself.

## Work of the Therapist/Companion

While I was working with CJ, I was also seeing another client (June, not her real name). They had some similar issues, but made different demands on my time and expertise. Some general counseling strategies applied, yet other areas required a customized approach. I found myself waking up in the middle of the night, unable to sleep, wondering if I could be the kind of counselor these people needed. I would pray, make notes, review helpful reading material, and worry about what I had said and how I had said it. My supervising psychologist, Dr. James Oraker, gave me some essential perspective. Not only did he show confidence in me, but he also talked about strategies and affirmed my concerns. I needed someone, appropriately detached from the intense clinical situation, who could listen to my feelings and perceptions, and help me make wise decisions.

At one point I became so overwhelmed that Dr. Oraker advised me not to take on any more DID clients. Chastened, I interpreted his words to mean that I had bitten off more than I could chew. Later he clarified things—he wasn't implying that I couldn't do a good job, but that dealing with two clients struggling with the same intense issues was enough. He reassured me that I was indeed capable and that my style was just what June and CJ needed. In my ongoing therapeutic relationship with them, I did have times when I literally sensed God's direction—as if I was in a "zone," speaking and acting with self-assurance and confidence.

This vacillation between confidence and self-doubt ("Do I really know what I am doing?") has continued throughout my career. I do not enjoy this tension, but it has kept me balanced, humbled, and dependent upon God, especially in crisis. One of my hardest times was when CJ was cutting herself and considering suicide. We are all prone to self-destructive behavior when we are overwhelmed, stressed, hurting, angry, lacking self-confidence and tired of coping with life. Rather than confront the problem in the beginning, we put off looking for a solution and hope for a quick fix. We avoid facing reality and self-medicate with our "drug" of choice: alcohol or drugs (prescription or illegal), overeating or eating unhealthy food, driving recklessly, not sleeping, spending money, taking poorly calculated chances, and other dangerous behaviors. We will use whatever diversion works to rid ourselves of unwanted pain and fear, even when we know that reality will catch up with us and that over time we'll make matters worse.

In CJ's situation there could be no "quick fix" because the fragments of her self were in opposition. Over time we found that many of her parts (or alters) were very young and immature, overwhelmed and discouraged. For example, Jill, one of CJ's alters, would become overwrought with despairing emotions and regress to wounding herself physically just to gain some relief. The problem was that it was CJ's body that she was maiming. Child alters and not CJ, believed that suicide would be a way out. There were moments when nobody could control them. Fortunately, as we will see, others of CJ's alters would inform me about what was going on.

Another dynamic at work was that the endangered alters needed some sort of protection; therefore, CJ would keep knives at hand. For a long time, unbeknown to her husband, she kept a butcher knife under her mattress. She would hide knives at work and in her car. She even gave me several she had been carrying in her purse. All these knives were too readily available when Jill (one of the alters) became upset and out of control. At times CJ would wake up in the middle of the night, feeling the pain where Jill had been cutting. This really frightened CJ, the other alters, and me. Even more unnerving to me than the cutting was the possibility that CJ could succeed in committing suicide. I've seen that great crises provide great danger but also offer great opportunity. The very real danger now was that Jill or some other alter would kill CJ. But I still believed in the possibility of limitless discovery and personal growth.

Later on in therapy we discovered an alter named "Knifer" who had been indoctrinated by satanic cult members. She was trained to keep a specific number of knives, in exact order according to size and function. Because "Knifer" was very obsessive and compulsive, reasoning with her did not work. Other alters had been indoctrinated to kill CJ if she ever disclosed satanic, ritualistic secrets to outsiders. Yes, if they killed CJ, they would also kill themselves and the others, but they were not rational. Coping with all the alters and their memories brought CJ to the point of collapse, and pushed her counselor to the limit as well.

## Detachment and Responsibility

Often my clients or acquaintances ask how I have managed to stay in the counseling profession so long. It's been more than 37 years—50 if I count my stint with the State of Colorado. Friends puzzle over my ability to sleep at night when I listen to so much pain. How do I maintain my own sanity and my ability to care? As I attempt to write from my heart about CJ, I want to be open and transparent and to offer our readers some attitudes, values and strategies that have helped. First, I continue as a therapist because I love my work and feel "called" to it. Beyond that, I have learned over the years to practice three sustaining mentalities. I constantly practice being appropriately detached, being "responsible TO and not FOR others," and being assertive.

## Appropriate Detachment

So far, this account has discussed detachment and being dissociative (DID) as detrimental, a disorder. For her first two or three years in therapy, CJ was detached and dissociative, cut off from her past and from all the internal parts (alters) of herself. Refusing to accept the alters or acknowledge that they were parts of herself, she could not grow emotionally. However, another kind of detachment, her strong intellect and capacity for objectivity, did eventually help her see the overall picture. Detachment can be detrimental when used as a defense mechanism, but positive when used appropriately.

Appropriate detachment is necessary in order for a person to gain a comprehensive perspective on life. The scientific method requires scientists to detach from their preconceived ideas in order to gather data, research objectively, join little pieces of a puzzle, and arrive at valid conclusions. Typically, scientists do not allow their emotions and personal bias to prevent them from discovering and verifying the truth.

In the realm of psychology, detachment is deemed inappropriate when a person suppresses the past, refuses personal responsibility, denies the truth, and is unable to feel. Appropriate detachment, on the other hand, helps us see what is going on around and inside us with a degree of objectivity.

Destructive detachment causes us to feel like victims. We believe nothing can be done about our situation, we have no choices, and we let others control us. In such detachment we abdicate our responsibility to change. While CJ was a child, her multiplicity worked to protect her. Detaching from all the parts, their memories and their feelings enabled her to survive the trauma of abuse. She was able to maintain her sanity, but after she became an adult, she suffered relationally. Now being detached/dissociative was counter-productive.

Appropriate detachment allows us to separate, disengage, and withdraw to a place where we can think through our reactions and emotions. When we are somewhat disconnected from an immediate problem, we can gain greater objectivity, seeing beyond our prejudices. Admittedly we become a bit aloof, but at the same time we are less enslaved by our biases. We discern more effectively when we are appropriately detached.

Discernment is the ability to distinguish one perspective from another. A detective's task is objectivity, remaining detached enough to recognize the clues that lead to solving the mystery. Discerning people have "the quality of being able to grasp and comprehend what is observable," they can discriminate, distinguish, and differentiate, using sound judgment. Likewise, discerning folks are both perceptive and insightful in their observations. They have the ability to see "into a situation" and intuitively sense "the inner nature of things."

It has been popular in some Christian groups to claim the "gift of discernment." I have become somewhat leery of this common church language. Such self-appointed discerners are often not as insightful as they think. Truly discerning people are humble: they observe and say little, seldom admit they are insightful, and lay no claims to having a corner on the truth. Capable discerners ask excellent questions, reflect back the responses to those questions, and are slow to impugn motives. People who vaunt their own "gift of discernment" are often quick to judge and correct others, and will even tell people what their motives are. I have to say that it's hard enough to discern our own motives, let alone another's!

Appropriate detachment enables a capable counselor, friend, or spouse to discern what the real issues are. When we are "lovingly detached," we will attempt to do the loving thing for all concerned. Counselors and friends lovingly detach by being empathetic: they listen to what is being said, and they reflect back what they intuitively see and hear. If the speaker validates that they feel understood, truth has been discerned.

By being appropriately detached, we are able to maintain a loving, non-prejudiced, open, empathetic heart. It is easier to be gracious and merciful when we do not take what is being said personally. We understand at times that others do make **US** the problem; they can blame, criticize, argue and complain, but we in our objectivity can know "we are not the one who is causing the problem." In this relational mode, we are outside our feelings and perceptions, we set aside our expectations and personal desires, and we demonstrate understanding by our demeanor and tone. We take IN the speaker's emotions without taking them ON. This is loving detachment, a kind of "sanctified indifference" which creates a therapeutic environment for the counselee. No small order, but this is ultimately our goal in all relationships, and this was my aim in therapy with CJ.

## Responsible to, Not for, Others

A simplified and practical phrase sums up the "how" of this loving detachment. I heard it first in the early years of my career. I wrote this sage piece of advice on a 3x5 card and attached it to my bathroom mirror so that each time I shaved and combed my hair I would see it:

<u>I am responsible TO but not FOR</u><br>my clients, my friends, my children, my wife,<br>and any other human being

Perhaps this has stuck with me because, for the first 35 years of my life, I thought I was responsible <u>for</u> others. My father taught me by example that if Mom was unhappy, I was responsible to make her happy again. If my Dad was upset and angry, then my responsibility was to pacify him. If my wife was hurt, my responsibility was to make her feel better. If my peers thought I was a dork, my responsibility was to convince them I was cool. I was responsible to care for others, and if I did, they would care for me. I even made myself responsible for my children; I assumed that if I were a good father, they would grow up to be happy, successful adults. I took the book of Proverbs to heart, quoting, "Train a child in the way he should go and when he is old he will not turn from it."(KJV) (I have since learned that these Proverbs are not promises but basic truths, philosophical generalities. I have also learned that the meaning of Proverbs 6:22 when more appropriately interpreted means to train up a child in the way he is bent, a very different slant on this often-quoted Scripture). Overall, I believed if I pleased everybody, they would be pleased with me. (By the way, our children did grow up to be happy, successful adults, but by taking personal responsibility **for** their own lives.)

I must admit I am a slow learner, or maybe I should say a slow "unlearner." Realizing that I am not responsible for other people's feelings, perceptions and behavior has been an eye-opener and a relief. My knee-jerk response is to take on more responsibility than I should, but seeing I can't be responsible for others helps me be more appropriately detached. Not even God is responsible for our decisions, emotions, responses, or behavior, because we have been given the freedom and responsibility to choose. God cannot make us do or feel anything we do not choose. Why would we imagine we are responsible for others? Certainly we are responsible to others: to model integrity, to listen empathetically and to love and accept. But we are responsible only for ourselves and nobody else; we are responsible for our choices, for our emotions, for our behavior, for our perceptions, for our self-esteem, for being the best employee, parent, spouse or friend possible.

Many years ago I noticed a bumper sticker that read, **"To Err Is Human, To Blame Others Is Even More Human."** Blaming someone is one of our most common defenses. If we are honest with ourselves, however, we must admit that we contribute in some way to virtually all our problems. We are responsible only to work on our piece—correct our behavior, change our attitude, forgive rather than resent, care instead of hurt, and ask for forgiveness when we fail. Our choices cannot be conditioned on the expectation that the other person will change or apologize before we do. Even realizing objectively what our choices are requires that appropriate detachment.

We can take initiative in communicating to others how we feel, how we think, or what we expect, by using clear "I" messages, but we can not make another person hear us. If others choose to blame, be angry, misinterpret, resent, or break off communication, they are responsible for their words and their actions. Then our responsibility is to avoid arguing, debating and making matters worse.

When we take responsibility for how we think, how we feel, and how we behave, we are on the road to freedom. When we refuse to take on responsibility for others' emotional responses, their perceptions, or their behavior, we are actually empowering them to run their own lives. We don't view them as helpless victims who are unable to change. I know instead that my clients do all of the work and initiate change. I can take very little credit for my clients' success; I can only facilitate, educate and mediate. I'm responsible TO and not FOR.

## Being Assertive

Assertiveness is one of the most effective skills I have learned over the years. This strategy and way of communicating sets appropriate boundaries so that relationships thrive. I assert myself when I get my needs met without disregarding the needs of others. Assertiveness has improved my marriage, relationships with my children, and my counseling practice, so much that I long to model this way of acting and responding. In the truest sense, I cannot be too assertive, any more than I can be too loving.

It may startle my readers to learn that when we are not being assertive, we will act aggressively, passively, passive-aggressively and/or a combination of all three. My intent is not to write or teach a course on assertiveness, but to give the reader a taste for this invaluable skill.

### *Aggressiveness*

Aggressive people display physically inappropriate behaviors. They may physically hit, throw things, kick, drive recklessly, glare and provoke. Verbally they are loud and obnoxious. They attempt to humiliate and depreciate others by name-calling, snide remarks, slander, gossip, teasing, blaming, talking down to others, snickering, interrupting, insisting on having the last word, intimidating, and speaking for others. Their stance is "I'm okay, but you are not." They tend to be "externalizers" of blame. Aggressive people appear to be self-confident, but inwardly they experience low self-esteem and a poor sense of worth. The illusion of controlling others gives them a false sense of security.

### *Passivity*

Passive people act inhibited, presenting themselves as helpless and powerless. They show anxiety rather than self-confidence. Rather than express how they feel, they let others make decisions for them. They don't rock the boat because they fear hurting others and want peace at any price. Many passive people take the stance "I'm not okay but you are." They tend to be "internalizers" of blame, and like aggressive types, suffer from low self-esteem.

### *Passive Aggressiveness*

It is said that passive aggressiveness is synonymous with "indirect aggression." Some people seem passive on the surface but generally "get back at" others, particularly aggressive people. Instead of dealing forthrightly with issues, they use hostile humor, sarcasm and ridicule. To punish others, they often withdraw attention and affection, or use the "silent treatment." The passive-aggressive stance is "I'm not okay and you aren't either." Again, like aggressive and passive people, they too have low self-esteem and sense of worth.

Whether people are acting aggressively, passively or passive-aggressively, they are attempting to manipulate others into doing what they want. They may use indirect, unfair fighting methods to get their needs met, such as whining, shaming, or inducing guilt. Or they may try controlling others by evoking fear. Manipulative people beat around the bush in their communication and make hostile comparisons to motivate others to do what they want. Their motto seems to be "My needs will be met at the expense of your needs."

The alters within CJ displayed all four stances. Rarely could the younger, more immature parts be assertive. During the abuse some alters would remain passive. Other alters would respond passive-aggressively, while internally they were extremely angry and aggressive. Actually, the more aggressive alters attempted to intimidate CJ, other alters and me. The more mature alters (named Truth and Keeper) were able to be quite assertive, unless they were experiencing their own terrifying memories.

Non-assertive people tend to fall into one of two camps—dependent or co-dependent. Neither is conducive to having intimate relationships. Highly dependent and co-dependent relationships are non-assertive, bouncing back and forth between aggressive, passive and passive-aggressive attitudes and behaviors. By contrast, healthy relationships happen when each party takes responsibility for his/her feelings, perceptions and behavior, and both persons are willingly inter-dependent. Such co-operation builds community through mutual encouragement, challenge, support and nurture.

I realize that my own relationships are not always totally healthy. With aggressive folks, I can lean toward being passive and/or passive aggressive. With passive people, I tend to be overly kind and sensitive to their needs, which is a form of co-dependence. Passive-aggressive people frustrate me most, overly dependent on me to give them what they want, yet resistant to identifying exactly what their wants are. Depending on the dynamics of a given system, we all find ourselves using various manipulative behaviors to get our needs met.

Assertiveness puts a stop to all of these dysfunctional games. Assertive demeanor and behavior mean that I'm learning to:

- say specifically and directly what I want
- express my feelings directly and spontaneously
- give and express compliments
- make and keep contact with others
- insist on fairness and justice
- say no without feeling guilty
- and above all, attempt to be loving in my behavior, attitudes and talk.

To recapitulate, healthy assertive people refuse to be victims; instead they make conscious, responsible choices. Their words and actions are open, non-secretive and authentic. They are able to appropriately detach, take responsibility to and not for, and maintain a healthy self-esteem. As listeners, they are attentive and non-defensive. In short, they assert themselves by attempting to be loving in all they do and say.

## Dealing with Suicidal Threats

When a client of mine seriously considers suicide, I rely heavily on these skills—being appropriately detached, being responsible to and not for, and being assertive. Suicidal threats must be taken seriously, especially when a person has already made an attempt. Wanting to die means that we have reached the end of our rope; we've exhausted every possibility of finding peace. We want to be DONE with all the pain of this life. My first responsibility as a counselor and friend is not to panic, but to listen and empathize with the one who wants to end his life. I reflect back what I am hearing, identifying and connecting with the feelings and the situation. My own fear must be put aside, since my job for the moment is not to discount what is being said, but to convince the person that I understand.

In dealing with CJ and the alters as they threatened suicide, I was able to reduce the anxiety by being calm, cool and collected. When we could have a more rational conversation, I would begin to confront what the alters were telling me. I tended to be lovingly blunt: "So you want to KILL yourself." "Self-murder is a serious act." "If you succeed, you're dead forever." "What do you think will happen to you after you're dead?" "If you choose to kill yourself and succeed you will no longer have any choices." I would argue for the preciousness of life, reminding them that life has purpose and value, even though they couldn't see that at the moment.

I would ask how they intended to kill themselves. The more thought-out the plan, the more seriously I would take the threat. Sometimes I would tell them about failed suicide attempts—how others have been left incapacitated, mentally and/or physically. My goal was to help CJ and her alters to de-romanticize death and face reality. Some people speak in awe of the courage it takes to kill oneself. I don't see it as courage, but as a temporary lapse in thinking. I warn clients against being totally irrational and impulsively doing something stupid. Too many times people take pills, attempt to hang themselves, use the car exhaust to consume the oxygen, put a gun to their heads, or crash a car into a concrete wall—and try at the last minute to abort their attempts. Sadly, even though people may change their minds, some of these attempts succeed, or do so much damage that the person's quality of life is never the same.

As my clients and I reflected in therapy about their despairing feelings, I would explain how temporary feelings are. I assured them that these feelings could pass and happiness be present in the future. I revealed that I, too, had been suicidal at times in the past. Learning to deal with depression and discouragement had helped me survive, so I could find my life to be happy, enjoyable, and purposeful over all. I asked them, "What if I had succeeded in killing myself? What is happening right now wouldn't be happening." This seemed to be a strong argument, because we could not imagine living without the vital relationship we had established.

Since many of the alters, including the one called Jill, were so young, immature and irrational, I would ask CJ and the adult alters to "listen in" while I appealed to these child parts. I am convinced, frankly, that anyone who is suicidal is thinking and feeling like CJ's self-destructive alters. Therefore, it is imperative that we draw on the more rational interior parts. If an alter succeeded in killing herself, "everybody" would be dead, so some of the happier alters had a vested interest in staying alive. Not only were INTRA-personal relationships affected by the actions of one part, but INTER-personal ones were also. CJ had to be faced with consequences for her husband, her daughter, her friends, and me if she murdered herself. She might be "at peace," but the rest of us would be devastated. We would always miss her, and never get over the grief.

I had to repeat that suicide is a very, very selfish act. Nobody else is considered. The self-destroyer has no empathy for others. It's like saying, "I don't care what you think and feel, I'm the only one that counts." I also pointed out that suicide would mean that CJ's perpetrators would win once again, and the rest of us would lose. All along I kept checking to see if the other parts were "listening in".

(Another motive for suicide is to make others pay. The attitude is, "I'll show you! You'll be sorry! Once I'm dead you will wish you had treated me differently." Such people are highly manipulative and very angry. Again, their actions are selfish, thoughtless, and self-centered. They use what power they have left abusively.)

## Contracting

Having people agree to sign a "Will not kill" contract can help everyone manage a crisis. When clients give me their word that they will not harm themselves—and especially when they put it in black and white—they will usually follow through. At first the contract is for a short period of time, a few days or a week. For example, "Do you agree not to hurt or kill yourself until our next session?" If the immediate crisis has passed, I will extend the contract to a month, then six months, with periodic "updates" in the months following. In Jill's case, (or with any other alter who was bent on suicide) I had her sign the contract along with CJ, making her responsible to stay alive and not "chicken out" on the process. Most of us can keep our vows if we don't make them forever. Short-term goals are more realistic and help us to reach longer-term goals.

The contract included a promise that any of the alters or CJ would call me in an emergency. If the suicidal alter wouldn't call, then another alter or CJ agreed to call. CJ protested that this was imposing on me, but I made the request for MY sake so that I wouldn't worry. Fortunately CJ was able to put herself in my shoes and saw my request as "reasonable."

(A little addendum. From the very beginning, I tell clients that I do not take on suicidal people because I'm not equipped; I can't dispense medication, nor am I fully qualified to deal with these situations. Interestingly, even though a client may have talked suicide in the past, he or she will consent to avoid it while we are seeing each other. I suspect that even the threat of being sent to another counselor may help arrest suicidal thoughts. Setting these boundaries is not just for my benefit, but also for the counselee's. I will not allow clients to emotionally blackmail me with the threat of suicide. They must be willing to talk about their problems and discuss options other than suicide, or they must seek help elsewhere. Most people feel safer with this kind of approach and are willing to deal with their feelings of hopelessness another way.)

I told CJ and company that I would be forced to call her husband if they refused to sign a contract. I was backed up by my supervising psychologist, who now insisted CJ see a psychiatrist for a medical consult. Further expertise was needed to

- prescribe an appropriate medication
- insist she remain on the medication until the doctor said otherwise
- tell me if we were on the right track
- validate my ability or lack of ability to handle CJ's case

I had to be informed when CJ followed through with seeing a psychiatrist. She also had to give me permission to call her husband in her presence (or she would call in my presence) when she was feeling suicidal. We could not afford any compromises on these agreements, because CJ's life was at stake.

Of course CJ and many of the alters were furious at these boundaries. I was extremely upset myself. I'd spent over four years gaining "everybody's" trust, and now I was worried about losing all we had built together. I had to keep telling myself that I could not counsel a dead client. Keeping CJ alive was far more important at this juncture than completing our work at integration together.

Overall, my insistence on a contractual agreement turned out well. CJ's husband was updated on her state of mind. He was supportive and understanding; he insisted his wife see a psychiatrist, no matter what the cost. Neither he nor I would allow CJ's hurt, anger and feelings of betrayal to prevent us from getting her the help she needed. In time the alters would also come to understand why we had done what we did.

I've wanted my readers to see a counselor coping with the stress of counseling a DID client. I offer the toolkit which enabled me to handle this particular situation in CJ's life: having appropriate detachment, being responsible to and not for, and practicing assertiveness.

## For Further Information

Glasser,William, ***Reality Therapy***, Harper and Row, 1965.

Burns, David, ***Feeling Good: The New Mood Therapy***, Harper Collins, 1980.

Alberti, Robert and Emmons, Michael, ***Your Perfect Right: A Guide to Assertive Behavior***, Impact, 1978.

Cloud, Henry, and Townsend, John, ***Boundaries***, Zondervan, 1992.

Weeks, Claire, ***Hope and Help for Your Nerves***, Bantam Books, 1969.

Steven Levenkron, ***Cutting,*** Norton, 1998

CHAPTER

# 11

# All Talking at Once (CJ)

*All psychological defenses are means of survival; they become neurotic defenses because they have outlived their usefulness.*
–Alexander Lowen, ***Fear of Life***

I don't remember a time when it was quiet inside me. There have always been one or more simultaneous conversations going on in my head. I took this as normal. Didn't everyone dialog back and forth inside himself?

## Attending to Internal Chaos

I told Jerry I sometimes felt very disconnected from myself, sort of out of my body. More than once, Jerry asked ask me if I had "lost any time." Lost time, he explained, was any period when I could not remember what happened. I emphatically said NO! I didn't like him asking me that; in fact, I probably wouldn't have told him if I HAD lost time. But I did say I sometimes felt as though I was watching myself go through certain situations. I was surprised when Jerry explained the concept of dissociation to me, but it made sense. Learning about the dissociative state also made me more aware of times when I was dissociating and helped me figure out what was pushing me to do so. One particular day I remember dissociating at a deeper level than I'd ever experienced before. I seemed to be on the edge of unconsciousness, not just looking on, but actually separated from myself. The experience was frightening, yet I also felt great peace and safety in that state of mind.

In one journal entry, I wrote,

*I just went inside myself to that inner place. It feels so good—exhilarating, yet peaceful—surprisingly peaceful. I'd like to keep trying to go there. I want to know what else is there—in that inner place. It intrigues me, but it does tire me out to go inside that far. I wonder what would happen if I went in there and had a memory?*

Another time I likened dissociation to drowning.

*I sort of drowned within myself. It was like I got smaller and smaller until I almost disappeared. It was a little frightening because I felt like I almost got stuck inside. I had to somehow crawl out of myself. It was difficult and I was unsure I could get out.*

I became more aware of voices in my head. Although I had assumed that everyone had voices similar to mine, now I feared that I might actually have multiple personalities. I tried to convince myself that there was no way I had Dissociative Identity Disorder (DID). Absolutely not! I did not want to be labeled with any kind of illness or disorder especially not DID. It seemed to carry a certain stigma—it was a disease of crazy people—and I didn't want anyone to think of me as crazy—even if I felt crazy! My journal entry showed my rationalization:

*Am I multiple? I really doubt it, but sometimes I do wonder. I've not lost chunks of time—so I feel pretty confident that I'm okay. Yet incidents of extremely deep dissociation make me a little wary.*

I was becoming very concerned that my "normal" voices might be a symptom of DID.

## Acknowledging and Living with the Many Selves

I asked Jerry if he thought I was multiple. He didn't say yes, nor did he say no. If I were truly a multiple, he assured me, then we would find out together. If I really trusted him, and if the potential alters or different parts of me trusted him, they would eventually reveal themselves. Jerry put my concerns in a very practical light. He asked me, "What if you are DID?" I guessed that then I would feel more fragmented and crazy. And the diagnosis would mean there was something else in me that needed to be fixed. Jerry really helped me by explaining what it meant to be DID. In order to deal with traumatic events in childhood, a person could split off into parts (different pieces of one's self), with each part holding one or more memories of events as they were happening. Jerry made everything seem so normal—not weird and bizarre like it felt to me. Over and over he had to assure me that I was not simply a nut case!

In October 1992, I began to experience audible voices, that is, the voices normally inside my head began to talk through my mouth. Strange, I know, but that's exactly what it felt like to me—that they were using my mouth when they wanted to. In the beginning, there were just two or three distinguishable voices. Somehow, I knew their names. I just knew! I felt entirely weird when this occurred and would frantically fight to get back control because I didn't want to relinquish any amount of control to any one part. Sometimes I felt as if I would shatter into a million pieces. At other times I seemed to be splitting off into someone entirely different, with "me" just disappearing. It was extremely difficult for me to acknowledge the voices and listen to their stories. It sapped my strength and energy.

During this phase, after long and agonizing indecision, I decided to begin taking antidepressants again. Any use of drugs is problematic for me. To this day, I fight against taking medication, even when I am as informed as possible. Jerry and I learned that one of my parts (Sharon) had been forced to take some type of drug in the past, and she went ballistic whenever I had to use antibiotics, antidepressants or even vitamins! My journal records the depth of my emotional struggle and the great distress Sharon and I experienced when we took medication:

> *This has been a difficult week for me. I'm not sure if I've had a crazier one. I've felt great, wonderful, and peaceful at some times and at others I've felt crazy, wild, out of control, and really scared. I'm not sure if any of those feelings are real or if I manufactured them. I feel exposed to far too many people. It feels dangerous. I'm tired. I would like to give up, yet I struggle for the last bit of control I think I have. I feel helpless and I hate feeling helpless! There seems like there is just too much ahead of me to face; it's far too overwhelming, yet if I can stand back far enough, I wonder what the problems really are—why can't I function like I'm supposed to?*
>
> *I'm degraded by the fact I'm forced to take antidepressants. Intellectually, I realize I have agreed to and choose to take them, but I feel forced into it by circumstances. Somehow this only adds credence to the fact I AM crazy! I'm deathly afraid to take the drug. What will happen to me? I had bad dreams last night and woke up shaking with fear. Is this just one more step to total breakdown? Will I ever be able to handle life on my own again? Am I just giving up?*
>
> *One of the major things on my mind is my session with Jerry yesterday. He suggested I am at a standstill because I will not accept the parts, validate their memories and own the experiences as my own. He is accurate in his assessment. I guess I realized I was disconnected from the parts, but I don't believe I realized the potential impact of being disconnected. I understand the importance of this in other people, other abuse survivors, but somehow I don't want to know the significance of it in my own*

*life. First of all, I don't want to be DID. Secondly, I don't want to believe the memories. Thirdly, even if I did admit the memories are mine, I don't want to experience the feelings that will go along with them. I ask myself, isn't the pain the parts originally suffered enough? They are me. Doesn't that mean I've already suffered through these memories? Like everything else in my life right now, this makes me feel overwhelmed, so I must try to break it up in small manageable pieces. Strange, but even small pieces seem huge—a big mouthful to swallow right now. Perhaps the best way to start working through my denial is to select one part and work with that part, accepting him/her, the memories, his/her existence along with validating his/her feelings and experiences and the value the part brings to the entire system (me). I guess I need to try. I may fall short of my goal, but I guess that means I would have to try again. I do really want to get beyond this stuff, get on with my life. If these are really my desires, then I must decide the struggle is worth the effort and pain and forge ahead anyway.*

*I feel beaten down, trod on and totally out of control. I just forced myself to take the Prozac. I hate myself for submitting. Sharon [one of my parts] is extremely upset! Even some of the younger parts are frozen with fear. God, help us! I hope I am doing the right thing. I'm doing what I think is best for all of us. I'm not trying to hurt or scare any of the parts. Sharon, I'm sorry I'm stealing some of your control. I know how important control is to you. Quite frankly, it is important to me too. I feel like I'm killing your spirit and I'm sorry. I want to vomit up that stupid pill! Is there no middle ground? Must I be totally ripped apart to be whole? God, why all this agony and confusion? Even in my surrender, I will not surrender; at least that's what I would like to say. I don't want to defuse Sharon. I need someone inside to fight for us. Even though Sharon would like to destroy us, I believe that is her strange way of trying to defend us—the only way she knows how. I'm so very weary. It would be so easy just to lie down and die. If it were only that easy! My heart is broken, my spirit is stamped on, and my hope is dim. God, I hope you are satisfied! You've accomplished what I believe you've set out to do—destroy my will. You've had to take it, because I won't give it up easily!"*

During this time, Jerry got permission from another client (June) for me to talk with her about some of her story. June had also been diagnosed with DID, and I found it encouraging to hear from someone who was experiencing the same weird things as I was. June was ahead of me in her process, so she could give me some valuable information on how to deal with alters.

I needed every bit of her help, as I discovered that the voices in my head had names and personalities. All the parts seemed like enemies to me, out to ruin my life and drive me insane. If my life had seemed out of control before, now it was shattered and wrecked. I felt stunned, frightened, and crazier than ever. Now I knew I was a monster, some type of weird creature, like an alien in the movies! Almost instinctively, I realized that some of my parts wanted me dead, or wanted to be dead—the end result being the same.

The first voice I heard talking through me was very angry. Bill (yes, alters can be both male and female) expressed his dislike for me (the host). He seemed to want to break out of the confines of my less-than-adequate body, yet he would back off at times, because he knew he must be discreet. His power lay in being unknown, hidden. To be seen or known often proved dangerous to us. Bill confused me in the beginning. It seemed so unlikely that he was a separate personality, that I tended to ignore him. I put his voice down as my own self-loathing.

That same month, I went out walking one day, an activity I undertook when my anxiety became intolerable. I was walking as fast as I could, nearly running, trying to escape or find release. I remember telling myself that I could not return to the house. I was so distraught that I wouldn't be able even to answer the phone if it rang. At that moment, Anita revealed herself to me. She simply said, *"No problem. I'll answer the phone and tell whoever is calling that CJ is not in right now."* As strange as it may seem, I accepted what she said. She was immediately familiar to me; I knew she had helped me in the past and could do so again.

After those two encounters, the inside of me quieted down for a couple of months. Then alters surfaced again, this time in Jerry's office. When I became uncomfortable during a session, I was in the habit of simply leaving (becoming quiet and not responding to him). However, on this particular day, Jerry chose not to ignore my silence. He simply asked, "Who is there? Tell me your name." The presenting alter was Bill, and he was terribly upset at being discovered. For a while he refused to acknowledge his presence, but Jerry persisted. Then Bill got very angry at being "called out" by Jerry, and argued loudly with him. It was only a few minutes, while I was in the background listening. I hated to hear what was taking place. It was absolutely mortifying to lose control of part of myself.

I dreaded anyone finding out about my parts. I begged Jerry to promise he wouldn't tell anyone. He promised to tell no one, except his supervising psychologist. I could accept that because the supervisor seemed distant and not threatening to me. What did scare me was what others would think of me, if they learned about all my crazy parts! How would my husband and close friends treat me if they knew? I was isolated from everyone else—different, weird. I wanted to stay home all by myself—with all my "bizarre selves."

Jerry sometimes asked me the names of my parts. At first I would not tell him names, because that seemed like a betrayal. I strongly felt that something internal was stopping me from revealing names. Jerry explained gently how much he wanted to talk with the alters, to hear their stories. In our sessions, Jerry would tell the alters they didn't have to be afraid of him. He encouraged me to talk with my internal people and let them know that he was safe.

Now an even more disconcerting experience began for me: I noticed that the parts were writing in my journal. Sometimes I would find messages written in between my regular journal paragraphs. At other times, entries showed a distinct change in the handwriting. I didn't recognize either the writing or the content. Bizarre!

Jerry wasn't shocked when I told him about the journal writing. He advised me not to fear the journal entries or try to stop them. Instead, I should allow the parts to write and to try to communicate with each of them. He encouraged me to be bold when I heard a voice or when a part took over my journal—to ask the voice what it wanted to say, what it knew. He explained that I couldn't rescue my parts from past experiences, but I could reassure them about the future and take care of them now.

Still, I was unnerved and scared by the different handwriting and separate parts using my journal. Increasingly, their journaling took the form of conversations going on among themselves. They would speak of themselves as "we," and normally I, CJ, was not included in the group. In one journal entry the parts wrote,

> *We don't let her come out often, because we can't trust her. We don't know what she'll do or say. She must stay in her place. She's mad and angry and she can hurt us." In response I wrote, "I'm NOT we. I'm me, singular. There's only one of me! I may act in different ways, but there's only me. I feel crazy. I'm afraid to let my hand write by itself.*

Often the parts introduced themselves through journaling. Sometimes their writing would bring up a memory, whether I wanted it or not. My once safe journal now became a dreaded object. I felt compelled to journal, yet when I did, I felt intruded upon and exploited by the parts. Frequently, in the middle of my journaling, I would find a statement or question written repetitively, such as, “What happened on the boat?” The parts were great at introducing a memory and allowing little remembrances to sneak out in the journaling, making me frantic until I allowed the parts to freely journal. On rare occasions I broke down and allowed them to come out in Jerry’s office and talk through their memory out loud.

Following are a few pages from my journal, illustrating what was happening.

41

Dear JD → This is a funny name. It has a j like my name.

I like you. You are a very nice man.

I will draw a piture for you

This is me

this is the big mean boy

I draw pretty good. This paper is funny with the lines.

I am a boy. Can you tell by My piture?

I am not good all the times. I try hard to be.

I really like ice cream. Sometimes she bys Me some. I likevenilla. the white kind.

Jack

I was fraid of that boy. He was very Mean and big

harmed ~~that~~ were okay. That may not be true.

What are you talking about?

The children were terrified – re-traumatized.

I'm sorry I didn't intend for that to happen. I'm very sorry.

What was accomplished?

Not a damn thing – Nothing.

I hate you!

I'm sorry I made a situation happen where you felt scared and out of control. That was not my intention. I wanted to fulfill an obligation by visiting and not have to feel guilty about that. Maybe I put my feelings and wishes above yours. I'm sorry. We won't have to go back for a while. You must have felt pretty helpless and powerless. Actually you weren't but I understand that you may have felt like that. I'm sorry to put you in that position again. It wasn't fair. I would have protected you though, if necessary. It's okay to get angry with me about it – it's also okay to let go and cry about it. Crying doesn't mean you're weak. It feels like you're weak – but you're really not.

I hate you.

Do you? Or is it those mean men that you really hate? They did such awful things to you. They treated you so badly. They are bad people – bad men. They deserve to be hated – they should be punished for what they did. They committed crimes and have gone unpunished. That's not right – or fair.

Don't talk to me anymore. I don't want to listen.

I know. Why don't you talk to me? Tell me what you're feeling?

NO.

Why not?

NO, NO, NO.

It's okay to talk about it. It really is.

NO.

Occasionally, a part that was very angry would emerge. Those parts terrified me. I was sure that if I let them express themselves, they would rage out of control. I felt that encouraging them would destroy my own control. In order to allow the angry parts to communicate, I had to remind myself that I WAS in control and the "voice" was an invited visitor. In one journal entry I wrote about a particular angry part who scared me:

> *I would like the voice to be a part of me. I would like to take on her anger and for her to take on parts of me too. I don't understand why she is so irrational. I would like to understand why all her anger is directed at ME. I want to talk to her. I'll listen and try to understand. I really will. Talk to me angry one, please, I'll listen.*

I didn't get a response because the part was simply far too angry to be rational and discuss things with me.

I thought some of the parts were just plain crazy! Then I would wonder what that said about me? Sometimes the parts mirrored me so well that it was uncanny. I saw so much of myself in them, some things I liked, but mostly things I hated about myself. Some of the parts were very wimpy, ugly, fat, too talkative, or unwilling to talk at all. From my perspective these parts were weak and uncontrolled—qualities I could at times see in myself. I didn't like any of them, but those who couldn't control themselves were the worst.

## Inviting Participation of the Parts

Jerry encouraged me to let the parts keep journaling. He suggested I step back and listen as the parts spoke. He said there was no need for me to be afraid of my parts (easy for him to say!) and challenged me to communicate directly with them (fat chance!). If I were to be nonjudgmental, I could ask questions and find out what they knew. I shrank from such a direct approach, but I was intrigued that I might find out the truth of my past through these misfit parts inside me. Once again, I was reassured when Jerry didn't seem to be upset at all about the parts. He explained that as we accept our different parts and become congruent, we become whole, healthy and truthful about ourselves.

I wrote in my journal:

> *Everything seems like it's changing—the ground is shifting beneath my feet. I don't feel like I'm the same person—I don't know who I am! I'd like to run. What's real? I don't think I know, but everything seems so strange. Everyone seems alien. I wonder if this is normal? I don't know, but it is certainly disconcerting. I need desperately to speak to someone else who is*

*multiple and can confirm that I'm okay. I desperately need stability right now—secure stability.*

At the same time I still struggled with believing my own memories and those of the parts. Off and on throughout my therapy process I would bounce back and forth between believing myself and not believing myself. The following journal entry shows my doubts—about myself, my memories and the parts' memories:

*I believe that in some way, shape or form I (we) were abused. I know there is at least one alter (Doris) who does not believe, and that's okay. I too have difficulty believing it sometimes, actually most times. But there has to be some reason why I (we) struggle like we do. I've prayed that God would remove the memories if they are false and the memories have never been removed. They seem to only grow in number. There is really no other reasonable explanation for the struggles I have, unless I'm just completely nuts, and if that is the case, I don't think I would be able to function as well as I do. Therefore, I must come to the conclusion that I was abused and because of the abuse I am a victim of crime against my body, mind, and my soul. This is so very difficult for me to say, perhaps because it says so much. I can't deal with listing my abusers at this point; for now it has to be enough to admit that I have been severely wounded.*

*When I think of someone who has been severely wounded from an accident, I think of someone with bleeding wounds and broken bones. These wounds and broken bones must be cleansed and bandaged, and the bones set to promote healing. The wounds are then un-bandaged and allowed to continue to heal. I guess that describes my parts and me. Because of the brutal wounds of my body, mind, and soul, I must have my wounds cleansed and bandaged and they must be allowed to heal. I believe that's what is happening (slow as it seems), but perhaps I have neglected to completely acknowledge the way the "accident" happened in the first place. I have been attempting to care for my wounds, but refusing to acknowledge what actually caused those wounds. It seems so simple and yet such a huge mountain to climb. I must say it again to reinforce it within my parts and myself: I have been abused (physically, emotionally, sexually and spiritually). I have been horribly wounded. Now that my wounds have been acknowledged they are in the process of being cleansed and on the way to being healed.*

*Even though it seems like the abuse is my fault, it couldn't have been my fault. If I had a choice, I would not have chosen that way. I would have chosen a life free of physical, emotional, sexual and spiritual abuse. Even as I write these words, on the tip of my tongue are the words "but I should have done something to stop that abuse."*

It's strange how even in the presence of intellect and fact those words refuse to die.

*Maybe this will only change as the alters each have an opportunity to work through their memories and have a new frame of reference. Whatever, I cannot honestly say that I relinquish myself from all guilt. Maybe one day…*

*I'm sure Doris is feeling very upset and betrayed right now. "Doris, I know you have no memories of the abuse and I'm so glad you don't. But unfortunately, you are one of the very few of us who has not been abused. Just as most of us find it hard to believe you have no memories of the abuse, you must find us extremely hard to believe too. But that doesn't take away or diminish either of our truths. We must accept you as having an ideal childhood, and you must also accept the fact we had an abusive and traumatic childhood.*

*I will continue to speak these truths over and over to myself and my parts. I'm sorry it has taken me so long to get to this point. And yet I must say I'm sure there will still be times of doubt. At those times, I will reinforce the truth by repeating the facts and hope the truth will someday take firm root in my spirit.*

*There is so much turmoil inside me—a twisting and turning deep inside, a bottomless, black hole of pain and agony. My mind seems overtaxed and exhausted. My emotions are being kept on a tight rein to insure that I can manage to get through each day. My spirit is confused and afraid. My body is weary and craves the nothingness of sleep, only to be haunted by evil and frightening shadows in my dreams.*

*I have great concerns that all hell will break loose while Jerry is away on vacation and there will be no one to understand what is happening to me. No one who will be able to help me see reality. I feel like there is a huge tidal wave inside me ready to cut loose and completely roll over and consume any sanity I may currently possess and replace it with an evil entity that must be destroyed. Even now, I am so frightened that I must stop and take deep breaths to ground myself. I don't think it would be God's will for something like that to happen (me falling apart), and yet was it God's will for a child to be brought up in the horrors of hell? No, probably not, yet it was allowed to happen. Perhaps God would also see it tolerable to allow me to have an emotional collapse, or even worse to be possessed by the evil that I seem always to be only one tiny step ahead of. Can I trust God now as I seemingly trusted him years ago as a child?*

When the parts were recalling memories, or when I wasn't responsive enough (allowing them to talk and really listening to them), the confusion inside became pretty intense. The conversations got louder and more complicated. The parts would all start talking at once, and I couldn't get a handle on who was saying what. The following writing was done after I had kept the parts boxed up for quite a long period of time. Notice how everything runs together. It's hard to discern who is speaking. I struggled to understand what was going on, but felt overwhelmed. The parts seemed to be punishing me for not listening.

The journaling reads:

*I need to focus on the inside. I know that, yet I seem to keep avoiding it. I'm tired and wary. I'm on the verge of depression. I need to let go. I'm opening up the floor for anyone who needs to talk:*

*It's about time. Take it easy, she's been busy and otherwise occupied. That's great...we don't matter at all. Get Paula out of here. She's making things worse. Not really, for now, I think it's helping all of us. I don't want to see him; he scares me. I just want to sleep. I don't want to work on anything. It's too difficult. You're mean, it hurts. That too. I just don't want to do this anymore. There is no alternative. There is too. That's not an alternative and you know it. Why can't things be normal? What is normal? Would we recognize it if we had it? I don't know, but I'd like to try it. Take away the man. He's bad. What's his name? Just take him away, we don't want to see him anymore. Who is he? You need to tell me who he is so I'll know who to get rid of. The man, just get rid of him! Take him away! Are you the one behind the door? Just take him away. He's a bad man. Why is he bad? What happened? Please, take him away. I will, but first I need to know who he is. Leave her alone. She asked for help. Just let her be. Don't ask her any questions. Why? Because she doesn't need to remember. Remember what? She doesn't need to remember anything. It's not necessary. It is, if it is bothering her. Do you know what she knows? I don't want to hear any of it. Do you know any of it, even just a piece of it? I won't listen to you. Does the memory involve you too? I won't listen to you or anyone else. I don't have to. You're right, you don't have to do anything you don't want to. But sometimes as bad as it feels, it's better to get it out.*

*There's the hole. Don't get near it. Stay away, stay away. But someone's crying in the hole. Stay away. Don't get near the hole. Look at the doors over there, stay away from the hole. Open the doors instead. See what's behind the doors. I'm afraid. I don't want to open the doors either. Just turn the door knob and let the door slip open by itself. No, no, stay away from the door too. We can't ignore everything and be afraid of everything. Sometimes we must step forward even though we're afraid. Just turn the door knob and unlatch the door, let it slip open. Then you can peek through the crack and see what's inside. You can always close the door back up if it gets too scary. Stupid, you know once the door is open, it's difficult to get it shut again. It might be difficult, but you can do it if you really want the door shut again.*

Distressing as this was, I could also sometimes see a kind of humor in being multiple, that is, when I could escape the memories long enough to see it. Different parts would come out during a session with Jerry, who was always willing to speak to each part. Abby, a very engaging part, really enjoyed the freedom to be out and seemed to relish talking to him. She held some memories, and at one session Jerry probed for more details. Abby said she didn't know what he wanted to know. Later, when I came back out, Jerry asked me also for more details. I couldn't answer either. Jerry then said he would ask Abby the next time he talked to her. I did not want to deal with that memory at all, so I told Jerry that Abby would not come out to talk with him again. Jerry replied that Abby WOULD come out. I resented this. He seemed too darned confident about that fact. I sniped back that Abby wouldn't come out, because I wouldn't bring her with me! Jerry chuckled… and so did I, when I really considered my statement.

Nevertheless, the parts and I were essentially at war. I was the outsider. The parts thought they were more important than I was. In their opinion, I had simply messed up our life and was inept at just about everything I tried to do. One part wrote this in my journal:

*I don't like you. You're weak. I want to hurt you. You're stupid. I'm not going to tell you what happened in the boat—you should know what happened yourself. You LET it happen. I could kill you. I would like to kill you. You're a jerk. You're sick and I hate you. You're a fake. I hate you. I HATE YOU. I HATE YOU. You've ruined everything. You can't do anything right. You screw things up. You're messed up!*

Another part wrote the following to me:

*You stupid girl. You deserve everything you got. I wish I could cut you up right now. You're ugly. Did you hear me! I said you're ugly and fat and you've always been ugly and fat. Why do we even bother with you? I'd like to scratch your eyes out!*

Sometimes I could remain logical and in control during these journal exchanges, but at other times the anger and rage of the parts terrified me. I was afraid one of these angry parts would gain control of me and cause trouble. I would resolve not to allow these parts to come out, but that resolution was usually short-lived. The parts could cause my life to be absolute hell. They tormented me with such turmoil inside my head that I couldn't bear it and had to allow them to speak. They believed I was ignoring them and keeping them in prison deep inside.

Some of my parts could "out logic" me! They were very astute and wise and could get me caught up in my own words. Keeper was one part who was both empathetic and logical. When I tried to hide because processing memories became too difficult, Keeper would always help me find myself and continue on with the process. The following journal entry shows how Keeper pursued me when I didn't want to do any more work. Her logic was far too reasonable to ignore:

**CJ** *Why has everyone [the other parts] gone away?*

**Keeper** *Because you sent them away.*

**CJ** *I did not.*

**Keeper** *Didn't you? Think about it.*

**CJ** *It's always my fault, isn't it?*

**Keeper** *Fault? I really don't think that's the important issue right now. I think denial and avoidance are the problem.*

**CJ** *I don't want to talk about this. I have a headache.*

**Keeper** *I'm sure you do. It takes a lot of energy to shut everything down.*

**CJ** *I'd like to tell you to just shut up!*

**Keeper** *I know. It's difficult to hear the truth. It's difficult to accept it too. And it's even more difficult to act on it.*

**CJ** *I don't think I know how to act on it.*

**Keeper** *Yes, you do. If you listen to the other parts, you'll know exactly how to proceed.*

**CJ** *I can't hear them.*

**Keeper** *You have to want to hear them.*

**CJ** *I don't know if I can do that.*

**Keeper** *Yes, you can.*

**CJ** *I'm afraid.*

**Keeper** *I know. We've all been afraid at one time or another. It's okay to be afraid, as long as your fear does not control you.*

**CJ** *I think it is controlling me.*

**Keeper** *Then you have a choice to make.*

**CJ** *Can't you do this for me?*

**Keeper** *I can help you along. I can be there with you, but I can't do it for you.*

**CJ** *I just want to quit.*

**Keeper** *I know. You think it would be easier if you quit, but it really won't be. Do you want us all to be like this for the rest of our lives?*

**CJ** *No.*

**Keeper** *Then the course is clear. You need to move forward. We can't do it without you. You think you don't know how to do this, but you just need to let go and let it happen.*

**CJ** *No, I don't want to.*

**Keeper** *Then things will stay the same. If you choose to ignore us, sooner or later it will become overwhelming. Remember what JD [Jerry] said*? *The struggle not to deal with things is far worse than actually dealing with the feelings and memories.*

My parts and I could always feel our separateness from each other, and we couldn't see that we had anything in common. They did not want to identify themselves with me in any way, and I absolutely refused to believe that these eccentric out-of-control rebels were connected to me!

Most of the parts hated my parents. They pretty much ignored my mother, but they couldn't stand my dad. The parts called him "the father." I think keeping that distance from him calmed their fear of him. Also, their anger and fear helped to keep them safe—actually kept all of us safe! I didn't hate "the father." He was my dad. I often defended the father to the parts, and that would really set them off!

Generally speaking, the parts didn't have much use for Jerry either. Initially, they were skeptical of him, and trust in him took time to develop. The parts always referred to him as "JD." There were a few parts who truly loved the father and related to JD as a father. After considerable discussion, the parts agreed to allow Jerry to read their journaling. The journaling was one of the main ways Jerry knew what was going on within the system. Occasionally, one or more parts would write and mail a letter to Jerry between sessions, exposing a new memory or telling him about situations that were going on within the system. On other occasions the parts had conversations with Jerry during our sessions.

One part, Snow, a young child, was generally a happy child and dearly loved to talk to JD, especially while we were in his office. Another part, Janice, asked JD if she could leave a stuffed animal, a teddy bear, in his office. He already had some sort of stuffed animal, but Janice didn't like it because you could put your hand inside its body (it was a puppet). Jerry agreed to the addition of Janice's teddy bear. That bear stayed in his office until I ended therapy and at the date of this writing continues to reside in my home office. The bear was comforting to many of the parts as well as to me.

In January 1993, I made a real effort to come to terms with my diagnosis. I wrote in my journal:

> *I need to think of the diagnosis of DID as a ticket to freedom instead of a prison. I need a more positive attitude. If I am multiple, then I need to quit fighting the diagnosis and let the process proceed. I need to concentrate my energies on getting well instead of fighting the inevitable. I need to allow the alters to help me. Certainly, they will eventually leave, but for now they can help. I need to trust them to help me. I don't have to feel like a freak of nature. I'm okay. Everyone has their own unique coping mechanisms.*

I was afraid that dealing with my parts in therapy would make me too dependent on Jerry. I was always concerned about that, but the parts heightened my concern. I wrote in my journal:

*I don't need Jerry in order to live, just to get through the process. I don't want to become too dependent on him. I'm afraid of being too dependent.*

Being dependent on anyone, even my parts, was not a good thing in my opinion. However, when memories of ritual abuse began to surface, I found I was forced to depend on others in order to make it through sometimes even a single day.

CHAPTER

12

# A House Divided (JD)

*...any town or family that divides itself into groups that fight each other will fall apart.*

–Matthew 12:25 (***TEV***)

As CJ became less embarrassed and more accepting of the discovered alters, the alters in turn became more trusting of me. They would directly interact with me, both in the office and on the telephone, especially when in crisis. And now CJ's crises increased and discoveries poured out. We learned that each alter had his or her view of the past memories, and we both needed to understand the various alters' views as well as the over-all system.

## Discovering Alters—Understanding the System

The number of alters we knew was increasing regularly, and I now suggested that CJ periodically construct a map, a kind of organizational chart, that would show the power and influence they had on each other. I wanted CJ to prompt the various parts to dialogue about their thoughts and feelings, and to write in the journal if possible. In all my therapeutic relationships, I challenge clients to dialogue with the parts inside. Earlier I referred to every person's "child within." It might be better phrased "the children, adolescents and adults within." If we deny, ignore, and refuse to listen to all the parts inside of us, we remain a divided house, and as Jesus said, that house cannot stand.

Our negative self-talk can become a continual inter-forum. I hear parts of me saying things like "Grow up!" or "If you just had a daily quiet time, you'd be a more spiritual person," or "You sure blew that $100.00!" or "You're going to be late again," or "Just control your libido and you won't lust." Nurturing statements are few and far between. Rarely will we say to parts inside, "Good job," "You're making progress," "Lighten up, you did the best you could," "That was a loving thing to do," or "So you failed—you're getting closer to success." Instead we are more at war, divided, than at peace, because we find some of the parts unacceptable, insensitive, selfish, immature and failing in many areas. Anything we do to open up dialogue within ourselves will help unite the parts and create a healthier system.

CJ did not value the role each part, each personality, had played in getting her through the abuse. Neither did they! Her maps attempted to control the alters, but in fact, the "organizational charts" indicated that the parts would compete with each other, compare, argue, defend, excuse, and use every possible defense mechanism to get their own way. They didn't trust each other, they were rarely affirming, they did not see the importance of the roles each played, and they were usually unwilling to give each other credit.

CJ let the alters who were willing write in the journal. Out spilled anger, hurt, fear, and jealousy. Each alter seemed to have distinct handwriting: some writing was bold and expressive, some small and lightly written. Some wrote beautifully in cursive. The young alters, who hadn't learned to read or write, drew pictures or had older literate alters write for them. Older child alters would misspell and awkwardly print their thoughts and feelings. CJ was disconcerted to see entries in the journal with all the different kinds of handwriting. Embarrassed and uncomfortable, she began to type up the journal entries before giving them to me.

The journal revealed angry parts, childish parts, vindictive parts, hurtful parts and gross parts. Many of the alters were unattractive and unpleasant to be around. Rather than expose them to others or me, CJ would keep them incarcerated deep inside. When she let them express themselves and experience a bit of freedom, she felt as if she had opened the gate to a bunch of unruly kids storming into an amusement center.

My process was to normalize CJ's discoveries. I let her know that I was no different in rejecting childish, negative sides of myself. Like her, when I focused on the negative, I would lose sight of the invaluable part each piece of me plays. The up side of our "alter egos" plays out in the more mature and wiser parts aiding the more child-like alters to act more appropriately. Inside me, parts can be easily provoked, then over-react and become self-destructive. An adult side can reason, be more tolerant, and calm down the immature parts. It is only when the various alter egos are in conflict with each other and fail to cooperate, that I become a house divided.

Gradually CJ and I learned that identifying and naming the alter egos would clarify with whom and with what we were dealing. We couldn't understand her situation or determine a game plan unless we had all the dates, memories, thoughts, and feelings of each alter as they were discovered. Ultimately all of the alters had to learn to trust, cooperate, compromise and empathize with each other. Otherwise the intra-personal relationships would fail, just as inter-personal relationships will. The alters needed a merging of the minds, a willingness to integrate with each other, and consensus that all of the alters deserved to be heard and not discounted. The only way CJ could "make sense" of it all was to know the whole story, and each alter had his or her chapter within that story.

CJ was becoming more willing to know and understand each alters' function. Disturbing though it was, she was becoming more proficient at appropriately detaching, just enough to remain in the "background," so the various alters could speak. She could determine what memories and feelings the alters had only by permitting them to "take over her body"—since, after all, it was their body too. Even though her body would then be "taken over" by the alter who was "out," she maintained control of her mind and will. She could "come back" whenever she felt it was important to do so. This remarkable way of hearing from one's interior parts has been called co-consciousness.

Most of us have experienced this state at one time or another. Often we notice being co-conscious when we realize we have "lost time." For example, I can be driving a familiar route and suddenly I "wake up," wondering how I got from point A to point B; I have no memory of what has just transpired. This usually happens when I am in deep thought and my "driving alter" takes over. Realizing I have "lost time" jolts me. What kept me from getting into an accident? My co-consciousness did—but I am still responsible for my actions. (Once, when I was a teenager, a cop followed me for miles through the hills in southern Michigan. He gave me ample opportunity to slow down, but I "didn't see" him, and got a speeding ticket.)

CJ had already been somewhat co-conscious, and she rarely, if ever, "lost time." She had always been aware of "the voices," the "noise inside." Now, as she progressively became more aware, she began to realize that each voice had a name, and eventually she let the parts speak for themselves. Very seldom would the alters take over total control, and when they did, CJ and/or the more mature alters learned to prevent them from getting out of hand. CJ refined her ability to be more co-conscious, more aware, and therefore more responsible. Over time, she became able to remain in the background as a somewhat detached observer. It could be "weird, scary, embarrassing," but ultimately she remained in control as the host personality. When she felt uncomfortable or threatened, CJ would "come back" into total consciousness.

In the co-conscious state, CJ learned a lot about each alter—how they thought, felt, and perceived each memory. She continued to discover different alters and would add them to her organizational chart. The mapping took on different configurations as various names were added. Because CJ's abuse was so extensive and prolonged, many alters were involved. Her pain needed to be spread out, because it would have been too much for one or two parts to bear. We concentrated our attention on the major alters, realizing that there were many "fragmental alters," those who were less involved, who usually were very young and carried only pieces of a memory, and who depended on major alters to support, encourage, and keep them in line. We had to know the roles of the major alters in order to understand their functions but also to help them manage life more reasonably. Each alter needed to increase his or her ability to reason, to analyze and to cope more appropriately with the emotions of fear, mistrust, pain, and anger that assailed them.

Now CJ needed to learn to communicate, empathize and accept the limitations and strengths of each alter. In a sense, she was learning growth development, because she, as the host, the instructor, was required to know and understand K through $12^{th}$ grade students. Any teacher must teach at the level at which her students are functioning. You cannot reason with a third grader as you would with a junior in high school. To manage her students and herself, CJ had to grasp the differences between conscience, consciousness and sub-consciousness, and the part they played in each alter.

## Conscience

To have a conscience is to be aware of guilt, to have a sense of moral goodness, to have a desire to do the right thing. The dictionary says it involves "conduct, intentions, or character, together with a feeling of obligation." The conscience keeps us aware of our need to conform our actions to our internalized value system. When we violate these values—for example, if we lie, cheat, or steal—the conscience prompts us to feel guilty. That guilt can motivate us to seek forgiveness or reparation; but we may also respond by denial or excuses. We can ignore the conscience's signals of guilt or defend ourselves from taking responsibility for our behavior by many different mechanisms. If we realize that we **are** guilty, and refuse to forgive or ask for forgiveness, we override conscience to the point where we no longer **believe** we are guilty. We human beings can become so seared and indifferent that we have no conscience at all.

Younger children have not developed a conscience; therefore, they don't feel guilt. But you might say, "My 7-year-old looks guilty; I can tell when he's been up to no good." What we observe on the faces of children is "guilty fear" or "a fear of being found out" or "a fear of consequences and /or punishment." From birth to the age of 10 or 12, most children conform to authority figures, learning that misbehavior has repercussions. Children who aren't disciplined when they "do wrong," who continually get away with destructive behavior, easily turn into tyrants. Developmentally, negative behaviors of children are dealt with most effectively by behavior modification, reward and punishment.

Despite some popular parenting advice, reasoning with children doesn't work. Cognitively they are unable to "make sense" of what is being said. When parents rely on logical persuasion, children will learn that the longer they can keep the parent talking, the less they will need to do what the parent expects. We've experienced "word games" with our children, trying to make them understand and choose logically to do as we ask. Generally they will repeatedly ask "why," ignore what we are saying, look bored, and resist our requests. (As a grandfather, I notice the bad habit of ending our directions with, "Okay?" –to which our child responds," No, I don't wanna!") This pattern ends in adult frustration and anger.

Though they don't recognize logic, children unconsciously know—by the tone of voice and body language—when a person is being serious. When our daughters were little, their mother did not play those "word games." Allegra was clear about stating what she wanted. She would not argue with the kids, but briefly explain the consequences, both positive and negative, of their choices. On the other hand, I, their father, would attempt to be kind, flexible and reasonable. All too often, the girls would take advantage of my appeals and push back until I got angry and yelled commands. Then they would jump into action and do what they were told, but because of fear. That wasn't my intention, and I'd feel guilty afterward. Over time (Did I mention I'm a slow learner?) I learned "to say what I mean and mean what I say." Giving directions became less confusing to my daughters and more satisfying internally for me.

Because children have not yet developed a conscience, they will take the path of least resistance or make knee-jerk responses. They don't think things through—they just react. There is little or no morality involved, so their actions come more from habit than from reasoning. The parents' behavior teaches them by cause and effect. When the expectations of one parent are confusing and wishy-washy, and those of the other parent are rigid and hard, children cannot develop a reliable conscience. Inconsistency, poorly defined expectations, and the lack of follow-through can keep children stuck at a low maturity level, relationally and cognitively.

Why go into such detail about the inner growth and development of children? It was key in working with CJ's alters. Even as grownups, every one of us still has this kid within. When push comes to shove, when we are cornered, when we've lost control of our emotions, we will respond in a very childish manner. Far into adulthood, when we run into unresolved issues, we regress to a seven-to-twelve-year-old level, and behave accordingly.

Because CJ had many child alters, in a sense she had to parent each one. I, too, had to be kind and direct, relate to their perspectives and emotions, and subject most of them to the behavior modification approach. The whole process was even more complex because we learned that each child alter had a different temperament, mode of operation, and maturity level. I can compare this situation to the challenge of parenting my three daughters. In a given confrontation, one daughter could overreact, another could seem oblivious, and the third become super-sensitive. My wife and I learned that to treat them fairly might mean treating them differently. Styles of discipline needed to be individualized, because what worked with one didn't work with the other. But with each of them we needed to be <u>firm</u>, <u>fair</u> and <u>friendly</u>.

CJ was learning to manage her internal family, the multiple personalities, the kids and the adults within. With the child alters, it didn't work to deny their presence, or to be critical, condemning, or negative. What did work was good parenting: being nurturing, supportive, assertive, and clear about age-appropriate expectations. Dealing with dozens of amoral personalities was no simple task, but we began to realize each part had a name, a job description, a way of dealing with the abuse, and an encased, relatively simplistic memory. As CJ and I worked with each alter, the "organizational chart" became clearer.

We who are not dissociative (in the clinical MPD sense) experience our inner parts as somewhat enmeshed and overlapping. We can, however, identify the major parts according to need and modes of operation. For example, I recognize in myself a sensitive, caring, loving part, which I view as "good," but that same part can behave badly when feeling rejected and/or abandoned. The once-tender part becomes angry and defensive, and can move into acting cruel and uncaring. Sometimes the uncaring part develops into a colder, more indifferent part. This child part gets highly agitated when he perceives he's being told what to do. He becomes surly, or may shut down, or defy authority.

As I write about my inner parts, I notice how hard it is for me to identify clearly separate parts. They seem to metamorphose from one state of my mind to the next. Even though I am aware of these different parts, I am really one person. When I nail down my parts as being purely good or bad, I tend to split myself. In reality, all of the parts are mixed. They contain aspects that are good and bad, right and wrong, open and closed, trusting and mistrusting, respectful and disrespectful. My strengths carry with them weaknesses.

When I am in the mode of reacting to some outside stimulus, I am apt to see from my inner child's perspective. I am more mature and adult when I handle my emotions and perceptions by choosing to act, being proactive. It is not fair or realistic to hold the kid(s) within us to the same standard as we expect of ourselves as adults. When CJ was a young person, she did what she needed to do to survive, to get through the emotional and physical pain. Inside her were the child alters who held her past. But neither CJ nor I could hold the children responsible as if they were adults. Now CJ needed to treat her inner children as she would treat her own daughter—by nurturing, having compassion, listening, and being supportive. This is what functional parents do.

All of us can improve family communication by being loving. When we default to judging, being critical, or making evaluative statements, we only cause defensiveness, create negative stress, and hinder necessary connectedness. Yes, at times we must be tough lovers—set limits, draw boundaries, clarify expectations and discipline poor behaviors and attitudes. Remember, real love is responsible **to** others. CJ was learning to set those boundaries, especially with the destructive child alters. Since they didn't have an internalized value system, it was necessary for CJ, in a sense, to impose hers upon **them**.

For instance, when "Jill" began to cut, CJ had to take over and stop her. CJ had to step forward and relegate Jill to the background. When "Sarah" was raging, CJ as parent acted to calm her down. When "Jill" was suicidal, CJ took initiative to ask for an antidepressant from her doctor. When "Richard" was freaking out about snakes, CJ set up an emergency plan to follow, in case a real snake crossed her path. Boundaries, limits, strategies, attitudes and behavior: all needed to be in place for CJ's internal system to be functional and healthy. Only a loving context could grow them.

## Consciousness and the Subconscious

The main purpose for and value in counseling is that we become more aware, more conscious of why we do what we do. To be conscious, we must be aware of what is going on outside us, of our own actions, and of our own thoughts. A conscious person notices with "a degree of controlled thought" what is happening inwardly and outwardly. This awareness offers us insight, alternatives and options—insight about why we do what we do, alternatives to the way we act, awareness of other options.

CJ was becoming more and more aware through her memories, alters and emotions. She had not yet discovered everything within. The subconscious held these experiences just below the surface of her mind. Intuitively she knew this, but they remained confused, unclear. She insisted that she wanted me to push her into making the necessary discoveries.

It took real courage for CJ to go forward when she was afraid of what she'd find. Fear is the de-motivator of being aware. The subconscious does protect us and can intuitively assist us in dealing with danger, especially when we are vulnerable. Likewise, the subconscious accumulates information and has a "sense" of doing the right things. However, fear keeps us ignorant. If we don't trust ourselves, we cannot consciously access this protective part of our minds.

In CJ's case, the alters were her subconscious who protected her throughout the years of abuse. They could not prevent the abuse, but the various parts intuitively learned to outwit her abusers, or at the very least, diffuse the pain. They kept themselves/CJ sane and alive, able to function in word and action. However, having limited information, they often made poor decisions. The adult CJ was unable to enjoy intimacy because the protective alters blocked her. Like all of us, CJ's alters resisted being aware; we think "ignorance is bliss" because we don't want to be responsible to act on what we discover. Working without the pertinent data, CJ kept making the best choices possible under the circumstances.

During our meetings, it was my responsibility to ask the probing questions, and to observe the cues given through her body language and the tone of her voice. Once the subconscious was overwhelmed and unable to contain the information, the thoughts and feelings would work their way to the surface of her consciousness. Awareness would allow growth to continue.

The alters who were angry had suppressed their rage, but in fact the energy of anger had helped them contain damage from some of the abuse. For example, when CJ was about 12 years old, her father would hold her under water for long periods of time. Sharon, the alter who held that memory, became so angry about her terror that she was able to keep her cool, hold her breath, and refuse to drown. She was determined to not let "the father" win.

Sharon and her twin alter, Sarah, ended up not trusting others, especially men. They often took their anger out on me. I determined not to take the anger personally; instead I tried to demonstrate that I cared and could be trusted. Being sensitive to Sharon's limited experience, I attempted to remain lovingly assertive, being empathetic yet maintaining an appropriate firmness. Most of all I wanted to gain her respect and trust. She watched me as I dealt with the other alters, listened with a high degree of skepticism, and rarely gave me the benefit of the doubt. When she felt I had blown it, I attempted to be undefended, reflect back to her what I was hearing her say, and apologize for my part. Since I seldom defended myself or threatened her, over time Sharon softened, though without losing her vigilance.

I hope I'm not setting myself up as a model of positive detachment. It is certainly easier to be objective when I'm "on the job" counseling, than when I'm with my own loved ones. The closer I am to a person—like my wife!—the harder it is for me to be objective, and the more apt I am to take the disagreement personally. "Sharon/Sarah" and the other alters taught me a great deal about conflict resolution, because I was invested in improving my skills as a reflective listener.

My hope was that CJ could build respect and trust with each alter, not by defending, arguing or enabling, but by the same kind of reflective listening that I was attempting to model. For both of us it was more important to relate than to debate or analyze.

## For Further Information

Erickson, Erik, ***Identity, Youth, and Crisis***, W.W. Norton, 1968.

Kohlberg, Lawrence, "Kohlberg's Theory of Moral Development"—see his writings.

Braun, Bennett, Editor, ***Treatment of Multiple Personality Disorder***, American Psychiatric Press, Inc., 1986.

Carter, Rita, ***Multiplicity: The New Science of Personality, Identity, and the Self***, Little, 2008.

CHAPTER

# 13

# Too Terrible to Recall (CJ)

*Evil is present when there is a profound absence of empathy, shame and goodness.*

–Dr. Dan B. Allender and
Dr. Tremper Langman III, ***Bold Love***

*...we must not pursue the kind of sex that avoids commitment and intimacy, leaving us more lonely than ever.*

–I Corinthians. 6:1(***The Message***)

When I was a young girl, we lived on a farm. Though it was fun to keep small rabbits, ducks and chickens, I hated the times when the animals were slaughtered. I remember watching as my father either chopped off their heads or wrung their necks to kill them. Once I had a black cat appropriately name "Blacky." When we moved from the country to the city, my parents told me we would have to "get rid of Blacky." They said he was used to running around the countryside, and we could not allow him to run outside in the city. So my dad killed Blacky by knocking him in the head with a hammer. I distinctly remember choosing not to acknowledge that act or think about Blacky being dead. I don't even remember feeling bad about his death. The same with my pet rabbit, Phoebe. She became irritable and began biting for no reason, so my dad killed her too. Although I could not pinpoint the exact day, I know we ate Phoebe for supper one night. As was customary for me, I did not allow myself to think about Phoebe being dead. I kept myself from feeling any pain.

## Remembering Ritual Abuse

I'm not exactly certain how old I was when I was introduced to a cult and rituals. However, I do remember that I was "trained" in my paternal grandparents' home—usually in their basement. These memories were so horrible that I had carefully stored them away for many years. While I was in therapy with Jerry, these memories began to gradually steal back into my consciousness. I remembered seeing animals being abused, tortured and killed; watching rituals using knives, blood, water, an upside-down Christmas tree, a paper cutter; and having communion using real blood and meat. I was forced to drink urine and to perform sexual acts with both my grandparents. Both of them abused me sexually. If I was not compliant, and even when I was, my grandmother devised mean, evil ways to torture me. Once when I resisted, she put me in a closet with a snake. The snake was harmless, but I didn't know that. I was petrified with fear, and screamed and screamed for her to let me out. But she made me stay in the closet until I was quiet and acquiesced. At other times I was required to sit at her kitchen table and alternately forced to hold food in my mouth without swallowing or not allowed to eat at all until she gave me permission. I believe all of these incidents were knowingly contrived to prepare me for attending the cult meetings when I was older, to make sure I would be compliant.

## Extent and Effects on the Survivor

In the therapy process, I recovered a number of other memories involving my paternal grandparents. One of the first was my grandmother locking me in the closet because I had wet the bed. Another memory involved my grandparents taking me to their basement, making me remove my clothing, telling me I was bad—"the devil's child"—and forcing me to drink my own urine. Other memories of my grandparents' basement included their praying, and using silverware (mostly a variety of knives) to inflict pain and perform shameful sexual acts. I abhorred these memories! As they came, I vehemently denied them. I could not grasp that they could possibly be true, and tried to convince myself that I was crazy or had become some kind of habitual liar. But Jerry told me that some of these incidents were forms of ritual abuse.

In our counseling sessions, we learned that most of my parts feared my grandmother. She had died several years before, but the parts she had abused still believed she was alive—or that her spirit was alive—and they would never be safe from her. Even though I knew my grandmother was dead, I too was haunted by memories of her. Trying to break the stranglehold her memory had on all of us, the parts and I worked together to write a letter to my grandmother. Although the parts helped me write the letter, they insisted the letter come from me, which showed how much they still feared her. The letter read as follows:

*Dear Grandmother:*

*This letter is to share my perceptions and feelings with you. I would rather not have any contact with you or any thoughts of your existence, but that's probably not a very healthy stance to take and it certainly is not at all realistic or honest.*

*I suppose I should just begin relating to you what I remember. When I think of you, I shudder deep inside myself. I know you are dead, but I am still wary that you might still be here in some form. I guess in a sense you are still here as I know we live on to some degree in the people we have left behind. I know that I resemble you. I hate to even admit that. It somehow makes you even more real.*

*Amazingly, I do remember some good things about you. You were always a hard worker. I'm sure you would have had to be a hard worker because you lived on the farm for so many years. Your mother, Grandma Smith, always scared me. She, like you, was a very strong woman, a true matriarch of the family. You always kept a clean house and served good meals. I will always remember your cheesecake. It tasted so good.*

*I've seen you cry and laugh. I've seen you angry and sad. I've seen you unreasonable. I've seen you when you were mean and ugly, when you seemed like an entirely different person—not my grandmother, not anyone I knew at all. I've heard you talk in that low authoritarian voice that demanded attention and obedience.*

*I have no feelings for you whatsoever. To me you don't exist, except like a character in a book. I refuse to allow you to enter in or influence my life in any way. Yet I guess that's impossible, because there is no way I can erase the affect you had on my life. Unfortunately, I am connected to you, like it or not, and I don't.*

*In my mind's eye as a child, I see many little girls all with different colored hair, different eyes and with different names. All of them are alert and watching and waiting. Waiting to respond to the ever-changing situation around them when they were in your presence. They were trying so very hard to stay safe, unhurt, knowing that was not really possible.*

*It's so difficult to tell you how I feel about you. Nothing would be my first response, but I'm not sure that is even completely true. Fear is there, for certain. Perhaps I should just stay with telling you what I believe happened to all those little girls inside me. It is so difficult to speak the truth.*

*It seems I have been running from the truth for so long, first as a little girl and now as an adult, always running and avoiding.*

*What transpired between those little girls inside me and the woman I called grandma? There was a basement room, cold naked nights, locked closets, forced eating or deprivation of food and water, snakes, sex and scenes no child should have been forced to see. You were very, very mean and cruel. You took an innocent child and brutalized her over and over. You took out your own frustrations on all those different little girls and exercised your power over and over to prove your power and authority. You succeeded in persuading me you were all powerful, all knowing and one whom I should never, ever defy. You used brute force and any and all emotional devices to keep me within your power and influence. You attempted to make me the image of yourself. You misused me in all ways possible. Your warped mind knew all the intricate ways to scare all those little girls to death—over and over again. You created a reality and images of horror that had to be lived through time and time again. The sense of not knowing when and where these awful things would happen hung over the heads of these little girls for years and years. You cultivated an atmosphere of fear and torment, evil and mistrust, unhappiness and a true sense of continuous unreality. What horror you presented my sister with, I will never know. Whatever you did, I'm certain it was terrible, horrible, unimaginable, horrendous acts of evil and cruelty, because it left her an emotional cripple.*

*You are truly an ugly person. Your spirit is evil and ugly. Only a truly evil person could think up and perform the unspeakable acts that you did. Then when you became weary of the little girls you passed them on to your husband and aided in his additional torment and abuse of them. You taught these girls how and what to do to sexually please him and watched the events unfold in front of your own eyes. You passed all this off and justified it as "teaching." Why did we always have to go to the basement or watch you perform sexual acts or see animals horribly mutilated? Why?*

*I refuse to care about any of this. You mean nothing to me. I will never allow you to be a catalyst of any sort of emotion in me. You deserve nothing from me, not my love, not my hate. You deserve nothing.*

*What kind of thrill did you receive as you watched a small child being raped by a 200- pound man? Or as you pushed all types of metal instruments deep inside her most private body entrances? Did you truly understand the sense of fear that you generated inside her as you prepared the instruments that would probe at her very spirit and inner being? What rationale did you use for thrusting her small hands inside a small animal whose body was ripped apart by a bludgeoning weapon she was forced to hold? What were you thinking? What sick motivation could you have had? Did you ever feel any type of remorse? Did you ever want to stop doing those evil acts? Did you ever want to cradle those little girls in your arms and beg for forgiveness? Did you ever feel even an ounce of compassion or concern for them?*

*I will not allow you to evoke any emotion from me. I will not give you the satisfaction of even thinking of you other than as an inanimate object in my life. You mean absolutely nothing to me and never did. You will never be anything to me, never. You do not exist. You are a mere shadow in my past, a quick moving entity who just quickly touched the outside of my existence. Nothing more. I will not allow you to be anything more than that. I will not feel. I choose not to feel anything about you.*

*I am still afraid of you. You still hold power over me, even now. I hate myself because I look like you. I can't stand to be like you in any way. I'm afraid I will be like you in some way. I would avoid you at all costs if you were still alive. I'm wounded because I don't understand why you treated me like you did. I hate you because of what you did. You are evil, mean, terrible and I hate everything about you. I hate the way you look, the way you talk, and when you cry. I hate you so much that even the positive things about you pale into oblivion. You are evil, evil, evil. You deserve to be thrown into the pits of hell with all your cohorts.*

The unsigned letter was one way to expel the trauma and evil my grandmother inflicted on my parts and me, to begin healing the memories connected with her evil actions. Writing this letter took huge energy and courage, but it was a start, a move from feeling powerless under my grandmother's hand to being powerful over my past.

### Role of Parts/Alters

Many of the parts had experienced ritual abuse. However, most of those parts held only very small memories, or only a part of a memory, probably because most of the memories were so intense. For example, Noah was a young child part who had a particular love and concern for animals. In the cult, Noah's responsibility was to keep watch over the animals that were caged in anticipation of cult sacrifices. Noah wrote in the journal:

> *I don't feel good. I don't really want to be out, but I need to talk about the animals. I feel really bad about the animals. I feel sad about them. They keep the dogs and cats outside behind the barn in cages. Sometimes the animals get mad at each other and fight. Sometimes they cry, because they are hungry and want to get out of the cages. Mostly they're scared. I feel so bad for them. When they send me out to get one, sometimes I accidentally let one or two of them get away. I feel good for the free ones, but sad for the ones that will be dead. I want to let them all go, but I know I will get in trouble. I hear the cats and dogs all the time, crying, crying, crying. I want them to be let go. When I take the dogs and cats to the barn, they cry harder. Sometimes they scream and scream and scream.*

I honestly don't remember giving names to my parts, but sometimes I marveled at their creativity. This part named Noah was taking care of animals.

Just thinking about the ritual abuse made me feel evil. I sometimes wondered if I myself was the evil force behind all the rituals. I vacillated between the horror of my memories and wondering how I could be so evil as to slander my family by making up these cult activities. It was bad enough to admit that my father and grandparents had sexually abused me, let alone to acknowledge the ritual abuse. I constantly questioned my own spirituality in light of all the evil in which I (and my parts) had participated. My imagined childhood—picture perfect, fairy-tale—was crumbling into tiny pieces.

When I first began remembering the ritual abuse, Jerry's client June suggested I try her support group for individuals who were DID. She said that most of the group members had experiences with satanic ritual abuse. After hesitating for several weeks, I finally forced myself to go. At first I did not like the group at all. I wrote in my journal:

> *I'm not going back to that Friday night group. I did not fit. One of the facilitators asked me straight out at the beginning of the meeting during introductions if I had DID or if I was an SRA (satanic ritual abuse) victim. I thought I should have had the option of offering that information myself, not be forced to reveal it. That left a bad taste in my mouth, so I don't want to go back.*

But I ended up becoming a member of the group anyway. When I began having trouble with a part that cut me, I needed a place where I could talk about the cutting. The other members didn't gasp or shudder when I talked about my experiences. They just nodded their heads in understanding, and then we talked about other options to use when dealing with pain. As much as I didn't want to, I knew I fit in the group. I belonged, and the members were extremely helpful to me as I worked through the ritual abuse memories.

This process of recalling and working through the ritual abuse memories became utterly exhausting. Often I (and the parts involved) were left physically, emotionally, and spiritually drained. Sometimes it was necessary for one of the stronger parts to assist another part as he or she recalled the horrific events. The following journal entry (written mostly by Anita) is a good example of how the system worked:

> *Today is a difficult day. I [Anita] am at work. There's a lot of inner turmoil. I think I need to call JD for her [CJ]. She saw a movie last night and it set us all off—or most of us, especially Richard. He's in the snake bed with the lid on and he can't get out. Sarah's offering to make him feel better, but we all know what that means and we won't let her out of the locked room. She's [CJ] trying to stay completely inside, but hasn't been able to. She's afraid (deathly afraid) as we all are, of the snake bed. Not one of us seems to be able to help Richard (except Sarah). I fooled several people already today. I wanted to see if people at work could tell it was I—not CJ. They couldn't. Ha! It feels good to be in control and it's amusing to know I can fool other people. Back to the problem at hand. I'm not sure what to do about Richard. I know he's not doing well, but I'm not sure he could even talk to JD while he's in the box. Of course, none of us wants to let him talk either. It's far too uncomfortable. I suppose Victoria might be able to help. She [CJ] doesn't want me to call JD, but sometimes there's no choice. I can do this job for her very well and with considerable ease and effectiveness. I wish I could do it more often. She thinks I'm proud, a perfectionist, and emotionless. Those terms may fit me, but so be it. I am good at what I do. Without emotion! That's probably why I function so well. The movie last night reminded Richard of the snake bed. Sometimes they put the lid on and it was harder to move around than other times. It got pretty crowded with the snakes in there too. (Richard is telling me this.) The snakes are fluid and have a smooth, leathery feeling."*
>
> **Richard**—*They bite sometimes too. I can't do this by myself. It's too hard.*
>
> **Anita**—*It's very difficult to try and help Richard. I really don't think I can do it. I try to make him see that he's not in the snake bed now, but it's difficult for him to know that. I need to let JD know. It's almost 8 a.m., so I*

*can call him soon. I hope he's there. I know I need to be working for her [CJ] but there is too much going on. Janice and Victoria are upset too. They don't want Richard to remember because they were there too. We're not feeling good at all right now—cold and sick. I'm going to put on a sweater—that helped a little. Oh, things are NOT good! I'm losing control of this situation.*

After Anita made the call to JD, I began to journal myself:

*Jerry talked Richard out of the box. Actually, he helped Richard kick open the box himself. That's good because now Richard knows he can get out of the box by himself. Jerry said he and Richard would talk about his experience at our next session. He seemed pleased that Anita had trusted him enough to make the phone call. While Jerry and Richard were talking, I thought I was going to throw up. I didn't, but I still feel sick. I had my office door closed and after I hung up with Jerry, I almost fell asleep, but someone knocked on the door. I'm so very tired right now. I could curl up on the floor. I know I would fall asleep immediately.*

I suffered with horrible nightmares generally dealing with snakes. These dreams plagued me. Jerry now suggested that I could actually control my dreams. Every evening before going to sleep, I was to remind myself that I created my dreams and was in control of them. I didn't believe a word he said! Determined to disprove his theory, every night for a week I repeated the statement to myself before going to sleep. Nothing happened for awhile, but then one night I had a horrible dream about snakes. They were all over the ground—in fact, the ground seemed to be fluid with slithering snakes! Then right in my dream I said to myself, *"I am in control of this dream and I won't have any snakes in my dreams."* Immediately and amazingly, the snakes disappeared! Though I was mildly annoyed that Jerry had been right again, I was enormously relieved. To this day I rarely dream of snakes.

Jerry also encouraged me to map my alters, that is, devise a kind of organizational chart showing the relationships between the parts. Mapping was a daunting task. At first, even the parts fought against creating the map. However, as more and more parts began to emerge, with intricate and complicated relationships and connections, I gave in. As the map grew larger and larger, I switched from making an organizational chart to simply listing the parts' names, along with information about the major event or memory each part held. (See following pages; also see Appendix C)

Stepping back and allowing the parts to speak as I listened was excruciatingly painful and difficult for me. Jerry pointed out my high level of control (though I certainly didn't feel as though I was in control). In order to work through the process, I would have to let go and not try to control so much. Easier said than done! I did realize that Jerry was accurate about my strong control. For instance, one of the parts could recall a memory while I was at work, and (often with the help of one of the stronger alters) I was still able to make a presentation in a meeting that same afternoon. Sometimes I wasn't entirely certain about which part took over for me in those situations. Whoever they were, I was deeply grateful to them! I couldn't have continued to work and fulfill other life roles during this time if the stronger parts had not stepped in to cover for me.

Jerry was competent in dealing with my wacked-out out parts and me, but I truly hated it when Jerry talked to the parts individually. While I was just the listener to their conversations, I felt completely out of control. Often during a session there was a lot of switching between me and other parts, especially with the parts that were involved in the ritual abuse. Jerry could usually catch the slightest change in me that signaled when the switching occurred. He treated each part as an individual and with great respect. He allowed my parts and me to retain what small amount of dignity we could manage. Demanding and draining as it was, Jerry's therapy method provided me with the model I needed. Gradually I developed skills to deal with the inner parts myself.

Occasionally, some of the helper parts comforted me—that is, if I would allow them to. The helper parts were wonderful, especially when dealing with the young child parts. One morning I was particularly depressed. Bernice, a part who often took care of some of the child parts, comforted me. She held me on her lap. I needed the helper parts because there were so many ritually abused parts that were out to do us all in. Sarah was not only homicidal toward me, but once she planned to destroy all of Jerry's notes from our sessions, because, she stated, "It was evidence against us."

Because the parts so distrusted Jerry and what he wrote in our sessions, I asked him in early 1993 if I could read my file. Without any hesitation, he handed me his thick file of notes on our sessions! The parts were amazed that he would allow us to walk out of his office with the file. Of course, Sarah was gleeful, seeing a unique opportunity to destroy the file. However, Jerry had trusted me with the file, and there was no way I was going to allow Sarah access to all that evidence. I made certain Sarah stayed locked in her room with her twin sister while I read through the file. I must admit that deciphering Jerry's handwriting was a challenge! But several of the parts were comforted by the freedom to read the file, and I satisfied my own curiosity about what Jerry had written in his notes during our sessions. As it turned out, the notes were boring to most of the parts, and only slightly interesting to me.

When the ritual abuse parts became most active, I became more self-destructive, and more frequently thought about wanting to die. Some of this self-destructive drive came from parts that were created during the ritual abuse period of my life. A few of these parts felt a desperate drive to kill me, mostly because I was telling secrets. Adult cult members had repeatedly commanded all of us never to tell anyone anything about the cult. We were constantly threatened with death if we talked to anyone about the cult or its rituals. Jerry suspected that some of my parts had been specifically programmed by the cult to report back if any secrets were divulged. The intensity of the drive some of the parts had, to destroy me or other alters, confirms his idea. But sometimes the desire to kill felt mechanical, sort of like a robot simply doing what he/she was programmed to do.

The next few pages demonstrate various attempts to identify and systematize the complex relationships of my parts.

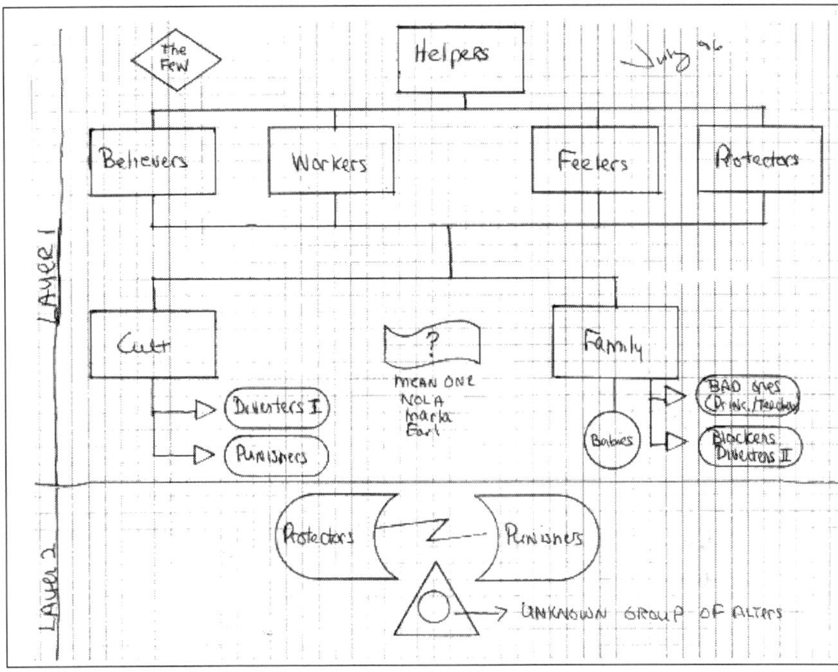


## Alter Map Key

| | |
|---|---|
| Helpers | Parts who provided assistance to the younger alters. |
| Believers | Parts with definite, strong spiritual beliefs. |
| Workers | Parts that helped me [CJ] in my profession. |
| Feelers | Parts that held many of the feelings from the traumatic experiences. |
| Protectors I and II | Parts that protected the system, especially the younger parts. |
| Blockers | Parts that blocked alters from talking about their memories. |
| Punishers | Parts that disciplined (generally verbal discipline) the alters that revealed their memories. |

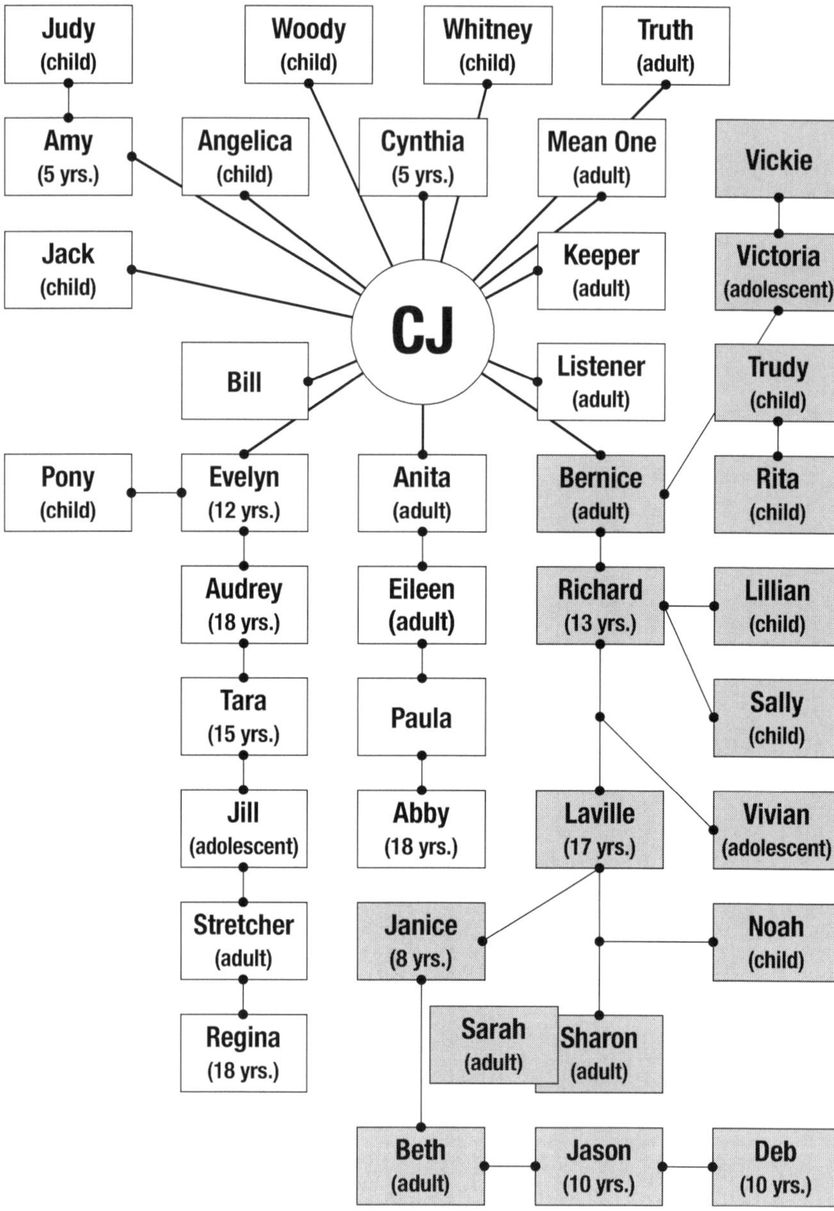
Judy
(child)
Woody
(child)
Whitney
(child)
Truth
(adult)
Amy
(5 yrs.)
Angelica
(child)
Cynthia
(5 yrs.)
Mean One
(adult)
Vickie
Jack
(child)
Keeper
(adult)
Victoria
(adolescent)
CJ
Bill
Listener
(adult)
Trudy
(child)
Pony
(child)
Evelyn
(12 yrs.)
Anita
(adult)
Bernice
(adult)
Rita
(child)
Audrey
(18 yrs.)
Eileen
(adult)
Richard
(13 yrs.)
Lillian
(child)
Tara
(15 yrs.)
Paula
Sally
(child)
Jill
(adolescent)
Abby
(18 yrs.)
Laville
(17 yrs.)
Vivian
(adolescent)
Stretcher
(adult)
Janice
(8 yrs.)
Noah
(child)
Regina
(18 yrs.)
Sarah
(adult)
Sharon
(adult)
Beth
(adult)
Jason
(10 yrs.)
Deb
(10 yrs.)

These journal entries record my feelings, approximately five years into therapy, as I faced my alters:

August 22

*I told Jerry I feel doomed, bad, and unredeemable. He said that was common for ritually abused individuals. He said to remember who had told me I was bad and who had called me the "devil's child." Jerry expressed concern for my emotional and physical well-being. He wanted me to promise to call him if I began to feel desperate. I did not promise. He mentioned medication again, but I told him what had happened with the first dose of Prozac. He encouraged me to talk to my doctor, but I don't want to take drugs because they make me feel out of control.*

August 23

*This morning I found myself thinking about overdosing. I was thinking of the bottle of Prozac I have but remembered that Jerry had told me overdosing on antidepressants didn't always kill a person but could leave that person severely impaired mentally. So I made myself quit thinking about taking my life. Those are not healthy thoughts.*

September 6

*I don't even care if I'm alive. I feel dead. Maybe I will always feel dead. Am I alive only to be dead? I walked 2.5 miles today trying to rid myself of the depression. But I feel useless and on the edge of the depression abyss, ready to plunge to the bottom of the pit.*

October 20

*Jerry gave me the phone number of his in-laws in Massachusetts where he and his wife will be staying. He said I was the only one he gave the number to because he is concerned for me. I've used the number—not to actually make a call, but just knowing I have it makes me feel good. Sometimes when I'm feeling panicky, I get the number out and look at it. I'm going to try very hard not to call and bother him. (I never did.)*

November 23

*I've been feeling very lethargic. I can't seem to do any housekeeping chores. Yesterday I just lay around all day. What a bum I am!*

March 10

*Jerry talked with Anita about the pills and asked her to dispose of them. She told him she couldn't do that, so Jerry insisted on speaking with me. It was such a strange conversation. He wanted me to flush the pills. I told him that I wouldn't use the pills but didn't want to flush them. He said that wasn't good enough, because he felt I was in a confused enough state (the others and I) that we could unwittingly take them. I'm not sure I believe that. He kept pushing me, saying if I didn't agree he would call 911 or Martin. The threat to call Martin always freaks me out. I told him I could simply lie to him, but he said he didn't think I would. It's so strange—there was a part of me that wanted to comply and be a good girl and there was another part that wanted to fight for my right to take care of myself, whatever that meant. At one point I agreed to flush the pills, and in the next breath I said I wouldn't. Jerry responded with, "Then I'll have to call Martin." I was backed into a corner, so I agreed to get rid of them. I don't think Jerry believed me, because he asked to talk to Anita again and asked her to be sure the pills got flushed. I did flush some of the pills, but not all. It's such a waste, plus I really need to have the pills here with me.*

April 3

*Jill, a new part came out this week. She's very fearful. Jill likes to hurt herself. She cut her arm with scissors the other night. I called Jerry and he got her to quit cutting until next week. He got her to sign a contract not to cut herself through April. Jill wanted to cut later but felt bound by the contract, so instead she burned her leg four times with the curling iron.*

Jill caused the system lots of problems. She was in awful pain, and the only way she knew to express her pain was to hurt herself (all of us!). Her preferred method was cutting.

Self-mutilation was a problem for several of the ritually abused parts. Of course, it became a problem for all of us. Audrey especially had an aversion to the cutting; she thought the cutting would disfigure her. She did her part in reporting any cutting to Jerry. As I've said, these self-mutilation and suicidal thoughts and ideas mostly came from the ritually abused alters. I know the cutting was troubling to Jerry, and he did all he could to get the parts to use other methods of dealing with their pain. Sometimes they complied; other times they didn't.

Cutting is such a strange problem. I know that my parts cut mostly because they were in such pain, and the pain of the cutting was a great diversion from the inner pain. Also, the ritually abused parts had experience with knives and felt comfortable using them to punish parts who told cult secrets. For a brief time after a part had cut, we all felt good, but soon after came the shame and disgust associated with cutting. It's an ugly and desperate cycle and difficult to break. I was grateful to my tattletale parts, who helped to keep the cutting to a minimum.

Halloween season was an especially trying time of the year for me. A combination of Halloween and a full moon could send me and my parts off the deep end. Many of the ritual abuse parts were absolutely certain that something evil would happen to them on or around Halloween. One of them thought the moon watched us. I could not bring myself to look at a full moon in the sky and was always relieved when it was hidden behind clouds. Another of the parts reported what the cult members had told her: Jack-O-Lanterns were their eyes to watch her and tell them if she disobeyed their orders. She fully believed this, and would do almost anything to avoid the Jack-O-Lantern's eyes.

Most of the parts hated being outside after dark. The intensity of their feelings made me avoid going places at night, especially alone. Attending the Friday evening group meant driving 15-20 miles from my home. Every Friday evening, the helper parts would accuse and undermine me, trying to protect some of the young alters who were traumatized by the dusk and night drive. Sometimes I would just stay home, to appease the parts, but at other times, I made myself emotionally strong and dealt with the inner turmoil. When I was deeply upset and felt really bad inside (with lots of memories and feelings), the dark time of day wasn't the issue. The parts pleaded to stay at home because it was the only place they felt safe. At those times, I usually gave in and stayed. I felt safer at home too.

Strange as it might seem at first, Easter was upsetting too. Our community staged an annual passion play, and some of our church people were actors, so I felt obligated to attend. However, I had to stop going, because it was far too vivid and barbaric, too close to rituals and cult activity I knew first-hand. Some of my parts went crazy even thinking about the events of the play. They acted out by engaging in self-mutilation, usually cutting. Their internal noise and objection was so strong, I surrendered to their desires to stay away. Fighting the entire group at one time was usually too much for me.

I would also become very upset about taking communion at church. I knew the theology of identifying ourselves with Christ, but the focus on blood, sacrifice, and broken bodies set off intense reactions. However, since I was the pastor's wife, I didn't think I should consistently abstain from taking communion. It helped that our particular denomination does not serve communion every Sunday, only 4-6 times a year. Still, even thinking about communion would make many of the ritually abused alters distraught

Even though I found every communion service difficult, I continued to participate. It took several years of intensive therapy for me to gain a new perspective on communion, as mirrored in my journal entry:

> *Communion was different for me today. Most of the time I just sat and listened to the voice of God speaking the word "beloved" to my spirit and allow it to simply soak into me. I realize the truth of my beloved-ness in my mind, but it seemed necessary to constantly hear God calling me his beloved CJ. Because I "know" the truth, communion took on the purpose of celebrating that new heart-realized beloved-ness and not concentrating on the blood sacrifice, but instead on the end result of God's acceptance of me because of what Jesus did on the cross. I believe, now that I understand my beloved-ness, I will be better able to communicate that to the other parts and to help them understand there is no further necessary sacrifice (cutting and abusing ourselves).*

At the height of my dealings with the ritually abused parts, Martin and I decided to visit the cities and towns where I had lived as a child and adolescent. This became even more distressing than I expected, because the ritually abused parts were convinced I was taking them home to die. Our trip was planned in the fall, which turned out to be a horrible time, ritualistically speaking, because the parts had many memories of satanic cult meetings during that season.

Jerry worked hard with me, trying all angles to prepare both the parts and myself for the visit home. Although I no longer had relatives in this area, thinking about returning to places where horrific events took place sent waves of anxiety through my heart and mind. Why then would I want to visit these places with Martin? First, I hoped to gain confirmation of memories to end my self-doubt. And then I wanted to begin to close the chapter of my past—to move on toward a future untainted by my past abuse. I intended for the trip to jump-start the healing process for me. I also hoped that the parts would see these places with new eyes and understand they didn't need to fear any longer. If some major integrations (merging of the parts) could take place, I could be propelled to the end of my therapy, toward being a whole person. My big plan was to go back home, see things, acknowledge them, and get quickly and miraculously zapped into a whole person!

Several weeks before the actual trip, I began to eat uncontrollably. I found myself stuffing any kind of food into my mouth as quickly as I could, and immediately craving more. It felt like trying to fill a bottomless pit inside me. Looking back, I think the eating binge was caused by the parts who were convinced they were going to their death. I myself also felt an impending death sentence. In addition to stuffing down food, I had trouble focusing, was very forgetful, and slept very little. Anxiety about the trip was building inside the parts and me. October seemed to be my death month, the culmination of everything bad that had ever happened to me. In September, I journaled:

> *I need to look at things more realistically—feelings versus fact. My feelings are all out of whack, but the facts remain intact. The cult is NOT in control. If I do die this month it won't be because of the cult, it will be because God has decided my time on earth is finished and there is no difference whatever month we are in. The death feelings are only that—something the cult programmed into me. Lies and deception. I'm so fearful that next Wednesday (October 1st) all hell will break loose. I even hate to write the date.*
>
> *I realize that trying to resist my fear and anxiety actually only makes the feelings more intense. I need to acknowledge the fear and then acknowledge the truth. The fear must be subjected to the truth, but that doesn't mean all my anxious feelings will disappear. I need to sit with the feelings and realize that they are simply that—feelings, not necessarily the truth. My feelings seem overwhelming, but they are not overwhelming me. A part of me believes I will die and my eternity will consist of the hopelessness of eternal rape. What a horrible concept! It's absolutely incomprehensible. Terrible, terrible. But that will not happen, because I am God's beloved. He has forgiven me, loves me and will take me to live with him in heaven. No matter what some of the parts were told, Jesus is NOT Satan's brother. It's simply not true. There is no family connection at all between them—they are exact opposites—holy and pure versus evil and vile—truth versus lies.*

Despite my inner turmoil, Martin and I did make our road trip back home. I took my camera so I could get pictures of everything: houses, schools, and other places where I remember living or visiting. Initially I was concerned about whether I could accurately find and identify these places, but I need not have worried. We found every one of them with absolutely no difficulty. The parts and I revisited the house where Tara was raped by the three men, the park by the river where Sharon was almost drowned by my father, and other places that held traumatic memories for me. Martin was blessedly patient with me, quiet and supportive, allowing me to spend as much time as I needed at each location. I was emotionally overwhelmed, feeling like I was falling apart yet still compelled to continue the journey. Even though we made only a few stops, some of my parts were utterly petrified by being in that country. We were all anxious to return to the safety of our home.

When Martin and I got home, I went to talk with Jerry. He said I would have to allow all the parts to talk about their experience of visiting the places of their abuse. Ugh. I wasn't eager to revisit the trip. But the good news was that we did not die that month as we had anticipated. We had all lived through another October. Though the trip had been hard, it was instrumental in my healing process. My memories were validated, I was affirmed, and I now had new energy and motivation to continue my journey of healing.

My alter Abby often gave voice to other parts, in the form of poems written in my journal. Her poems often expressed the experience of another alter.

## Children Are Born—Keeper's Story

By Abby

The air is cool and crisp
Wind blows through trees
Leaves fall silently to the ground
Feet crunch through brittle leaves.

A child is taken through the evening gloom.
To seclusion, to darkness lit only by candles.
In the dim lurks the devil and his people,
Animals, reptiles, and fire and blood.

The night is dark.
The stars are bright.
The moon is full.
A heart is fragile.

In the shadows, a child is born of a child, born to die.
A tiny baby, a brand new life,
Taken quietly and quickly
Placed on a hard, cold altar.

In the gloom, the mother child delivers yet again
An older child born to obey, born to survive.
The child brandishes the sacrificial knife,
Carves death into the tiny new life.

Two born there that night.
Three died there that night,
In the woods, in the dark:
The mother child,
The baby child born
And the child born to kill.

CHAPTER

# 14

# The Destroyers of Freedom and Safety (JD)

*Christ has set us free to live a free life. So take your stand! Never again let anyone put a harness of slavery on you.*

–Galatians 5:1 (***The Message***)

As we discovered more alters, CJ and I faced the awful reality of how extensively she had been abused—by her father, her grandparents and a number of other persons connected to her extended family. The splitting into alters, CJ's long ignorance, and her resistance to admitting the abuse are all products of that family system. Therapist Robert Becker sums up the dynamics of such dysfunctional and abusive families in his book entitled ***Don't Talk, Don't Trust, Don't Feel.*** I want to look at CJ's experience in light of these three traits. I call them "destroyers of freedom and safety." In these families, secrets are never shared, there is no trust, and feelings are not felt or expressed.

## Don't Talk—Keep Secrets

Abusers intimidate, threaten, bribe and use whatever forms of manipulation they can to keep the abused quiet. After all, if the victimized keep their mouths shut, the perpetrators will never be discovered. CJ was threatened within an inch of her life if she did not keep the secrets. Her father abused her and in all probability was abused by his own parents. They taught him not only to maintain the secrets but also to perpetuate them; he continued to be victimized and evolved into the perpetrator. He even victimized CJ's mother who, probably because of her own fear, also became a perpetrator. She too kept the secrets and made little or no attempt to rescue her daughters.

The essence of secrecy is fear; all secrets are constructed around it. The bigger the secret, the greater the fear; the greater the fear, the more elaborate the cover-ups and the rationalizations. All of us fear being "found out," because if our secrets are discovered, we could lose the reputation we've attempted to build. If our inner thoughts were displayed on a large screen, in color and surround sound, we would be overwhelmed with shame.

If someone published a scorecard of our violations of the Ten Commandments, no doubt we would be very embarrassed. In reality, most of us do covet what other people have. Like Jimmy Carter, we commit adultery in our hearts. We often lie (or at the very least deceive), steal (maybe not outright, but we "fudge" on income taxes, and "forget" to replace items taken from the library and work), and fail to love God with all of our hearts, souls, minds, and strength. We can't love ourselves, let alone our neighbors. We gossip, speak ill of others, consume more than we should, cover up our "mistakes," don't ask for forgiveness, and so on.

We hold these failures secretly inside, and if we are unwilling to admit them to ourselves, we certainly will not admit them to others. As the secrets increase, we become more and more enslaved to them. Our lives can become one big secret—to the point that nobody REALLY knows us, and we hardly know ourselves. When we compartmentalize these secrets, we compartmentalize our lives. We become one person at work, another with our friends, and still another at home. Our role-playing can increase until we fall into a particular role whenever different situations arise. It's like maintaining two or three secret lives.

CJ's family had learned this role-playing well. The parents and grandparents were all quite active in their local church. Yet, along with some other "upright" church members, they were perpetrators of the sexual abuse. They were "Christians" and leaders in the community, while at the same time they were occult practitioners and sexual abusers of their own children. These "secrets" were never revealed to the community at large.

My central purpose in asking CJ to share the secrets and uncover the shame was to let her experience the feelings that come with honesty and freedom. Once secrets are exposed, they lose their power. As each alter opened up to the other parts, the others could also experience the release of fear and be empowered by freedom. Once she had shared her secrets with me, I encouraged CJ to share them with Martin and intimate friends. As she felt safer speaking of her memories with me, I hoped she could extend her area of safety and freedom by sharing with close loved ones.

It takes too much energy to hide from others, and we end up hiding from ourselves. At this point I acquainted CJ with the "Johari Window," named after Joseph Luft and Harrington Ingham.

### The Johari Window

| | Known to self | Unknown to self |
|---|---|---|
| Known to others | 1<br>The public self | 2<br>The hidden self |
| Unknown to others | 3<br>The private self | 4<br>The discovered self |

**Window # 1 is "known to self and others."** **<u>The public self.</u>** For example, others and I myself know that I'm 6'2", in my mid 70's, with gray hair and hazel eyes. I work as a counselor, and I'm a Christian who attends church regularly. Whatever I choose to reveal about myself publicly is obviously known to others.

**Window # 2 is "unknown to self and known to others."** **<u>The hidden self.</u>** I can be unaware that I have mustard on my mustache or a tear in my shirt, or that I have a habit of juggling the change in my pocket when speaking to a group. These are aspects of myself which others can observe, and if they are gracious enough, point out to me at an appropriate time.

**Window # 3 is "known to self and unknown to others."** **<u>The private self (can also be secretive).</u>** This window can be quite large for those who do not reveal much about themselves. Such people are very closed and hard to read. CJ didn't know all the secrets that the alters held; her inner system was closed. However, all the information and secrets each held, when combined, made much to "be known." You could say that CJ had many windows inside window # 3.

**Window # 4, "unknown to others and unknown to self."** **<u>The discovered self.</u>** This part is fully known only by God. If we are growing, maturing people we can discover little nuances about ourselves almost daily. When we do not allow others to know us, if we choose to keep them and ultimately ourselves in the dark, window # 4 will also remain very large.

Secrets prevent discovery. If CJ had refused to open up and discover who she really was—her history, her story—nobody, including herself, would have known her. For my part, I had to practice openness, transparency and honesty, or our relationship would have never developed. I chose to be authentic rather than secretive, and I'm convinced that CJ helped me to expand my #4 window. I discovered thoughts, ideas and techniques that I never knew were in me. As I read books about dissociation, talked to my supervising psychologist, and shared with my wife about what I was learning, I too experienced more of who I really am.

## Don't Feel—Cover Up Emotions

Our sense of who we are is intertwined with how we feel. Emotions arise from our physical being. When we are angry, we can feel our bodies tense. Our blood begins to "boil," our jaws tighten, and we have a real urge to release our anger. When we are fearful, every cell wants to pull away, our stomachs tighten, and we may feel chilled or shake uncontrollably. When we are hurt, it's our bodies that feel the pain (i.e. we say that our hearts ache). The common question, "How do you feel?" forces us to examine the state of our physical being. To know how we feel, we check our bodies, our five senses.

Very early, CJ learned from her perpetrators, not only to keep secrets, but also not to feel. Over and over she heard these messages: "Feelings are not important. You shouldn't feel that way. That doesn't hurt. Don't complain or the situation will become worse. My feelings matter more than yours do. Love is not a feeling; it's obedience and sex."

Blocked emotions damage as much as uncontrolled emotions do. As CJ endured severe trauma, having to ignore her own body and emotions, her alters each learned different ways to cope. Some discounted their feelings, others learned to ignore them, others became angry and protective. Most of them realized that they had no power or say-so. Each alter dealt with their emotions a bit differently; when one of them could get past his or her fear, the repertoire of available emotions expanded.

We've known for years about IQ (intelligence quotient) but Goleman suggests that we have an EQ (emotional quotient) which, unlike one's IQ can be increased. Emotional intelligence is our ability to sense and manage our emotions. People with a high EQ do better at work and in their relationships and generally are happier. This is not the same as emoting all the time. Melodramatic people have a lower EQ They have tremendous highs and lows and display their emotions without control. Others of low EQ are indifferent to what they feel, are unaware of their bodies, and are therefore emotionless. Still others are one-dimensional. Fear, hurt, or frustration may be the predominant emotion, but such people can feel and express only anger. CJ's EQ was low. Her primary emotions were fear, hurt and frustration, but her perpetrators did not allow her to feel them. Her survivor alters did indeed feel anger, but could not "come out" or show themselves, because her abusers would then inflict even more pain. It is difficult to fathom CJ's position; she was damned if she did and damned if she didn't.

Against such odds, CJ was learning to feel more. As each month went by, she moved further into present feelings and appropriate feelings toward the past. Sometimes she could now get angry with her husband and me. No longer could she remain indifferent to those she cared about. CJ's anger felt contradictory to her desire to be more loving, but in fact, as she gained ability to express anger, her ability to love also improved. She still could not feel anger at her perpetrators, nor could she love them. She could remain a dutiful daughter, but there was no relationship, no emotional connection. CJ had been prevented from caring, and consequently, connecting with her parents did not so much as cross her mind.

Though most of us have not been forced into dissociation, we do have choices about what to do with painful feelings—numbing them, discounting them, giving in to them, suppressing them, or clinging to them (which can lead to bitterness and vindictiveness). We can choose a better way. To me, Victor Frankl embodies the better way. He was a medical doctor who survived the Holocaust without becoming indifferent or vindictive. Though he did not deny his emotions, he determined that no one could imprison his mind. His book ***Man's Search for Meaning*** shows not only how he managed to survive, but also how he strengthened others to grow through suffering.

CJ persisted in her quest to know the truth while bearing the pain. I could see her EQ steadily increasing.

## Don't Trust—Remain Fearful

Hallmarks of dysfunctional families: We don't talk (we keep the secrets), We don't feel anything, and We don't trust anyone. CJ's family had demonstrated these every day. Now she was learning to talk, open up, and disclose the family secrets. Likewise her feeling level rose as she became more emotionally intelligent. This was the time for her to open the gates to trust. From the very beginning of our time together, CJ had longed to be able to trust. We both knew the teaching of Jesus, that even faith the size of a tiny mustard seed would grow into a large, very fruitful tree.

My next step was to build a trusting relationship with each alter, and not let them down when they trusted me. As the alters began to disclose their memories and how they dealt with them, I saw how important it was to believe (trust) what they were telling me, and reflect their feelings so they'd know they'd been heard. Trust is most quickly built via understanding.

Empathy was crucial: if we don't feel understood, if our feelings are not heard, and if we are discounted, we will not open up nor trust. Only when we are allowed to talk and feel do we feel safe. We must trust that the other person has our best interests at heart before we can safely confide in them.

CJ's relatives used and abused other people to fulfill their own needs, and never vice versa. Their selfish desires, their self-centeredness, and their insensitivity prevented them from loving others. None of them were empathetic or even concerned about her. Such people are not to be trusted. Their evil, heartless, abusive behavior taught CJ not to trust at all. Each developing alter was programmed to look out for her or himself alone, in order to survive. The system inside CJ showed some cooperation, but trust among the alters was minimal—and trust of male counselors even less.

The importance of trust in our relationships cannot be over-emphasized. We often speak of "earning" another's trust, but I suspect that it's usually the other way around. We trust until another betrays that trust. CJ naturally wanted to trust her father, but each time he betrayed her, her ability to trust was maimed. History shows us how much human beings want to trust. Charismatic leaders win the trust of their followers by the things they say and the promises they make. Devoted followers often remain committed to cultic leaders, even when (for example) a person like Jim Jones directs them to drink poisoned Kool Aid. We want to believe. The Germans believed Hitler who led them to invade their neighbor states and to murder their neighbor Jews. We would like to think we could resist such leaders, but they reveal our deeply-rooted desire to believe and trust.

Trust is both naïve and skeptical. I see myself as basically a trusting person, with a little skepticism thrown in. In general, I'd say most people are well-meaning, but I also know that any given individual is capable of committing atrocities. I trust that most of the drivers will stay on their side of the road most of the time; however, I don't trust drunk drivers to do that. I don't want to be either paranoid or naïve. I'm a believer but I doubt. Without both I'd be foolish. In fact, my doubting and looking for answers can make me more of a believer. Trusting myself, trusting others, and trusting God require discernment. I make a commitment to truth as best I can identify it. Redemptive trust has to build upon truth. Since CJ was rarely told the truth, she could not trust others and herself. As she and I became acquainted with the alters, we learned that each one wanted to believe. Some naively believed and trusted; others had few or no experiences with trust. Each alter needed to balance reason and trust.

Trust is based on truth, so the framework of therapy offers honest talk, open expression of emotions, and a progressive testing and building of a safe relationship. My aim in quality counseling was to show CJ a functional relationship involving all three elements.

CJ was learning to talk, trust, and feel—with support from group members, her husband, a close friend and me. Now it was time to practice this "triad" inside, *intra*-personally. The divided house where CJ, the host, lived with the alters had to come together.

## For Further Information

Manning, Brennan, ***Abba's Child,*** Nav Press, 1994.

Smedes, Lewis, ***Forgive and Forget: Healing the Hurts We Don't Deserve,*** Harper and Row, 1984.

Ford, Marcia, ***The Sacred Art of Forgiveness***, Skylight Paths Publishing, 2006.

Becker, Robert, ***Don't Talk, Don't Trust, Don't Feel,*** Hci, 1991

Goleman, Daniel, ***Emotional Intelligence,*** 1995, Bantam.

CHAPTER

# 15

## Hearing the Alters Speak (CJ)

*I truly delight in God's commands, but it's pretty obvious that not all of me joins in that delight. Parts of me covertly rebel, and just when I least expect it they take charge.*

–Romans 7:22-23 (***The Message***)

A number of years into my therapy, as the parts of myself began to reveal themselves and the fragments of the past each one held, gradually I became aware that there were more than just two or three of them. These parts, or alters, were adults, adolescents, and children, male and female, angry, hysterical, calm or wise. Many of the parts held only one or two small memories. Others held some very traumatic memories and played major roles in the entire system. As I learned, I noted their names and what I knew about them. In the end, I had listed well over one hundred and fifty different and distinct parts. This large number sometimes dismayed me, but once their memories and stories were processed, the vast majority of them seemed to simply melt away, or be absorbed by the remaining parts. (This is called integration.)

Often I was overwhelmed by the intensity and volume of the parts' internal conversations. Then I had to either disassociate from all the parts or send the parts **away.** I would create places in my mind where they could wait. Once there were many ritually abused younger parts who cried and wailed at the pain they felt. I could not deal with them, so I placed them for weeks in a white room I created, until I had the energy to face up to their emotions. On another occasion I created a fence and told the parts to stay behind it and not speak. Another time I created a box where I placed some of the major alters (i.e., Sharon and Sarah). Abby wrote a poem about the parts' feelings while they were kept in it. Appropriately called "The Box," Abby's poem expresses the despair and pain of the parts at being separated and ignored.

The box is crowded.
Inhabitants are restless.
No air to breathe
No space to move.

No window to view
No door to open
No air escapes
No sun shines in.

Cry—it won't help.
Scream—it won't matter.
Curse—it's not heard
Pray—it's not uttered.

Pressed close together
Hot and sweaty
Hungry, thirsty
Tired and hopeless.

No one to care
No one that loves
No one to rescue
No one to help.

Sometimes when the parts were in the middle of telling their memories, the process became too much for them to bear, and they would actually dis-associate themselves by simply going away. Many times in my journaling, reference is made to particular parts who "were gone." Other alters would question why they had left, when they were expected to return, or if they were dead and never coming back. When the parts "went away," it was as if they had moved to a more interior place inside me, so deep that they were inaccessible to anything or anyone. Other parts and I might talk to them and plead with them to return, but they only came back when they were ready to face the memory or situation, not before. These times were respites where the parts regained the strength and energy to forge ahead in the process. Keeper explained this hiatus as a time of resting and regrouping. She reminded all the parts that the hiding one was not weak, but rather strong. Keeper told us that the parts knew themselves well enough to understand they needed time away, and that this was healthy. At other times, the parts' retreat was motivated by their intense fear. The helper parts spoke directly and constantly to the fearful parts, and eventually dispelled their fear. Then the hiding part would return and begin interacting again with the rest of the system.

## Identifying Some Major Parts

As I recognized these different parts, each one looked different to me—each one had a distinct face. One part had no face at all. They had different hair colors and styles. Their body shapes varied from slight and frail to large and towering. I've mentioned that each one had his or her own character; I learned to depend on some of the parts who had real strengths, rational knowledge of the abuse, and/or ability to manage my internal system of people.

The various parts often spoke amongst themselves. At first I was mostly just an observer, rarely involved directly in their conversations. When the inner chatter was very loud and intense, it was tiring just to listen. At one point when the parts became extremely vocal, Jerry suggested I let them write about themselves in my journal. So I stepped back and allowed them to talk among themselves. I don't remember whether Jerry asked to see the journaling, but soon after the parts began to journal, I took a copy to my session with him. I felt extremely uncomfortable about letting him read it; it seemed to be just one more way that I was making myself vulnerable. So as I placed the journal on his desk, I declared that he could have it, only if I forgot to take it home with me. If I remembered to take it, he was out of luck. Not until I was in my car on my way home, did I actually remember the journal. It was too late to go back for it, even though I wanted to. This showed me there were two camps inside me: one needed desperately to stay hidden, and the other deeply desired to be known, to end the isolation. The second camp had won this particular battle.

Most of the parts distrusted Jerry. However, a few of the younger parts were afraid that Jerry would leave us, either by firing us or dying. Often in long conversations between the parts, the younger alters would lament that we caused Jerry too much trouble. They were certain Jerry would stop seeing us. Over and over Jerry had to tell us (all of us!) that he would stick with us and not leave us. One journal entry shows this ongoing concern about Jerry terminating our therapy:

| | |
|---|---|
| **Nicky** | *Is JD going to make us quit coming to see him?* |
| **Keeper** | *He hasn't said that. Why do you ask?* |
| **Nicky** | *Because we bother him too much. Because he's tired of us. Because he doesn't like us.* |
| **Keeper** | *He hasn't said that. What makes you think he feels that way?* |
| **Nicky** | *He's tired of listening to us, I know he is.* |
| **CJ** | *I've asked him to be honest with us. He's never said anything like that.* |
| **Anita** | *He probably wants to, but thinks we'll freak out.* |
| **Sharon** | *I'm sure he'd like to dump us.* |
| **Keeper** | *We can ask him.* |
| **Sharon** | *He won't admit it; he'll just dump us one day.* |
| **Anita** | *Maybe we should fire him.* |
| **Keeper** | *Why?* |
| **Anita** | *Then we would have the best position. We can find someone else to talk to before we fire him, then we won't miss him.* |

Jerry was always sensitive to our fears. He would begin telling us weeks in advance of a pending trip or vacation. We all hated it when Jerry was gone. The younger parts would whine and cry about him dying and never returning. For this reason, I usually saved a phone message or two from Jerry, so I could play it back to the parts during the time he was gone. Just hearing his voice would generally calm them down.

An alter named Audrey, the seductive, feminine part of me, enjoyed sex and flirting. I was disconcerted when she occasionally flirted with Jerry, but I really kept tight reins on her. I never allowed her to behave inappropriately with him—not that Jerry would have allowed that, in any case! Audrey wrote in the journal:

> *My name is Audrey. I like life. I like men. I like flowers and perfume. I help her [CJ] with her husband. I know how to make Martin feel wanted. Today I got very upset with Jill. She was doing bad things; she burned us with the curling iron. I don't like scars and I think Jill gave us some scars today. Jill burned us four times before I could stop her. I was pretty pissed with CJ, Jill and JD. JD should have known better. Jill needs a stricter contract. Jill told JD she wouldn't hurt us anymore, but I don't believe her. She gets all freaked out and gets crazy. I do like JD, I think, even though he made a stupid mistake with the contract. He's pretty nice. He does help when we ask him to. He's not mean to us. I think he tries to understand. I could be wrong though, because I may just like him just because he's a man too. CJ is a wimp. She'll never make it by herself. I feel very powerful and important. I like to have fun too. But she doesn't let us have much fun. I love ice cream. I'm certain I do. I like the outdoors, warm sunshine and cool breezes. I like birds.*

### *Anita*

One of the first and most influential parts to emerge was Anita, one of my helper alters. When I was a child, Anita had often accompanied me to school, in case I needed her to intervene and take over for me. As an adult, Anita would on occasion call Jerry if she felt it necessary to do so. One journal entry reads:

> *Anita called JD and said she was worried about me. She told him I had freaked out about Evelyn and Richard. It was weird because she was talking and I was there, but only listening. It was kind of comforting to have her talk for me. JD said a lot. I could tell he tried to make her feel at ease. He tried to explain to her what was going on. He said everyone has parts—mine are just more clearly defined. Jerry told Anita he knew all the parts were scared, because they all had been treated so badly. He said the parts needed to know that kind of treatment was over. He told Anita he was concerned about Richard and Bernice and wanted to talk with them. I don't know if they will, but he wants to try.*

Jerry had several conversations with Anita. He enlisted her help to get introduced to other parts. Most of the parts felt Jerry was dangerous and needed to be watched very carefully. Anita, in her usual helper way, made Jerry promise not to physically touch any of the parts at any time. When

Jerry promised, Anita gave him names of several parts who were ready to meet him. One part (Bernice) was convinced that Jerry intended to get all the parts to come out, and then would just leave them. She was convinced Jerry did not want to treat another DID but didn't have the guts to tell us or to terminate therapy. As therapy progressed, however, Bernice had opportunity to watch Jerry work with some of the other parts, and she came to trust that he really cared and wanted to help all of us.

Sometimes I was unable to function, not even to get out of bed. Then Anita would get us all up and started for the day. Often I could take over later, but she was very near throughout the day, to step in immediately if I became too overwhelmed to function. Here, some initial journaling done by a few of the parts reflects a typical conversation:

**Anita** *I think writing in this journal is stupid. I really don't have anything to say. I take care of her [CJ] when necessary. There is nothing I want to talk about. I don't have any problems. Sometimes the others cause me some concern, but I don't have any needs myself.*

**Victoria** *I like to have fun too. I don't like remembering things. I don't like blood and skin. I don't want to talk anymore now.*

**Jill** *I don't feel good today. It hurts inside. I want to cut, but I promised not to.*

**Audrey** *Don't cut and I mean it! JD said there are other ways to take care of feelings. What else can we do? I don't know right now.*

**Sarah** *I can make everyone feel better. I can bring all this misery to an end. She's [CJ] just messing everything up for all of us. She doesn't know what she's doing. She's telling all the secrets to everyone. That's bad, VERY BAD! It makes everyone feel bad too. Everything is out of control. We will all suffer because she tells so much. It's trouble—bad trouble! I don't like it at all. I need to stop her before it's too late for the rest of us, but I signed that stupid contract. We can't trust him [JD] either. Can't be deceived by him. He's no good, no good at all. I don't like the idea of writing in this book either.*

**Bernice** *Actually, I don't think writing in this book is very wise either. It gets everyone stirred up. That may not be a good idea since things are already out of control. But maybe we should* *trust JD for now, that is until he really blows it—then we can reconsider. He has helped. CJ trusts him. He seems careful.*

**Jill** *NO, no, no, no, no! Men are bad! They are bad! They do bad things! BAD, BAD, BAD, BAD!*

**Audrey** *Stop it! You're upsetting the others. JD has NOT hurt us. He made a mistake with your contract, but he didn't do it on purpose.*

**Laville** *DON'T TRUST HIM! IT'S STUPID TO TRUST HIM!*

**Sharon** *I'm confused. I don't know whom to believe. Who is right, who is wrong? I don't know. It's too tiring to figure it all out—too confusing.*

**Judy** *JD, Jack would like to talk to you, but he's too little to write. He likes you. She (CJ) let Jack have ice cream once. Jack is only 5. He has a memory. It's not a bad memory. It just scares him. He's a nice boy. I don't care what the others say, I think you are a nice man, JD.*

**Abby** *I like the idea of writing in this book. I can say <u>exactly</u> what* **I** *want. I'd like to say that the Father is a <u>jerk</u>. He is a <u>mean</u> man. He hurt a lot of us. He hurt CJ too. I don't like him much and never will.*

**Anita** *I hate being late. We were 10 minutes late for the doctor's appointment. Late is irresponsible. She [CJ] should have started earlier.*

**Audrey** *Lighten up, Anita. It wasn't her fault she was late. Anyway, they always make us wait to see the doctor.*

**Unidentified part** *The Father always said NOT to be late. He ALWAYS gets mad if anyone's late. Hurry up, hurry up! Don't be late! The Father says there's no excuse if you're late. You should leave early enough not to be late. You leave a bad impression when you're late. There's NO excuse—NO excuse for being late—none whatsoever!"*

**Jill** *You get punished when you are late. You get into trouble so you won't be late again.*

**Bill** *The father is unreasonable. He won't listen for explanations. He doesn't listen at all to anyone. He thinks he's always right. No, he IS always right!! But not really. He's stupid. And he's wrong a lot of the time. He's worthless…*

**Evelyn** *That's not true! He does do things wrong, but nobody is completely worthless. The Father does love her [CJ] sometimes. Sometimes he can be good and kind.*

**Bill** *You always defend him! But it doesn't matter. He's NOT good and kind. He's bad and mean.*

**Anita** *This is useless conversation. We can't change him no matter what. Let's just forget him.*

**Evelyn** *She [CJ] can't. She loves him. She needs him.*

**Bill** *No, she doesn't! None of us need him, ever, never!*

**Jill** *He hurts us.*

**Anita** *Not anymore. That's why this conversation is ridiculous. It doesn't matter anymore.*

**Bernice** *It matters to some of us. Some of us need to talk about it.*

**Vivian** *But he's bad. Did he make us all bad too?*

**Victoria** *I feel bad. I think I'm bad. But it's because of what I did. I did bad things. Bad, bad things!*

**Janice** *Me too, but I didn't mean to. I didn't do them on purpose.*

**Laville** *We're all bad. ALL OF US.*

**Evelyn** *I don't think so. JD says we're not. Bad things just happened to us.*

**Keeper** *I'm beginning to think that IN (the inside place—described later in this chapter) is not such a wonderful place anymore. CJ came out today and then went right back IN. I think Anita may be right. We need to find a new way to handle trauma rather than to run and hide. If I really care for CJ, I want what's best for her, no matter if it's painful. If CJ keeps running from the pain, she won't work through it. Do you hear me, CJ? You need to face/embrace our memories, emotions and pain. We need to lock the door to IN for a while.*

*I will find out how I can help you go through this without going IN. IN will not be destroyed. We will just shut it up for a while, like a summer home is shut up in the winter. I promise I won't abandon you. I never have, have I? You need to listen to Noah. You need to hear what he says and feel how he feels. It's okay. Really. I can sense you are pulling away from this. You must be strong! I'll be there for you. Just think about it. Think it through. You'll see that it makes sense. I don't think I want you to give my journaling to JD. It makes me feel uncomfortable.*

**Anita** *I don't think your talking made very much difference. She's back IN. You need to lock IN up and hide the key! I agree, I don't like JD to read our writing. I can't think it helps very much anyway.*

## Understanding Their Places

### *Abby*

It seemed that the parts identified themselves in my journaling mostly for Jerry's benefit, though this was often helpful for me as well. Abby was one of my more delightful parts. She was born when I used to take piano lessons from my aunt as a child. Abby loved my aunt and grieved horribly when she died. She was engaging and creative. Abby had a great sense of humor and loved to play piano. Abby also sang and wrote poetry. She even managed to get several poems published (under her name, of course!). After that she was very proud of herself and I must admit I was proud of her too. Even though I often ridiculed her writing, because it evoked too many feelings for me, I did notice that her poetry always told a story, usually about one of the alters or a memory. Now I see her poems as contributing to our search for truth (see the poem titled " Truth" in Appendix A).

One time when I was going through a particularly difficult stage, I had been scheduled to sing with a friend at a concert. It seemed impossible, since I was severely depressed and having trouble concentrating. So I asked Abby if she would sing for me at the concert, if I needed her to stand in. She eagerly agreed! As it turned out, I was able to sing myself. Later Abby let me have it! She had been looking forward to performing and was very disappointed that I hadn't let her.

### *Sarah and Sharon*

Sarah and Sharon were twin parts born out of the ritual abuse period of my life. Sharon was the stronger and more dominant of the parts, although she took longer to emerge than did Sarah. Sharon held many more memories and feelings than most of the other alters. She was also my last part to integrate.

When I first met Sharon I described her as "unemotional and driven" in my journal. Later I realized Sharon WAS driven but also had a very emotional side. Again and again she warned me that I had broken the cult's rules of secrecy. She was trying to protect us from the cult, but she didn't know that most of its threats were lies. Sharon was the watchdog over all the parts and could quickly move into the role of executioner. When one of the parts told Jerry about a particular memory, Sharon would immediately make threats, seeing indiscretion or just plain stupidity in telling cult secrets. In the beginning, Sharon was convinced I had to die because I was revealing those secrets.

Sharon also had a high level of distrust for Jerry. She often baited and ridiculed him, calling him a pathetic therapist. If Jerry made a mistake, no matter how small, Sharon was the first to point it out, and in very graphic terms. It might be as simple as Jerry saying something that upset one of the other parts. Both Sharon and Sarah would blame Jerry for all the problems that arose in the system. It wasn't fair of course, but they reacted out of their extreme distrust for people, especially men. In the following journal entry, Sharon resists seeing Jerry:

**Sharon** *If you really want to help me out, you won't go back and talk to him [Jerry] again.*

**CJ** *I know you don't like Jerry. But I think you need to realize that you wouldn't be getting as much attention and consideration now if we weren't seeing him. It is his idea that I try to work with you.*

**Sharon** *I don't like him at all. He's dangerous!*

**CJ** *I understand you don't like him, actually that you hate all men, but why do you say he's dangerous?*

**Sharon** *He just is.*

**CJ** *How does he threaten you?*

**Sharon** *First of all, he feeds you a line of bull and you swallow it. Then he's just too damn nosey.*

**CJ** *He doesn't make any of us believe anything. He simply discusses things with us. It is we who choose to believe or not believe. As far as being nosey, I've given him permission to ask questions and to help in any way possible. So you probably should blame me for that.*

**Sharon** *Oh, I do!*

**CJ** *So it bothers you when we give out information to Jerry?*

**Sharon** *No information should be given to anyone, at anytime.*

**CJ** *Jerry has never betrayed us.*

**Sharon** *That we know of. The bottom line is all men are bad. They cause nothing but pain and trouble. I hate them all. They are all a threat to us.*

Sharon also hated my father, and in this case, for good reason. He had once attempted to drown her. When my parents came to visit me and Martin, Sharon had a fit. She wanted to murder my father during one of their visits. There was no actual plan to kill, just an intense desire to protect the system and make my father pay a price for his actions. Finally I managed to convince her that keeping a knife under our mattress would provide enough protection.

Sharon could be very threatening and overpowering to all the parts, but to me especially, because she hated me so much. At one time, Sharon became so threatening that I put her and Sarah in an imaginary locked room, to protect the rest of us. I never gagged them; they could say whatever they wanted to say, but they could do no physical harm to the others. Sharon and Sarah were very tough. Even while locked in the room, they didn't seem the least bit perturbed, but continued to be extremely self-confident and self-assured. While she was locked in, Sarah wrote this letter to Jerry:

*Dear Mr. Donaldson:*

*This is Sarah. You've not met me, but I know you and the trouble you can cause. I was very angry yesterday after you talked with Sharon because of you and her [CJ]. Sharon is very confused. There is no need for her to be confused on this issue. The direction is very easy to understand. You confused Sharon with unimportant details. What matters is only our instructions.*

*Quite frankly, I want this whole business finished and done with. It's Sharon's job, but if she's too weak to follow through, then I'm quite capable of stepping in and won't be easily deterred from my mission.*

*I'm sick and tired of being subjected to her [CJ's] every whim. I have a life of my own and I want to be free to enjoy it. If Sharon chooses to conform, so be it, but NOT me! CJ can't keep me locked up forever. I'll get out and get my way once and for all. I wonder who you think you are that you can come in and destroy things? Actually, maybe I should thank you. The secret is out, we can get rid of her [CJ] and be free. But it would be much easier if you and her would just butt out and quit feeding us crap.*

*You really piss me off. You try to make her [CJ] think you're different. But you're not! You're just like the rest of us—out to get the best for yourself. We trust NO one. And you are not an exception. You've not only messed up Sharon, but you've confused the little ones too. You don't care about any of us. That's why I must look out for myself. You are right in one respect—these people were bad people, but they were just like everyone else. So what difference does it make? We either listen to one group of bad people or another group of bad people. It's just a trade off.*

*You do understand what I'm saying, don't you? I intend to be in control of this situation no matter what. So back off!! We don't care to listen to your words, because that's just what they are—WORDS—nothing more. Worthless and meaningless. A mere waste of time and energy.*

*You know, if you'd just stop with the rescue service, we might be friends. Probably never good friends, but we don't have to be at war. On second thought, it won't ever work. You're far too pushy. Just leave us alone. You're NOT helping things at all. Sarah*

### Keeper

I believe that Keeper was my most interesting part and had the greatest depth. I knew she was directly linked to me. From the beginning she told me she was a helper for the little ones. Keeper was wise and comforting, yet not afraid to speak the truth as she saw it. She was the one who explained "IN." She said it was a place I had created when I was a very small child. She described IN as a room filled with sunshine and white fluffy pillows and blankets. When someone lay in the pillows and blankets they sank in deeply and felt really safe. Keeper used to accompany me to IN when I was a child and would hold me and comfort me. However, she told one of the other parts that as I got older, I didn't want anyone to hold me, so she stopped entering IN with me. Instead, she entered IN before I did, to be sure the curtains and window were open ever so slightly, so that I could see what was going on outside if I wanted to. She stood guard at the door, a locked door, so no one could enter while I was there. When I was ready to come out, Keeper would unlock the door. She never again entered IN while I was there, but respected my privacy and need for a safe place.

I loved Keeper, probably because she cared deeply for me and took such good care of me when I allowed her to. While I was inside IN, Keeper, along with Anita, handled my life and managed the other parts. Some of the other parts would be afraid that once I entered IN I might never come out. Keeper told the other parts not to worry; she understood me well and knew I simply needed a retreat. On several occasions, she did express her humanness. Once she wrote about worrying that she would not be needed if I got well. Keeper acknowledged that when she took over for me, she felt powerful, needed and in control.

On one occasion when I was completely overwhelmed by memories, I felt the need to go into IN. On this particular occasion, Keeper walked with me. She had already prepared the room. The situation was different this time, however, because after Keeper locked the door, I cried out for her to open it and keep it open just a crack. I also asked her to sit just inside the doorway while I slept. Keeper was truly surprised. When I woke up, she and I had a wonderful conversation—I let her know how much I valued her and appreciated her. Keeper wrote later in the journal that I had made her feel loved and needed. She considered locking IN, so I wouldn't go there again, but she guessed I would soon be able to leave IN behind all by myself. Keeper was right. In due time, I no longer wanted to enter IN, because the place felt claustrophobic. I had outgrown IN.

Keeper was a great mediator between the parts and me, and also between the parts themselves. In the midst of my most difficult and exhausting therapy, when I was too distressed to carry on a conversation, Keeper kept her watchful eye on the other parts. She often alerted me or Jerry when parts were upset or if new parts were emerging. When the twins Sharon and Sarah were enraged, she often stood between them and the other parts to keep peace. Like Anita, Keeper would sometimes make phone calls to Jerry when a situation became too chaotic or dangerous. She defended me to the other parts and pushed me to work harder.

My relationship with Keeper was not perfect. It was nearly impossible for me to accept Keeper's memories. In one of her memories, Keeper believed she had been impregnated by a cult member and that the pregnancy with her baby (whom she believed to be female) had been terminated early and the baby killed in a cult sacrifice ceremony. Jerry never questioned this memory. However, I know I sometimes was drugged at cult meetings. It is impossible for me or anyone else to know if Keeper's memory is completely accurate. It is conceivable that the cult used an animal fetus and made Keeper believe it was a human baby. But it is interesting to note that Keeper's name means "keep her" and that Keeper deeply mourned the loss of her baby. She also blamed herself profusely for not being able to save the baby. For weeks, even months, I refused to believe Keeper's very intense and painful memory. So Keeper simply left, for a long time. In my journaling I agonized over her departure:

> *Keeper, I need to talk with you. I feel at a loss though. I have so much respect for you. You seem to always be in control of the situation. I wish I could be more like you. I sometimes stand back in awe of the way you so ably manage the different parts with such perceptive insight and wise actions. I guess in many ways I would like to emulate you. I learn so much by listening to you and watching you interact with the parts. I have a deep affection for you too. I don't know that you've ever told me you loved me, yet I feel loved and respected. I think I love you too. I know that I miss you when you are gone and dread the thought of losing you. I feel devastated when I think of you leaving me. You probably ask, after all I've said, why then don't I believe your memory? That's a very fair question. As much as I care for you, I think I also hate you when you are overtaken by the feelings and emotions of your "memory." I want you, of all the parts, to be above being affected by all this crap. I want you to be entirely free of it and because you aren't, it somehow taints you. Perhaps I don't want you to have any problems so that you can always take care of the rest of us. Maybe I just want you to be perfect and okay in every way. It's not really that I doubt your character and think you are making an attempt to deceive me. It's more that I don't want anything to be wrong with you. The other thing is, your memory is so outrageous, that quite frankly it's difficult to believe. And I don't want to believe there is even a possibility it could have happened. I DON'T WANT YOUR MEMORY, KEEPER! I want you just to somehow get rid of it. I guess I'm being pretty unfair to you. I don't want to deal with your memory at all. I just want you to fix it, get over it. I don't want to be understanding and empathetic. I don't want to even consider that your memory has any validity. I don't*

*want to be involved in your memory. I don't want to talk about it or be affected by it. I understand my wants aren't practical or in any way compassionate toward you or your feelings. Sometimes all I want to do is protect myself. Even though I don't want to, I will try to listen to you and accept what you say as truth. I'm sorry. I'm sure I've disappointed you and made you feel as if you don't matter. That isn't my intention. Jerry says that you are me and I am you. Intellectually I know that's true, but it sure doesn't feel true. Everything within me wants to scream out, "NO, you are Keeper and I am me!" I believe if I become a part of you, I will somehow contaminate you and if you become part of me, I will have to own your memory.*

The parts often fought among themselves, long and hard, but at other times they helped each other cope, as revealed by the following journal entry:

**Noah** *Who knows how to cry? I want to learn. There's a big bag of cries inside me that need to come out.*

**Bernice** *I don't know how to cry either. We need to ask the others. Who does know how to cry?*

**Anita** *Maybe Abby.*

**Keeper** *Maybe Amy.*

**Judy** *No, Amy can only let a couple of tears get into her eyes at a time.*

**Bernice** *Well, that's more than most of us can do. Maybe Amy is the place to start. Maybe she can teach Noah how to just get a couple of tears up into his eyes.*

**Keeper** *Sometimes CJ cries when she is sad or happy. How does she do that?*

**Noah** *I don't think that's what I want. It doesn't seem to let much out. Her tears don't seem to make her feel better, and besides she hardly ever cries. I don't think she is the one to teach me. I think Amy is the best. Will she help me?*

**Judy** *Amy doesn't like to have tears come to her eyes. She says it makes her feel bad.*

**Noah** *Can you talk to her and get her to help me?*

**Judy** *Maybe, I don't know. Not sure I want to, 'cause when she feels bad, I do too.*

Around the time of this conversation, Abby wrote the following poems:

### A Tear

What is a tear?
A wet place on the face?
A water-filled eye?
A salty moist spot?

What makes a tear?
A hurt deep inside?
A crude, cruel word?
A strike on the face?
Love for a child?
Joy from a hug?
Peace in the heart?

That is a tear.

### Tears

The face is wet,
The heart is sad.
The eyes are filled
The hurt is bad.

The sob is muffled,
The day is bleak.
The body is shaken
The soul is meek.

The spirit is closed,
The mind is slow.
Visible or not
The tears, they flow.

### *Beth*

Beth was my major spiritual part. She loved and trusted God with a simple child-like faith. I wondered if Beth was created when I was a very small child, because my mother told me I had accepted Jesus into my heart when I was just three years old. It's still very interesting to me that even though Beth was part of the ritually abused family of parts, she maintained such an unshakeable faith in God. Beth was one of Jerry's allies. She felt a distinct bond with him because of his spirituality and religious beliefs. Even though most of the parts did not believe in God, or were afraid of God and didn't trust him, they respected Beth for her belief. The alters seemed to hope that Beth's spirituality could somehow provide additional protection for all of them. Beth reminded the parts that even though God didn't always protect them, he had never left them and he had preserved their spirits. The parts argued with Beth, saying God did not love them. She adamantly insisted on God's abundant love, and pleaded with them to trust God. Trusting anyone was a huge jump for most of the parts, me included. Those who had been ritually abused believed that they were too evil for God to love, that God only wanted to punish them. Beth was the catalyst for many deep and intense discussions about God and our spirituality. Sarah openly opposed Beth and called her 'preacher,' arguing that God was just as barbaric as Satan, that there was no difference between them. Beth in her gentle way encouraged all the parts to move to a place where they could at least have hope that God loved them. This is only one example of Beth reassuring the other parts (and me) about God:

**CJ** *At first I was upset to know there were more parts, especially on the SRA side. But then after I learned about Beth, I was somewhat relieved. Beth loves God and trusts him. As far as I know, she is the only part who does. All the other parts either don't believe or are apathetic. It seems strange that Beth is one of the SRA parts. Beth, how are you connected to the satanic abuse?*

**Beth** *Why shouldn't I be. There must be some good to balance out the bad.*

**Keeper** *That's for sure. We all need Beth. She is important to us. She helps keep us all safe.*

**Beth** *I want to help all I can. I know it is important to have faith in God to be able to go through bad times. I have always been able to have faith for all of us, even though some of us didn't want to have faith or trust in anyone. God has never left us. He has preserved our spirit.*

**Bernice** *That seems too good to believe. It doesn't seem like he was always with us. It doesn't seem like he was anywhere around.*

**Beth** *Oh, but he was. That's how we managed to survive. I'm going to start reading the Bible more and praying. It's what will get us through this. It will get CJ through. It's really the only hope we have. Most everyone else has left us, but not God.*

**Laville** *I don't know about this crap. It doesn't make much sense to me. I'm not sure God, if he does exist, would ever want to help me.*

**Sarah** *I KNOW he wouldn't. Anyway, he doesn't exist. If he did he would have helped before this. I don't need his help anyway, even if he is there.*

**Janice** *I don't think God would help me either.*

**Noah** *Not me either.*

**Beth** *Oh yes he will. He loves all of us. He knows all of us. He wants us all to be okay. All we have to do is trust that He will help us.*

**Bernice** *Trust…I don't know about that. That's not too smart.*

**Victoria** *I would like to trust God, but I'm afraid. I would like him to love me, but I don't think he would. I did some very bad things. I think he knows I did bad things. I don't think he could love me because of what I did.*

**Sharon** *Why would God love us?*

**Sarah** *He wouldn't, he can't, because he doesn't exist. No God would let someone he loves suffer, right? So, either he doesn't exist or he doesn't care anyway.*

**Beth** *No, that's not right. He does care. I know nobody likes to hear it, but God sent his son, Jesus, to earth because he loved all of us.*

**Bernice** *Beth, don't start talking all that religious stuff, you're just upsetting everyone.*

**Lillian** *I don't want to hear it! I'm not going to listen! No, no, no, no.*

**Sarah** *Now see what you've done! It figures…*

**Laville** *You know we don't like to hear about that stuff.*

**Bernice** *That kind of talk only hurts and confuses us.*

**Sharon** *I don't get it. I still don't understand why any God would love us. It doesn't make sense. What do we have to give God?*

**Beth** *He only wants us to love him and do what he wants us to.*

**Laville** *That sounds all too familiar, huh?*

**Beth** *No, wait. He never asks us to do anything he wouldn't do himself.*

**Victoria** *But I did bad things, very bad things.*

**Beth** *Someone made you do those things, Victoria. You didn't do them because you wanted to.*

**Victoria** *But I knew what I was doing was wrong.*

**Keeper** *Yes, but you didn't have a choice either. If you didn't do those things, you would have been hurt, maybe killed.*

**Laville** *I don't want to talk about this stuff any more. It's all crap and I won't listen anymore.*

**Beth** *That's okay, Laville. God loves you no matter if you want to listen or not. He understands.*

**Sarah** *Oh brother, give me a break. The preacher is on her soapbox again.*

**Bernice** *Sarah, Beth is only giving her opinion. You give your opinion any time you wish. Give her some room to express herself. Besides maybe some of the rest of us want to listen.*

**Sarah** *God is just as barbaric as Satan. He does all the same stuff Satan does. There is no difference. Even if there is a God, it doesn't change anything for us.*

**Beth** *You're wrong, Sarah, it changes everything. It is our reason to go on. It is why we have hope.*

**Sarah** *Give me a break! Who has hope? We all know that it's hopeless, futile.*

**Bernice** *It does seem hopeless sometimes. But we want to have hope.*

| | |
|---|---|
| **Beth** | *We can have hope. God preserved us in the past and will not leave us now. He cares.* |
| **Vivian** | *Does God love everyone?* |
| **Beth** | *Yes, he does.* |
| **Vivian** | *Does God love the father too? And the grandfather and the grandmother?* |
| **Sarah** | *There! Gotcha, Beth! Answer that one.* |
| **Beth** | *Yes, God loves everyone. He doesn't like what they did, but he still loves them. In fact, he hates what they did to us.* |
| **Laville** | *Then why didn't he stop it? He's God, right? I know I didn't want to do those things, so why didn't he help me then?* |
| **Beth** | *Actually, Laville, he did help you then. You're alive aren't you? We're all alive.* |
| **Sarah** | *Well, if you can call it that!* |
| **Beth** | *God saved our lives.* |
| **Sarah** | *It's all so simple-simon, Beth. You always have the answers, except that in this instance, your answers just don't fit. Oh sure we…well, not me, but the others, want to believe someone actually loves and cares for them, but that's just a fairytale. That kind of love just doesn't exist.* |
| **Keeper** | *What about JD?* |
| **Sarah** | *You actually think he cares?! Give me a break. We pay him to say the right things. He only has to be with us for one hour a week.* |
| **Bernice** | *That's not quite fair, Sarah. He has always been honest with us.* |
| **Beth** | *JD is a good man. He doesn't lie to us. He knows God loves us. JD loves God. JD knows God. Remember, he said he doesn't understand all about this either, but he still trusts God.* |
| **Sarah** | *This is all very confusing. It makes me very tired, too tired to think it all through.* |

Abby, too, was affected by Beth's God and wrote the following poem:

### God

God?
Who is that?
Who knows God?
Is He real?

Love?
What is that?
Who gives love?
Is it real?

Hate?
I know hate.
It is pain.
It is real.

Fear?
I know fear.
It is dread.
It is real.

Doubt?
I know doubt.
It is questions.
It is real.

Hope?
I know hope.
It is belief.
It is real.

Trust?
I know trust.
It is faith.
It is real.

I know God.
God is hope.
God is love.
God is trust.
He is real.

CHAPTER

# 16

# Coming Together (JD)

*The different parts make up the whole. What the parts know the whole knows, even if the whole doesn't know because it is made up of the parts.*

–CJ's alter, "Truth"

This stage in CJ's therapy became intense and bewildering for her. She discovered an increasing number of alters, and trying to "map" them all was confusing. The destructive parts, like Jill, were becoming more active and dangerous, and the internal conflict was acute. CJ experienced too many voices vying for attention, as the alters' intra-personal conflicts intensified. All her adult life, CJ had managed to stay in control, but now, the more she attempted to control the alters, the more they rebelled. Once the alters were out of the closet, they were trying to individuate and become their own persons. The lack of order multiplied the crises, intensified the fear, and broke down the team effort to a level of the survival of the fittest.

I observed that the situation wasn't totally chaotic. There was some cooperation among alters, but it took effort, time, patience, and persistence to gain some semblance of order. From CJ's perspective, her inner life was totally disordered. She was coming to terms with DID, Dissociative Identity Disorder, also known as MPD, Multiple Personality Disorder. All of the alters needed to be "on the same page," going in the same direction, striving for the same end, but how could each alter maintain his/her own identity and still reach a cooperative state?

## Quest for Congruency

CJ wanted to integrate each of these personalities into who she was. Integration generally means "blending separate elements into a unified whole." However, everything that I had read had implied or stated that total integration was not necessary to mental health. Nevertheless, the alters would at least have to become teammates, stop the in-fighting, and pursue a common goal of trust and acceptance. Healthier integration can only take place if the person with DID really wants it, and CJ was ready to go through the process.

Rather than aim for integration, I used the term "merging," hoping the parts would find this more acceptable. I likened the merging process to a highway. As we approach a city, traffic increases; one road merges with another and becomes a highway, and those highways merge with other highways, and then the driver is on a major freeway with hundreds of cars all around. The bigger the city, the greater need for ramps and merging lanes.

CJ's internal system was in total chaos. Each alter had been functioning reasonably well in his or her role for twenty to thirty years. As we recognized in the previous chapter, each alter had a task and a responsibility. Some were stabilizing and functional. Others were very immature and impetuous. Still others would undermine and resist. But now CJ realized the system had become archaic. The infrastructure had become unmanageable. Country driving would no longer work in a large urban area that offered many and sometimes conflicting choices.

There was only one vehicle, CJ's body, but several parts of her wanted to be in the driver's seat or drive their own car. Those who were in the same car were constantly doing backseat driving. Some wanted to move along in the fast lane, and others wanted to take it slowly and carefully. Major alters were jockeying for position, because some were ready to merge; others found the idea very threatening, and still others were determined to do their own thing. The alters were journaling their thoughts and feelings about merging.

> *"It feels like dying." "I'll merge when I'm ready." "No merging for me. I'm just getting out."(Sarah) "I want to live."(Claudia) "I don't want to merge 'cause I'll have to give up my anger."(Bill) "I'm afraid of merging. I feel like I'll never be again. We have unfinished business. It's not a good time."(Bernice) "I don't want to merge with any of you. I want to be me."(CJ) "We ARE you. Intellectually you can't deny that we are you, but emotionally you are not ready to accept it yet. I think a merger would indicate that you have accepted that we are you and if you merge with one of us, you would have to own our memories as well."(Truth)*

Even for the alters who were willing to merge, the question was "Who with?" A few alters were self-destructive, "ugly," "too angry," "too immature," so no-one else wanted to incorporate them. I explained that nobody HAD to merge; it would always be their choice, and nobody HAD to take on another alter until they were convinced it was best. The main principle for CJ and company to consider was to get all the alters to flow and merge in one direction, while staying in their own lanes and following the rules of city traffic. Otherwise there would be accidents and traffic jams.

No matter what analogy I used, the concept of merging was very threatening. The child alters just wanted to be happy and have their way. The rational, adult alters needed to parent the child alters appropriately, by empathizing, confronting, encouraging, and challenging them to trust and respect "their elders." Doing this required the older alters to be patient, loving and assertive; however, many of them were too hurt, too angry, and too frightened to consider merging. It seemed easier for the fragment alters to think about merging with the more known alters. For example, several fragment alters would carry memories together—about a specific abuse situation, concerning a particular individual. At that time, the pain had been so great that several alters had been created to deal with that emotion. Once all of the alters associated with a specific memory could combine their stories, they could see the whole picture. Then they would not need to be separate, so they could merge and become one, like several small gravel roads merging onto a paved road.

A key element of mental healthiness is being congruent. This term refers to the state of agreement or coinciding, when the different aspects of the self come together in harmony. Ideally, human beings experience themselves as being the same person, over time. CJ suffered because she was divided within herself, split and incongruent. All of CJ's alters were occupying the same space—her heart, mind and body—but there was very little agreement or harmony. We humans do not deal well with in-congruency. CJ's house was too divided. It would self-destruct without a common effort to come together

I explained to CJ, and the listening alters, that when the alters merged or integrated, they would not be lost or dead. Instead they would become part of each other and part of CJ. Merging would be like many cups of water (alters) poured into a single large container, or a drop of ink into a quart of water. In this latter picture, the ink would add its own color to the larger whole. This metaphor had helped me facilitate a session with June, the other DID client with whom I was working. June's 5-year-old child alter was sweet and affectionate, but frightened about merging with June. So I told her that merging would be like a small sweet marshmallow (her) dissolving into a cup of chocolate. The hot chocolate would be even sweeter as the marshmallow became part of the whole. The child alter then decided to merge.

People with DID are not the only ones who need inner integration. As I have suggested earlier, we all have parts, and if we refuse to accept certain ones of them, we too become incongruent. Denying parts of ourselves will prevent wholeness and guarantee intra-personal conflict. Inner harmony and peace require that we accept, trust, respect, value and team up with those seemingly undesirable parts of ourselves. For example, I might have a part that is greedy and doesn't want to share. I'd prefer not to acknowledge this part, let alone integrate it into the whole. But the greedy part is there for a reason. Perhaps that part is tired of being poor, or perhaps the biological family fought over money, so if that part had more money or possessions, he/she would feel less vulnerable. Thus the greedy part is in survival mode. I must deal with the fears of the greedy part, so that he/she feels heard and understood. Then this part of me is more apt to cooperate with the giving, sharing part.

Another example: One part in me loves the excitement of taking risks, but I also have a rational part, who will caution that "we" could get hurt. If the cautious part ignores or dominates the risking part, life can become pretty dull and boring. It isn't that one part is right and the other wrong. Both parts have needs, and if they can dialogue (by making a pro and con list, for instance) and understand each other, they can cooperate, and both can win. When both win, they accept one another.

I've quoted earlier, "You can't love whom you don't know." Therefore, it is essential that we know all the parts of ourselves. It is also true that "You can't love whom you don't understand." Therefore, we must empathize intra-personally, in order to understand. Finally, "You can't love whom you can't accept." If we feel that some of our parts are totally unacceptable, we will not be able to love ourselves. The same principle operates interpersonally. In order to love others, we must know, understand and accept them.

In order for CJ to love herself, she needed to <u>know</u> each alter (part), <u>understand</u> their roles, functions and memories, and ultimately <u>accept</u> with gratefulness the contribution each part had played in her life. She was "tired of all the conversing, not sleeping, putting up with too much noise," and the dissidence which prevented order. She had found it counter-productive to criticize, condemn, reject or ignore these parts of herself. Integration cannot take place without trust, and building that trust can take years, especially in a DID person whose trust has been broken time and time again by family and "friends." Honesty within the system was imperative for the merging and integration process—honesty not only among the alters, but also in communication among the alters, CJ, and me.

### Necessity of Honesty and Trust

> *When praying…be there simply and honestly as you can manage.* –Matthew. 6:6 (***The Message***)
>
> *…those who are simply and honestly themselves before him in worship.* –John. 4:23 (***The Message***)

Most of us see ourselves as honest. We don't cheat, lie or steal. When we find something that doesn't belong to us, we usually attempt to return it to the rightful owner. We lose respect for people who cheat, especially if they cheat us personally. The word honesty comes from the root word honorable. Honorable people are free from fraud and deception. In what they do and say, they are genuine, forthright, and sincere. They are authentic. As the late comedian, Flip Wilson, used to say, "What you see is what you get."

Even when honesty is a high value, though, it is difficult to be absolutely honest. I wonder, am I really an honest person? Probably most of my friends and my wife would say "Yes." But in fact, fear prevents me from being totally and completely honest all of the time. I worry about what people will think; therefore, at times I won't express how I honestly feel, or what I honestly think fearing that I will be disliked or rejected. I find myself continually checking people's body language and facial expressions, to see if they are responding positively to my words and actions. Sometimes I also hide my feelings and thoughts to avoid upsetting another person: for example, when a friend is deathly ill or when I fear my opinion will offend someone. Being honest about my emotions is particularly difficult, because expressing my feelings makes me vulnerable. I am afraid of being judged, discounted, or not heard at all.

When someone asks me what I think or feel, conscious and sub-conscious responses flash through me. Does this person want an honest response, or a specific answer? Why is she asking the question? What is her motive? What will she do if I'm honest? If she asks, "How do you feel?" but expects only an "appropriate" response, if she isn't happy with my true feelings, or wants to "fix my feelings," I'm unlikely to be totally honest. I have painful memories of trying to answer questions from my late aunt. My repeated attempts at honesty got me nowhere. Finally my wife pointed out the frustrating and hurtful dynamic: my aunt was not questioning me to find out who I was; instead, she was baiting me. She wanted to argue with my feelings and beliefs. In fact, she wasn't interested in communicating what SHE thought or felt. My aunt only wanted more information about me in order to "prove" that I was wrong or didn't know what I was talking about. Ordinary as this may seem, my aunt's questioning helped to shape my life-long anxiety about expressing my feelings.

Can we possibly imagine what it was like in CJ's family? My fears about emotional honesty are minimal compared to hers. She was taught—no, forced to be dishonest in order to survive or to even lessen the abuse. No matter what her response, she was going to be hurt, disregarded, and treated badly. As the abuse continued, the number of alters increased so that CJ could survive the trauma. At this point in her therapy, more than eighty alters had revealed themselves to CJ, although only about twenty were journaling. I was thankful that at last they were expressing what they honestly felt and thought. My job was to make it safe for CJ and the alters to share their journaling with me. When the alters "came out" and talked, I encouraged honest dialogue, without being critical and condemning. I worked to listen well and reflect back what I had heard. Not only did I want them to trust me, but I also hoped to model for CJ how to become co-conscious from within.

At first, the alters themselves were unable to be totally honest with each other. They didn't trust themselves, let alone each other. They interacted with fear, anger, bickering, put-downs, condemnation, misunderstanding. Their overall lack of safety kept getting in the way. This chaos among alters, whose numbers were increasing almost daily, was almost intolerable for CJ. As she tried to hear, to understand and to accept all of the parts, she questioned her own ability to be honest. I valued her integrity and that of the alters'. When they began to share, they tried hard to be honest about their feelings and perspectives. I had come to believe them, but CJ couldn't. She could not even believe herself. Even at this advanced stage in counseling, CJ would still tell herself that she was "making all of this up." I had to remind us both that honesty and trust cannot be rushed, especially for someone who has been taught not to feel, talk or trust. CJ's goal of being totally integrated would still require a long and arduous process. Only honesty could build the trust which was our major goal in therapy—CJ's trust, not just in me, but especially in herself and in the alters.

A friend of mine embodies this value of blunt honesty, (in some ways, almost to a fault) I can trust what he says, even when he speaks angrily and forcefully. He doesn't mince words, and he isn't afraid how others will take him. You never have to guess what he is thinking or feeling. He seems freer than most people I know, because he doesn't hide behind passivity and overly kind words. He's a what-you-see-is-what-you-get kind of a guy. Most of our friends see him as refreshingly honest. He's not perfect—he's sometimes sneaky, doesn't want to stop what he's sneaky about, and doesn't like being lectured! But I enjoy our freedom to be open and honest with each other in almost everything. We are good friends because we are not secretive. As I got to know Sharon, one of CJ's alters, I found that she was kind of like my friend—candid, surly, argumentative, willing to say what she thought and felt. This angry part of CJ was not only refreshing, but essential to her survival. Sharon managed to keep everybody alive during some nearly fatal abuse, such as the time when "the father" tried to drown her.

Sharon didn't like me, for a number of reasons. I am a man, I was winning the hearts of some key alters, and I was a therapist. (She said that "they just mess with your head.") When she attacked and accused me, I refused to be baited by her. I didn't take her negative remarks personally. Over time our trust in each other increased because, I believe, we were both honest. I wasn't trying to make her think I was a good guy, so deep down she was beginning to like and respect me. As our mutual respect became unshakable, Sharon and I developed a functional relationship that included talking, feeling, and trusting.

In my therapeutic work with CJ, I sometimes made "honest mistakes." I'd choose what seemed a good and right course of action, based on the information I had gleaned, but I still blew it from time to time. Sharon and other alters would be quick to point out my "mistakes," assign negative motives to what I did, and generally write me off. My response was to own up to what I had done wrong, to apologize, and to ask them for forgiveness. None of them were used to apologies. Their perpetrators had never, never apologized nor asked for forgiveness. Now the alters could learn a different mode of operation for dealing with conflict: honest acceptance of responsibility, and mutual willingness to give and receive forgiveness.

Sharon was only one of the alters whose trust I had to earn. The more the alters could trust me, the more honest they would become, and the greater their honesty, the more trusting and trustworthy our relationship would be. I cannot emphasize too much that "You can't love whom you don't know," and this knowledge is impossible without honesty. Likewise, "You can't love whom you don't understand." How could I possibly understand CJ without knowledge based on honesty? And, "You can't love whom you don't accept:" such acceptance required my understanding based on truthful knowledge. My responsibility was to know, understand and accept each of the alters. Even more important, each one of the alters would have to come to know, understand and accept each other. And finally it was CJ's job to incorporate—to know, understand, and accept every part of herself. Only then would integration be possible.

Being honest and truthful is absolutely essential to good mental health. Truthfulness and honesty may seem to be synonymous, but they are not always the same. It's possible to be honestly wrong. Rarely do we remember things as they actually happened. Our emotions can be so interlaced with our perceptions that both our emotions and perceptions become distorted. To make recovery even more complicated, if years have passed since the events have occurred, some of the actual details are either forgotten or distorted. Twenty to forty years after CJ's experiences of abuse, the alters still believed that they had the facts straight. To them, the events had just "happened yesterday." Because of the severity and duration of the abuse, many of the alters actually went through the same experience, but each had a different take on what had actually happened. They were certainly honest, but factuality had become somewhat warped.

We know what often happens when the police are asking what happened in a car accident—you are going to get as many views as you have witnesses. Can all the witnesses be honest, be telling the truth? Certainly. But sometimes the police wonder whether all the witnesses saw the *same* accident. It's the task of the police to objectively gather the data, analyze what everyone has said, and decide what is "true," what best explains what has actually happened.

## Truth Personified

CJ and I were the police here. We had to listen to the "truth" of each alter, put it all together, and come up with a more accurate truth, the real truth—not denying the sincerity of each alter, but taking all pieces of the puzzle and putting together a larger and more accurate picture. Astonishingly, CJ actually had an alter called Truth. In her summary of roles and memories and definitions of the known alters, CJ reported that "Truth was an adult and told only the truth. When things got confused about the truth, or what to keep secret was confusing, Truth knew what to say, yet maintained the knowledge of the truth of each situation." Somehow Truth had been there for CJ almost from the beginning. This is the genius of a tortured little girl who created an alter who kept the facts straight and who could offer true, pithy statements in the midst of chaos.

Following are some illustrations from CJ's journal around this time. As the old system of multiplicity broke down, CJ was becoming aware that a new system needed to be created. However, moving from the old to the new was very threatening to everyone.

- Truth: "*Sometimes the present structure must collapse before a new building can be erected. The inside is in turmoil. This is the time for revelation. The ground is shifting to a new order.*"
- After CJ said she "*hated all of the alters,*" Truth replied, "*Hate is directly related to fear.*"
- When CJ was attempting not to listen to another alter at one point, Truth said, "*A voice will find its way out in the end, either helped out or by bursting its way through the barrier.*"
- Once when CJ did not want to deal with the memory that was working its way out to her consciousness, Truth admonished, "*Sometimes the face of something is overwhelming and must be looked at slowly. There is no shame in knowing your limitations and working within them. The danger comes when we choose to ignore things. You can't run away from things forever. Someday you have to stand in one place and face the truth.*" Fearing that CJ would not be able to distinguish the truth from lies, Truth said, "*You must believe us. What other choice is there? It's been painful to believe in the past and it will be painful in the future. Pain does not kill.*"
- At another point Truth spoke to another alter, Jill, who was in great pain and wanted to die: "*Pain can seem unbearable, but we can bear it, we have each other.*"
- A month later, CJ was still looking for proof that she had really been sexually abused. Truth stated, "*Some things cannot be proven or unproven.*" Truth was suggesting that CJ must trust, believe that the alters were being truthful.
- One and a half months later, Truth remarked, "*We are all the whole. The parts make up the complete whole.*" CJ said, "*I won't allow any more parts. I just won't.*" Truth answered, "*Do you think you have any choice in the matter?*" CJ: "*<u>I'm</u> in control.*" Truth: "*Control of what? You can't make something disappear by willing it away. What exists will remain unless destroyed or consumed.*" Sarah (angry alter) "*Don't you get tired of her (Truth)?*"
- Most of the alters were very fearful. Truth tells them, "*The truth resides in all of us, individually as well as corporately. If we are to be whole, we cannot separate ourselves from the truth. The truth remains, whether we acknowledge it or not. Fear comes from the unknown. When the truth is known, the fear can be eliminated.*" Then for almost a month, Truth was quiet, probably because CJ was facing the feelings, thoughts, and memories of the alters. Truth prodded Sarah,

> who had yet to disclose her memories, *"What's your reality?"* Sarah: *"Stuff it. I'm perfectly sure what reality is,"* to which Truth replied, *"Are you? There are extremes on both sides of reality."*

I found that Truth seemed to have more insight than I did. She had learned valuable lessons throughout the abuse, and she had become a vital mediator within the system. Over time, she had discovered how to facilitate interaction between the alters. Her wisdom and healthy emotional detachment allowed all the parts to deal with what had really happened to CJ.

I recognized Truth's role because it paralleled my job as a counselor. To all my clients, I explain that I am a mediator, facilitator and educator. My task is to empathize, to be realistic, and to lovingly accept them. I'm not there to rescue, to fix, to feel sorry, or to create an over-dependence on me. In therapy, as in daily life, we get into trouble when we become overly attached to our emotions, our perspectives, and our addictive behaviors. The therapist reminds us that our "truth" is rarely synonymous with the real truth. We all need a part within us who acts like Truth. Being empathetic with others' situations is much different than drowning in sympathy. When I get too close to a problem, I feel sorry for myself or choose to pity "poor me." But if I can pull back, detach somewhat, and empathize, I have a better grasp of the truth.

So the alter Truth was an invaluable ally. We might well ask how a person like CJ—who had so many parts driven by fear, anger, hurt, confusion, and disappointment—could also have a part, an alter, who was calm, logical, rational, wise and intelligent. I surmise that somehow a part of CJ had been able to pick up truth-filled thoughts over the years. Though Truth had been there for a long time, I don't think that she became wise overnight. She brought cumulative wisdom. When I re-read Truth's comments in CJ's journal, I wondered how we had ended up on the same wave-length. Had CJ subconsciously filed those truths away once she had heard them? Perhaps in all of her reading, valid sermons she had heard, and Bible verses she had memorized, certain truths stuck and were available to her later.

In any case, we humans have opportunities to accumulate wisdom. Throughout life we are exposed to enduring truths that can serve us well if we are willing to tap into that resource. Romans 12 is one of my favorite chapters in the Bible. I remember, very early on in my Christian life, reading this chapter dozens of times. In essence Paul challenged the Roman Christians not to be arrogant or be conformed to the world's way of thinking and behaving, but to be real, loving, respectful of others and ourselves, and to live in peace. We are to empathize with those we disagree, who are in a lesser position, and we are to overcome evil with good. Almost sixty years later, as I continue to read these words in various translations, I realize that I have come to live very much by the spirit of the passage. I also recall what God once promised Isaiah: "My word will not return to me void"(Is. 55:11). Whatever truths we incorporate into our lives will not disappear, but will be available to us during desperate times.

Next to my office doorway hangs a little motto that one of my DID clients, June, gave me. I often get a chuckle from my clients as they read it on the way out. "Please solve your problems in advance so I can help you more." Though it was a humorous gift, the saying is remarkably apt. Even before they come in to see me, many of my clients have gained tremendous insight about solving their problems. They have discovered valuable truths, or <u>the</u> truth, within. Now they really just want me to confirm their discoveries, and to assess whether their truth aligns with my truth. In our search for wholeness, we need others. We may actually know what is true, but we need help making the truth overshadow the lies. If we have accepted lies and distorted truth for a long time, it is difficult to separate the real truth from the counterfeit truth.

## Truth Frees Us

Therapy is founded on truth. Most counselors work to free their clients by guiding them to know the truth, deal with the truth, and practice the truth. Truth sets us free from enslavement to lies and deceit. This is a central teaching of Jesus: "*You will know the truth and the truth will <u>set</u> you free*" (Jn. 8:32, ***NIV***). The ***RSV*** uses a different verb: "the truth will <u>make</u> you free." ***The Message*** paraphrase brings it home even more vividly: "Then you will <u>experience for yourselves</u> the truth and the truth will free you."

Secrets keep the truth from others. CJ's perpetrators did not want the public or the authorities to discover their sexual or satanic ritualistic abuse, so they took great care to keep the secrets within the abusive circle. CJ's own experiences were kept as secrets by her alters. In fact, CJ had held the secrets for so long that sometimes even the alters wondered if they were true or not. What had happened seemed too bizarre and weird to accept as fact. Secrets had covered the truth like darkness **shuts out** light.

Most secrets conceal shameful and guilty acts. We keep truth hidden at all costs to keep our feelings of shame and guilt from spilling out. What we are ashamed of is unacceptable, and what we feel guilty about <u>seems</u> unforgivable. We'd rather keep our shame and guilt in the dark, hidden deep within, rather than risk exposure to the light. We fear being seen for who we really are, considered less than human, rejected, damned.

But secrets prevent deep relationships. The secrets held by each alter in CJ were preventing open, honest, truthful intra-personal relationships. These secrets were thus also keeping CJ from deeper intimacy with her husband. Secrets are the enemy of soul mates. Instead of enlisting the help of another, we often try to keep ourselves in line by being self-critical and self-condemning. We shame and guilt-trip ourselves to "do better" and "be" better. In fact, what we say to ourselves is often not true—"You are so...dumb, stupid, selfish; such a...pervert, s.o.b., insensitive jerk" etc. CJ was a master at being critical of herself and the various alters within. Shame and guilt were rampant in her mind. Such negative self-talk only sets up a self-fulfilling prophecy

We do make mistakes, we'd all like to be smarter and less selfish, but blanket condemnation never works. If we continue to use negative, critical self-talk, we literally undermine our self-esteem. For years I had nothing good to say about myself. Even when others affirmed me, I would discount what they said. This was totally counter-productive, both inter-personally and intra-personally. We need to tell ourselves the truth, to see ourselves in a more realistic manner, and believe that we have the capacity and capability to do "good." After all, we are created in God's image. CJ agreed with this principle in theory, but could not experience its reality. The secrets and her self-condemnation were in the way. But fortunately, Truth, her truth, persevered in refocusing on the facts and determining how to deal with the facts. The truth was being discovered, and eventually the truth would set her free.

That freedom would still require CJ's acceptance and forgiveness. She had to know and understand all of the alters, whether they were likeable or not. What was crucial for her quest to bring about unity and cooperation, was accepting, caring about and loving each part of herself. When truth is exposed, a person often needs grace and mercy in order to forgive and let the past go. Truth gives us the necessary insights and awareness, but going beyond bitter acknowledgement takes grace, the practical application of love.

As a Christian, CJ had the example of Jesus. According to his earliest followers, "Jesus was full of grace and truth," (Jn. 1:14) and "grace and truth came by Jesus." (Jn. 1:17) CJ now saw that before unity could be a reality, each part was going to have to come to grips with Jesus.

CJ's next chapter demonstrates the necessity of being honest, learning to trust, and maintaining a dialogue internally as well as externally, in order to reach a point of congruency. Would she have to "give up" parts of herself in this process? We all have parts that we would like to eradicate, ignoring how much hold they have over us. If we refer to these parts as "them" or "they," we will end up denying and detaching in such a way that we begin to believe "they" are not a part of us (just as an alcoholic denies that she/he has a drinking problem). If we keep ignoring and denying the undesirable parts, we remain highly defended and therefore limit our discoveries and ultimately prevent our personal and interpersonal growth. When we refuse to deal with the reality of who we are, we become dysfunctional.

Actually, congruency is not "giving up" parts of the self; rather, integration means letting go of the anxiety the parts tend to generate. For example, most alcoholics find that they can never completely give up or rid themselves of their alcoholism (the part that likes and wants to drink), so they refer to themselves as recovering alcoholics, no matter how long they have been sober. They accept that the alcoholic part/alter is always tempted to drink, and goes out of control when it does. Psychologists would say that "merging" or "integration" describes this process of coming to terms with the unsettling parts of the self—better than "giving up" those parts.

As you read CJ's internal dialogues, attempt to imagine having your own internal conversation with various parts inside yourself. We do something similar when we make a pro and con list to help us objectify a decision, but for a major issue, such a list oversimplifies the situation. Then we are not dealing just with the positives and negatives (the concerns of two parts within us), but with many parts inside, who have different issues, different lists, and different reasons for not coming to an agreement. We become argumentative debaters with ourselves. Sometimes the more convincing and dominant parts control what's going on, but then the "losing" parts, who have been ignored, "rebel," causing an insurrection. If those parts have been losing for a long time, the rebellion may show in our doing something "out of character." If this conflict continues to intensify, we feel out of control and even "crazy."

To offer an explanation of this lack of cooperation, the Apostle Paul refers to the "old nature" and the "new nature." Other authors write about the "ideal self" and the "actual self." These two-part explanations can help us understand the reasons we function as we do, but no matter what analogy we use, the "two part" examples fail to account for the many parts within any conflicted person.

Consider that CJ identified 150 alters inside herself. Reflect that each part had an old nature and new nature, an ideal self and an actual self. Each alter had retained his or her own isolated memories. Each had a distinct personality and temperament, and hence a different way of dealing with fear and hurt. CJ's integration required these many unique alters to become cooperative, unified, trusting, accepting, empathetic and congruent with each other. Now you can begin to see how daunting a task integration can be.

So as you read the following chapter, keep in mind how brave and persistent CJ was. May the integrity and courage that she had to have in order to integrate help us learn how to integrate our own various parts, especially those parts we have failed to acknowledge, understand, accept, trust, and love.

## For Further Information

Jourard, Sidney, ***The Transparent Self,*** D. Van Nostrand Co., 1964.

PART IV

# Integration Takes Place

CHAPTER

# 17

# Becoming One (CJ)

> *He who cannot change the very fabric of his thought will never be able to change reality and will never, therefore, make any progress.*
>
> –Anwar Sadat

In order to become a whole person, I had to completely accept each one of my parts, believe the memories they held, and own those memories as my own. It may sound simple, but it was horribly difficult. I absolutely hated some of the parts and believed them to be liars—mostly because I feared what they had to tell me.

## Meaning of Integration

In the eighth year of therapy, I found this integration process very intense. Many of the parts were resisting the process as actively as I was pursuing it. Earlier, the parts who held only small pieces of memories had left (integrated) at the moment when they revealed their memories. This informal unplanned integration often took place with little or no notice from me or to the parts who held the more major or intense memories. Now these strongly defined parts fought to save themselves.

Jerry often encouraged me to talk with the different parts and to listen to them without judgment, but doing so was a great struggle. I was bent against them before I even spoke to them. Many times I argued with some of the helper parts about how I was treating the ones I really disliked. One journal entry went like this:

**CJ** *I'm not sure I can do this.*

**Keeper** *Yes you can. Remember what JD said. Be empathetic and trusting of the parts. Also, be nonjudgmental.*

**CJ** *How can I be nonjudgmental, when I believe they are lying?*

**Keeper** *Remember Sally at the support group? You believed her story immediately. Trust and believe the parts just like you believe Sally.*

**CJ** *Even if their memories are outrageous?*

**Keeper** *Listen and accept their perceptions. You can always gently question them later. It's important to accept what they say at face value. Don't judge.*

**CJ** *What if I know beyond a shadow of a doubt that the memory could not be true?*

**Truth** *Logic and truth will always prevail.*

**CJ** *So what does that mean?*

**Keeper** *If the memory is completely off the wall and facts prove it wrong, there should be no question of the truth, but that still doesn't invalidate the part. I think it just means there is a distortion in their perception. We are strong. You are strong. We all have what it takes to face the truth.*

It was extremely hard for me to believe the parts, or myself. I continued off and on to tell both Jerry and Martin that I was simply making all the memories up. The internal wrestling seemed endless. In my journal I wrote:

**CJ** *Jerry is right. I need to quit riding the fence and simply make a decision to believe or to stop this process now. Easy to say, but so difficult to do.*

**Beth** *It's not a whole lot different from deciding to believe in God. The principle is the same. Faith. Faith in God. Faith in yourself and us.*

**CJ** *Trust yourself—that's hard to do. I do want to make progress; I don't want to stay in the same place for the rest of my life. I guess if that is truly my goal, I must step out and take a risk—believe myself. Then when the doubts come, which they inevitably do, what do I do then, just ignore my doubts and plunge forward?*

**Beth** *We can help solidify your belief.*

**CJ** *How can I face my parents, if I truly believe all these memories?*

**Beth** *You can face them with the knowledge of the truth inside you. You can be true to yourself and to us—admit the past and help us all deal with the present.*

In spite of my good intentions and all the goals I set, believing the parts' memories proved to be a difficult feat for me, throughout the entire therapy process.

I've pointed out that the parts often had a difficult time getting along with each other, and there was great conflict amongst them; however, at times they also experienced great unity. Early in the process, the parts wrote this letter for me when I was unable to write it for myself. It is addressed to my father, grandmother and grandfather. The "girl" who is referred to is me. The letter reads:

*This is a letter to the Father from all the parts. You are the Father, the Dad, the bad man. You have caused the parts a lot of pain and hurt. You and your terrible mother, the grandmother, did terrible horrible things to the parts. You are not worthy to be related to the girl. You are bad people and you associated with bad people. You promoted bad and sinful activities that were hurtful to many innocent people. Your father, the grandfather, is also a wicked man.*

*We do not understand why you chose to become active in the bad group of people. We don't understand what you thought you would accomplish. It is true that you could be like us—fragmented. But we don't wish to give you any excuses for your behavior. It is probably true that the grandmother and grandfather first introduced you to the group when you were a child. We feel sorry and sadness for that original child, but do not feel sadness for you, the father. You betrayed your child, the girl. You stole away her innocence and purity. True, you gave us, the parts, our life, but again, that is no excuse for your actions.*

*You, the grandmother and grandfather have caused the girl and the girl's sister much agony and distress in their lives. You should be shamed because of it. You should burn in hell for it.*

*We, the parts, have chosen to reveal the horrible and sinful activities which took place many years ago. We, the parts, are no longer subject to your whims, your anger, your abuse. Some of us hate you. Some of us despise you. Some of us disown you. Some of us still writhe in pain because of you. Some of us remain hidden because of your actions. Remarkably, some of us still love you. The girl remains uncertain about what she thinks of you. You have done the most damage to her. You have ripped apart her very spirit and we are the results of that horrible injury. Even now she questions her own sanity. We say that we are no longer subject to your whims, but even now the girl is influenced by you. But beware, because we the parts know beyond all shadow of doubt who you are, what you have done and know the sinful part you have played. We know that the grandmother is dead and we rejoice. We know the grandfather still lives, but we refuse to shrink back with fear. We will continue to reveal the truth. We will continue to help the girl because we have cared for her from the beginning and will always. We are trustworthy where you and the others are not. We will work together to bring order and peace to the girl, where you and the others brought chaos and pain to the girl.*

*At some point, we shall all be free of you, free from the memories and free to live, to be, to be as we should be. You still hold some of us, but not for long. When we are truly free of you, then perhaps we will also be free to forgive. But first your marks must be removed from the girl's spirit. She must be released from your shadow and released she will be!*

*(Signed) The Parts of the Girl*

Even though my weird parts drove me crazy and often wanted to kill me, I resolved to be fully integrated with every one of them. Throughout the therapy process I hated, ignored, criticized, and murmured against my parts—but I still realized that they were "my parts." Even as I continued to rail against the idea, they were still me. For a long time, though, I resisted fully integrating, because I still fought the reality that all these parts carried truth, that I had indeed experienced the horrible abuse and trauma. It was harrowing to accept the "dark side" of me; I didn't want to know I had been involved in such dark, evil things—even under duress. So I wanted integration and resisted it at the same time, because I did not want to own the parts' memories—my memories.

The parts didn't look very fondly on integration either. They didn't like me very much. They didn't trust me. They didn't want to give up whatever control they had, and they mostly feared that in integrating, they would "die." Like me, they didn't like change and hated it when the system was upset. Some of the younger parts didn't understand the process or idea of integration at all, as evidenced by the following journal exchange:

**Sarah** *Getting better—what is that?*

**Beth** *Becoming whole. Merging [integration].*

**Sarah** *Don't give me that crap. I don't believe in that merging stuff.*

**Audrey** *I don't want to merge. No, no!*

Some of the parts thought that merging meant that I would lock all the parts in an internal room and never allow them to come out. Others thought integration meant sudden and certain death. One part, Doris, was convinced she was the core personality (me). It took a lot of dialogue between Doris, some of the stronger parts and me to finally convince her differently. Even Keeper had a difficult time with integration in the beginning:

**Keeper** *Well I think I can speak for most of us that we are not wanting to be dissolved [integrated].*

**Anita** *Not me!*

**Audrey** *No way!*

**Claudia** *I want to live.*

**Bernice** *We have unfinished business. It would not be good for us to be dissolved.*

**Victoria** *Does dissolved mean killed?*

**Audrey** *More or less.*

**Beth** *Maybe just one or two of the parts should merge with you [CJ].*

**Anita** *Not me.*

**Audrey** *Me either.*

**CJ** *I don't want to merge with any of you. I just want to be me. No one else, just me.*

**Truth** *We are all you.*

**CJ** *No!*

**Beth** *Intellectually you can't deny that we are you, but emotionally you are not ready to accept us yet. I think if you merged with some of the parts, that would say you have finally accepted that we are you.*

Coming together was hard but rewarding. As each part's story unfolded, I assumed my appropriate role in the memories, and we formed a strong bond with each other. We always maintained our differences—we looked different, spoke differently, wore our hair differently, and sometimes had a different gender—but as the memories were processed, we understood that we were one being.

When some of the parts had told their stories, they seemed confused about staying around any longer. Their dilemma was not whether to integrate, but how. Several fragment parts (Laville, Adrian and Millie) were at this stage. They wanted to integrate but had no clue about how to do it. And neither did the rest of us! When Jerry had talked to all of us about integration, he had suggested a visual picture: pouring a glass of water (one of the parts) into a bucket of water (me)—or combining warm water with cold water. But many of the parts had bad memories involving water, so they worked on finding a different visual metaphor.

Since I was working in the computer field at that time, Anita suggested using a computer scenario. Her suggestion was to open a file (Millie), then do two file inserts (Laville and Adrian), and save the new file. However the parts were unanimous that the computer file scenario was too cold and heartless, so they continued to look for a better picture. The concept of integration was a very serious matter to my parts and me!

**Millie** *Can we do this [integrate] by ourselves or do we need JD?*

**Keeper** *It might be helpful to let JD assist us, especially since this will be the first merge, but it's really up to us. Does anyone have an objection to the merger and how or when it happens?*

**Anita** *I think we should wait for JD's help. What if something goes wrong?*

**Audrey** *What could possibly go wrong, except that it wouldn't work?*

**Adrian** *I'm scared. I think I would like it better if JD helped.*

**Anita** *But does JD understand the concept of merging files well enough to go through the picture?*

**Victoria** *I'm afraid.*

**Keeper** *You don't have to worry it won't affect you. We need to describe this better so it doesn't upset the younger parts. Can someone explain it better?*

**Mouth** *It's like a baseball fitting into a baseball mitt. After the ball goes into the mitt, both the ball and mitt are still there, but with the mitt folded around the ball, you can only see the mitt.*

**Keeper** *That's good. It's like Adrian and Laville are baseballs caught by Millie (she's the mitt). Millie folds around them. Adrian and Laville are still there, but they are inside Millie. Is that better?*

**Victoria** *I don't like it, I want them to stay separate.*

**Keeper** *Even if they don't want to? If they stay separate, they might be very unhappy. Do you want that?*

**Victoria** *No, but I want things to stay the same. Stay like they are now.*

**Millie** *I kind of like Mouth's idea about the mitt and baseball. I think it sounds like a real good way to merge.*

**Laville** ***Fine let's just get it done.***

**Adrian** *I agree.*

And so it happened, the first formal, conscious integration of my many parts. It turned out to be the only time when an integration used the baseball/mitt scenario! I rarely needed outside assistance with the actual integrations; the parts and I managed to come up with adequate integration methods for every major part. The integrations all seemed very private to me, and I was reluctant to involve others, even Jerry, in the process. Most of the integrations took place when I was alone. I discussed the integrations only with Jerry, and he did not facilitate any of them. Neither did Martin and Janelle have any knowledge of, or participation in, the integration of my parts.

Everything depended on the specific part and the memory he/she carried. Sometimes when parts merged, there was grieving and mourning within the system, for the parts who were gone. Some of the younger parts were afraid that the older, more mature parts would integrate and leave them alone. I myself was afraid of losing Keeper. Sometimes, when the parts were having a difficult time with their memories, they would "go away" for a while, until they were able to handle telling the memory. This happened with Anita, who could not tell a particular memory. Her going away upset us all. We had to face integration and what it would mean:

**CJ** *Anita has gone away [she didn't integrate, she just left for a short time] and I miss her terribly. Will you leave too, Keeper?*

**Keeper** *I'm not planning to go away. Anita will be back.*

**CJ** *I don't believe it. Anita has been gone too long and I've been lost without her.*

**Keeper** *Are you afraid if you are able to facilitate and work with the parts that I won't be needed any longer and will go away?*

**CJ** *Well, won't you?*

**Keeper** *I won't disappear, if that's what you are asking. I must admit I'm a little sad at the thought of merging, but there will come a time when you won't need me anymore. But even when I merge, I will still be with you.*

**CJ** *It won't be the same.*

**Keeper** *I know it won't. It will be different, but it will probably be better.*

**CJ** *Keeper, I don't want you to go!*

As I mentioned previously, some of the parts equated integration with death:

**Audrey** *I don't like the merging idea. It seems too much like dying to me.*

**Keeper** *No one has to merge until and only if they want to.*

**Sarah** *No merging for me! I've just finally got out and have freedom. Anyway there is absolutely no one with whom I would want to merge.*

## Coming to Consensus

Although Jerry and I documented more than a hundred and fifty parts, many of them were what we called fragments—that is, they held only tiny portions of a memory. These fragment parts tended to integrate quickly, and sometimes the actual integration wasn't even noticed until it was completed. This rapid change could be disconcerting to the system, but generally if the integrated part was happier, then the other parts accepted the integration with very little distress. Most of the time, however, integration of the parts was a slow process, and usually took place only when we were all ready for it. The exception was the surprise integration of Truth and Keeper. (I call Keeper and Truth's integration the "illegal integration," because it happened without our knowledge, approval or involvement—not mine, nor any of the other parts'). We, all the parts and I, became aware of the integration during one of the journaling sessions. I had just gone through an intense ritual abuse memory and was having a difficult time believing it. That is where the journaling picks up:

**CJ** *It's so difficult.*

**Keeper** *Let the truth permeate. Don't try to think it through, just feel the truth. Let the truth stand by itself. It needs nothing else. It's the lies that require defense. And that's what you are doing, defending lies and ignoring the truth.*

**CJ** *I'll try to listen to the truth. I will try to be open to it.*

**Keeper** *If you are, then you will truly be Red Baby and she will be you. You will be Snow and Snow will be you. You will be me and I will be you. Inside and out, we will be each other.*

**CJ** *Don't get inside me. Not yet. I'm not ready for that; I need you where you are.*

**Keeper** *There is no need to rush anything. There is time for everything to get finished. There is time to know the truth.*

**CJ** *Truth is inside you, isn't she?*

**Keeper** *Yes.*

**CJ** *When did that happen?*

**Keeper** *Recently, didn't you feel it? She has become a part of me. It was what she wanted. It has made both her and me more complete. Otherwise I wouldn't have been able to speak to you like I just did about the truth. Don't be sad. She's not gone.*

**CJ** *Don't leave me, Keeper. I need you to stay like you are for now, please!*

**Keeper** *I won't leave.*

**Sharon** *I want you to know that I'm totally against this sort of thing.*

**Abby** *I think it was beautiful.*

**Anita** *I suppose it's okay if that's what Truth wanted.*

**Bernice** *Can we talk to her like we used to?*

**Keeper** *She hasn't left. She has just changed her form. She felt we could work well together. She didn't want a predominate role anymore.*

**Abby** *It happened so quickly.*

**Bernice** *We should have been warned.*

**Keeper** *It was her choice and my choice. No one else needed to be consulted.*

**CJ** *I don't know about that, I would have liked to have been in on the decision process.*

**Keeper** *You would have just vetoed it without good reason. Integration is the decision of the integrating parts. Certainly it can affect others, but the choice to integrate was mine and Truth's.*

**CJ** *I miss her. How do we know something of her wasn't just lost forever? Maybe it got away before she went inside you?*

**Keeper** *I can't answer that. But if a part of Truth did get lost somewhere, where would it go? The only logical place it would go is inside me. I don't think there are tangible pieces of the alters that can break off and leave the body. Everything that is inside us, should stay inside us. No parts should be lost unless they are not really true parts of us in the first place.*

**Abby** *I can feel Truth inside you. She is there; all of her is there. She is not lost, she is just more complete now.*

**Keeper** *I think it is a good thing too.*

**Sharon** *Why wouldn't you? You didn't lose in the proposition.*

**Keeper** *No one lost. All is intact, nothing is lost.*

**CJ** *I miss her and would like to talk directly to her.*

**Keeper** *You are talking to her. She hears.*

**CJ** *It's not the same.*

**Nicky** *I want her back.*

**Keeper** *She is here. She has not left.*

**Abby** *Listen Nicky, you can hear Truth when Keeper talks.*

It may seem strange, but I was extremely angry about the merger between Keeper and Truth. In my rage, I ignored Keeper and kept her isolated from the rest of the parts as best I could. The other parts wanted me to ask Keeper to come back and help us, but I told them emphatically that if Keeper returned, I'd be gone. The parts told me they would rather have Keeper! That really torched me! I journaled by myself, without those disagreeable parts:

> *I have mixed feelings about Keeper and Truth's integration. It really took me by surprise. I guess I thought I would have had some input into the decision. I sort of felt left out of the whole process and in all actuality it affected me too!*
>
> *I was afraid something like this would happen without my knowledge. Keeper seems a little strange to me, different. I don't want her to change. For just a split second, I did feel Truth go inside Keeper. It was the strangest feeling, sort of like I felt my skin part and something slipped in through the parting. As quick as I felt it, it was over. It felt slightly intrusive. I guess I'm feeling angry because I wasn't in control; it was discussed and decided without me and I don't think that is appropriate.*
>
> *I feel like somehow I have betrayed myself by allowing this to happen, yet I wasn't even aware it was going to happen, so how could I have prevented it? Keeper seems different. I'm not sure I can explain it, except that she is more confident perhaps. Wiser? I'm not sure. That isn't too threatening, but just the change itself is threatening.*
>
> *I feel somewhat off balance, as if I've lost a little of my foundation. Keeper seems to be fine with things. Sharon is absolutely freaking about the whole thing. I do miss Truth.*

In some situations, the other parts did join up to ask Keeper to come back and help out. I was tolerant enough to go along with their decisions but always stayed in the background when Keeper was around. I didn't make connections with her; I didn't want to. I was still angry with her for taking Truth away from me without my permission and blessing. For several months no journaling happened. I simmered: if those lousy parts wanted to part company with me to run to Keeper's side, I'd simply ignore all of them! However, I could only ignore them for so long. I wrote in my journal that it felt like a huge river being held back by a dam. The river kept pushing harder and harder against the rotting wood and crumbling cement of the dam. The river also kept rising higher and higher and threatened to flow over the top of the dam. In the face of impending disaster, I realized that I needed some place along the river-bank for the river to flow out. In other words, I had to hear from the parts, whether I wanted to or not. I decided I would honor myself by listening and trying to understand them. The way to begin was to initiate a dialogue with Keeper, though I was still extremely put out with her:

**CJ** *Keeper, I'm so mad at you for taking Truth away. I really miss her and you just ate her! I think you were very selfish to take all of her and leave nothing for the rest of us. I don't even want to hear your reasons; I'm simply furious and disappointed in you. I don't want you to ever do anything like this again; at least not without letting me know it's going to happen before it happens. It's not fair. I didn't even have a chance to say good bye to Truth. She was just gone!*

**Abby** *JD said you could probably get Truth to come back if you want to. You need to make peace with Keeper so you can eventually talk to Truth.*

**CJ** *I want to talk directly with Truth. Truth, if you can hear me, I need you to come out. I need to talk to you. You can go back inside Keeper later if you want to. I won't stop you, but I need to see and talk to you first, please. Keeper, please let Truth come out.*

**Keeper** *This is not what we planned; we planned the integration to be permanent. Why do you need to talk to Truth?*

**CJ** *I never had a chance to say anything about the integration or to talk with Truth. I don't think that's fair. I don't want something like this to happen again. I've been petrified that you will integrate with other parts without my knowledge. I wouldn't even be talking with you if there was another way to get to Truth.*

**Keeper** *You hate me this much because of the integration? It seems like you might be overreacting. I agree with you that Truth and I should have talked the integration over with you and the other parts. We could have given some type of warning and time for everyone to adjust. We could have handled it better. I'm sorry we hurt and frightened you. That was not our intention. In spite of that, I really don't want to step backwards and then go through the entire process again.*

**CJ** *You're probably just paying me back for ignoring you.*

**Keeper** *I don't like to be ignored and put on a shelf. And I am hurt because of the things you have said, but I'm not trying to pay you back.*

**CJ** *I want to talk with Truth, please.*

**Keeper** *I need to think about it.*

**CJ** *Can't you just let Truth out to talk to me?*

**Keeper** *You ARE talking to Truth AND me. Truth would never have integrated with me unless she fully trusted me. I needed her unemotional, clear logic and truth to be able to balance out my own overwhelming emotion and pain.*

**CJ** *I don't want to talk about your pain.*

**Keeper** *Because it's your pain too. You try to shun the pain, yet you carry it anyway. Why not look it full in the face, take on the pain and agony? Embrace the truth. You recognize Truth in me, don't you? She has made us both stronger. We are both thinking and feeling now.*

**CJ** *I do hear her in you, but I want to hear her as she was.*

This dialogue between Keeper and me went on for some time before she would consent to my speaking with Truth. Keeper, in her brilliance, was using this situation to help move me in the direction of accepting the parts' memories as my own. Of course, I fought her at every turn, but Keeper held the trump card—Truth. Keeper had a bargaining tool I could not ignore. I desperately wanted to speak to Truth again, and the only way was to really listen and hear Keeper. Now Keeper made me go back to the very beginning of her creation. She wanted me to fully appreciate her contribution to the system.

**CJ** *Did you create Truth?*

**Keeper** *No, you did. She was created after me to know the truth and be able to keep the truth safe. Her logic and intelligence has survived. You did good to create her and she fulfilled her purpose. You understand that Truth integrated with me because her main purpose wasn't required any more?*

**CJ** *But I still need her.*

**Keeper** *You need her ability to see the truth. I have that now; she is not lost or gone, simply redistributed. She has given me so much. I can now cope much better. I feel strengthened by her presence. Before our integration I was becoming very emotional, almost out of control. Truth has pulled me back in the other direction. I now have Truth's objectivity and cognitive skills. Keep an open mind and remember we are both still here. Not one of us has been lost, just made more complete—whole.*

**CJ** *Does Truth ever talk to you?*

**Keeper** *Truth IS me. She is not separate from me. She doesn't "talk to me," we simply are each other and think like one person.*

**CJ** *I suppose it might be unfair of me to ask Truth to come back especially if the process is so involved and it was something she really wanted to happen. But I do miss her terribly.*

**Keeper** *I want you to understand me. I am very real and human. I have always fulfilled your purpose for me. Everything I have done is because you asked me to do it for you, consciously or subconsciously. Sometimes you just left and I knew what had to be done. Other times you specifically asked me to come and help and I did. It has all been done for you.*

**CJ** *I know you have done everything as well as you could. You are sensible and have compassion. I appreciate all you've done.*

**Keeper** *Listen carefully. All those times I helped out, it was really you doing the work. You just gave yourself a different name and made yourself look different. So any success or failures I had are also yours. I know we all feel unique and different, but we* *are all you. If you trust me and believe me you will be able to open up a whole new dimension of yourself, which up to now you have attempted to ignore and even deny.*

**CJ** *You're getting too close Keeper. I need you to back off.*

**Keeper** *I know what I am saying makes you feel uncomfortable. But you need to hear me. You need to believe me.*

**CJ** *I can believe your reality for you.*

**Keeper** *You need to believe my reality as yours. You need to slip inside me and be me just the way I have been you.*

**CJ** *You are asking me to take on a lot and I don't know if I'm ready or even willing to do that.*

**Keeper** *I understand what I'm asking of you. But you asked a lot of me in the past. I do understand the magnitude of what I'm asking you. I cannot and do not want to go on carrying this all by myself. It's time you share it with me.*

**CJ** *I'm feeling very overwhelmed right now and close to going over the edge.*

**Keeper** *Can't you hear there are other parts who are also upset?*

**CJ** *Yes, they don't want to know the truth either. You want me to look through your eyes and I'm so afraid to do that.*

**Keeper** *Think of it as simply putting on a pair of sunglasses, mine, and seeing things from my perspective.*

**CJ** *Honestly, this is not a good time to pursue this.*

**Keeper** *There is never a good time. Your fear keeps you from the truth.*

**CJ** *I'm feeling too vulnerable to look through your glasses.*

**Keeper** *That's exactly where you need to be. Put down your guard, and put on my glasses.*

**CJ** *I can't, Keeper, I just can't!*

**Keeper** *You are making a choice. A choice not to accept my history or me. You are not acknowledging who I am and what I've been through. You are not acknowledging who you are.*

Gradually, with some help from Jerry, I quit blaming Keeper and simply trusted Truth—that she knew what she was doing when she integrated with Keeper. If I couldn't trust Keeper's motives, I decided to trust Truth's motives. Truth had always been responsible and never made rash emotional decisions. I tried to allow Truth to speak through Keeper to me.

It was months after Keeper and Truth had integrated with each other, when a miracle literally happened for me. I was sitting through a regular church service, when I had a vivid vision/encounter of Truth and Keeper. I wrote about this experience in my journal:

> *God has temporarily given me back Truth! I saw her immediately today! She was with Keeper. In my mind, I saw Truth and Keeper both sitting in front of me. Truth was holding my hand and Keeper was holding me as I wept for relief and joy. To me the vision spoke volumes: Truth can surely help understand and see truth and the reality of situations, but Keeper is the one who has the compassion and empathy. I thought it was interesting in the vision that Truth had no desire to touch me, except for holding my hand and that seemed to be uncomfortable for her. She possesses very little, if any, emotion. It was through her wisdom that she understood the importance of holding my hand (for me), not because she felt any need or desire deep inside her. Yet Keeper knew I needed to be held. I know that I only have Truth back with me for a short time; that she needs to go back inside Keeper, but it has been such a peaceful time with her back. I haven't suffered from any anxiety since Truth has been back. I guess this says that I need Truth as much as Keeper seems to and the only way I'm going to permanently get Truth back is through integration with Keeper. I'm not ready for that yet. I don't know what will happen when Truth leaves me for good. I don't want to think about it, but I need to prepare for that permanent separation.*
>
> *I believe that God has orchestrated Truth's temporary return. I can only think that he has heard my silent and constant, distressed prayers and has worked with Truth and Keeper to allow this time for me. I must believe it's God's way of telling me he cares and that I'm valuable to him. I'm having a difficult time getting a grasp on that reality; it still seems a little illusive. But I must remember God's action and compassion to me. I know beyond a shadow of a doubt that it is through his action I have Truth back with me for now and I am extremely grateful. I believe there are many things I need to learn from this experience, but no, I simply want to savor my time with Truth! I don't want to waste a minute of it.*

*I will be devastated when she leaves me again. I know I will only be able to be back with her when and if I choose to integrate with Keeper. But if I take on their strengths by integrating, I will also take on their weaknesses, and most of all their history—admitting that their history and memories belong to me as well.*

Integration with Keeper and Truth was a turning point within the system, with major effects on me and potentially on all the parts. Our journaling had allowed Keeper, Truth and me to begin the pre-integration process. Now, on the verge of integrating, we wrote to each other again in the journal:

*Dear Truth,*

*I am so grateful for your pursuit of truth and the way you fearlessly communicate it—honestly and openly, realistically. I truly thank God for you. I believe you are God's messenger to me. I don't want to lose you! I desperately need you. Just in case this integration gets messed up I want you to know what you mean to me and how much I love and trust you. I wish I could selfishly keep you as you are, but that's not to be. I hope that I can give something back to you.*

*CJ*

*Dear CJ,*

*I am who you made me to be and have done what you asked of me, nothing more or less. You are fearful of losing the truth, but by creating me in the beginning, you determined to always have the truth. Don't worry about me. I am doing well. I enter you willingly and with full knowledge of what the result will be—and I am not afraid.*

*Truth*

*Dear Keeper,*

*I have treated you like dirt so often. I have willfully trampled you into the ground. I have mistrusted you and your intentions. I have judged you harshly at every opportunity. I have greatly wronged you and yet through it all you have stood by me always supporting me. You even hid your grief from me because you knew I could not bear it.*

*Finally, I have been able to accept your truth, Keeper. You bore our child, our tiny baby girl and you bore the grief of having her ripped away from you before you could even hold her in your arms, kiss her tiny cheek or touch her tiny hands and feet. You did this all and then bore the guilt of not being able to protect her. You did all this for me. And in return I pushed you away from me and called you a liar. I'm so very sorry. I deeply regret my actions and the needless additional pain I caused you. Even now you consider me more than you do yourself. You are choosing to give me the only thing you have left to give—yourself. I have often sung praise of Truth and been far too silent about you. I'm sorry. You too deserve to be honored. I love you dearly, Keeper. Now as we integrate, if things do not go as we think they will and you are somehow swallowed up into nothingness, I will grieve. I love you, Keeper. I thank you and I continue to need you. Please God, don't take Keeper from me.*

*CJ*

*Dear CJ,*

*I love you too. This final act of integration is simply to totally embrace you in my love. I know how much pain you are in now and I want to give you strength. Our life is important. We cannot, no matter how much we try, bring back our baby. We cannot breathe life back into her, but we can honor her by staying alive ourselves. After we integrate, you MUST strain and struggle to stay alive, no matter how much you may want to die. You will have Truth inside you, her strength and her reality. You will also have me. All of our strength combined will help us honor our history, our suffering and our survival! I cannot leave without saying thank you to JD. JD, you loved me, cared for me and looked after me. You are a godly man.*

*Keeper*

When Keeper (with Truth inside her) finally integrated with me, I knew it was the pivot of my healing process—I was becoming stronger and more whole. The actual integration occurred one day while I was at home, as I recorded in my journal:

*Well, today it happened! Truth and Keeper integrated with me. I am sad. But I know we did a good thing. It happened like this: In my mind I saw Jesus standing in front of me with Truth on one side and Keeper on the other. Jesus had his arms around Truth and Keeper. He moved Truth forward and her brain melted into mine. Then he moved Keeper forward. She moved toward me with her arms wide open as if to give me a hug. I moved towards her also with my arms opened and embraced her. For a mere moment we embraced and then she moved into me. All this occurred while Jesus stood in the background and watched, careful not to move forward towards me to frighten me. Since the integration, I feel a deep sense of sadness—my dear friends have moved on. I really didn't feel any different emotionally or physically right after the integration. I didn't expect that I would. But I don't seem to have the intense self-hatred that I had before the integration. I'm most certainly still wary and suspicious of myself, but I don't desire to harm or inflict pain or kill myself. For whatever reason, because of Jesus' participation in the integration, I have less fear and mistrust of him. I don't have all the answers for the healing that still needs to occur (even though I do now have Truth inside me!!!), but I don't think I need to have all the answers now, because I'm God's beloved. I don't feel holy, I only feel loved. I don't feel perfect, I only feel forgiven. Welcome, Truth and Keeper.*

I was nervous after Truth and Keeper's integration, dreading it might trigger a quick succession of integrations. The parts all loved Truth and Keeper. What if they wanted to join up with them, because they missed them so much? I wasn't ready for that. I initiated serious conversations with Abby, Beth, and Bernice about their intentions. It helped me to hear that they were dedicated to the system, wanted to keep things under control, and committed to remaining separate for as long as they were needed. Of course there were still some parts like Sharon, who refused point-blank to consider integration.

Abby asked me how I was feeling about Keeper and Truth being gone. I replied that sometimes it was okay and sometimes it was gut-wrenchingly painful. I vacillated—at times I wanted to fall face down and weep, because I missed them so much. On other occasions I could see that their integration was progress, and I felt honored they had chosen to integrate with me. And then I would feel very sad and depressed again, as if I could not continue without them.

Because Keeper was gone, it was now up to me to manage the system and care for the parts. The younger ones were having the most difficulty with Keeper's absence. Nicky especially missed Keeper and sitting in Keeper's lap. Our journaling went like this:

**CJ** *You must have felt very safe sitting in Keeper's lap.*

**Nicky** *Yes and warm and loved.*

**CJ** *Keeper was really good about showing us how much she loved us. Nicky, Keeper isn't really gone. She's just inside me. You can sit on my lap if you want to. I'll hold you.*

| | |
|---|---|
| **Nicky** | *But it's not the same.* |
| **CJ** | *I know it's not, but I would like to hold you. You could even lean back against me and rest.* |
| **Nicky** | *But I want Keeper.* |
| **CJ** | *I know you do. I miss her very much too. Sometimes I miss her so much that it makes me cry. I'm sorry you're so sad.* |
| **Nicky** | *You don't love me like Keeper did.* |
| **CJ** | *I know, but I want to. I just need to get to know you better. I'll bet if you sit in my lap and close your eyes it might seem like Keeper is holding you. It's okay to cry. I'm really sorry you're feeling so bad.* |

Nicky remained inconsolable this time around, but as I worked more directly with the parts, they began to accept me as Keeper's replacement.

Next I realized that Anita was moving toward integration with me. I could sense it in the way she talked and acted, and I grieved her loss before it even occurred. At one session with Jerry, Anita desperately wanted to say goodbye to him—to me, it was just one more sign she was getting ready to take her leave. She insisted on shaking hands with him, which I believe was important to her—to touch him before she left. I often balked at what the parts wanted to do, but this time, I didn't even question her desires and subsequent actions. My journal reads:

> *Anita is with me at work today, at my request. I know she will be leaving soon. I didn't think I would miss her so much because I didn't think we had a very strong emotional tie, but I'm grief stricken at the thought of her leaving. I wanted to have one last day at work with her at my side, watching or participating, whatever she desires. Just to have her physically near me seems important. To be able to touch her, watch her, listen to her, share ideas with her—that's the goal for today. I have begged her to stay separate for just a few more days to give me a chance to let her go. It doesn't seem to matter that she will be integrating with me; I still feel like I'm losing her. I wonder if the other parts will miss her? And if so, will they miss her as much as I will? She has always been so responsible, reliable and competent. It seems impossible to preserve any of her qualities. The thought of me absorbing them seems heathen and so wrong. In my mind, I know I can manage without her. The truth is she has had nothing to do for quite a while. I've been able to handle things very well without*

*her assistance. I know it's probably unfair of me to want to keep her just the way she is, forever preserved, just to make me feel more comfortable. I need to let her move on, grow and become what she is destined to be, which I guess is "us." Talk to me, Anita. Let me know your thoughts and feelings.*

**Anita** *It is time to move on. I didn't think I would ever want to integrate, but I honestly do want to finish up. You don't really need me any more, although you used to depend on me a lot. I have done my best. I have enjoyed working hard and presenting accurate, well-organized projects. It has fulfilled me and made me feel needed and useful. But you are doing all these things very well by yourself. I'm tired and bored. If there are no more challenges for me, then I am prepared to step aside permanently. Integration doesn't scare me. It is inevitable. The door is open and I am ready to walk through it. I am happy and content to be working with you today, simply because my journey is nearly complete and I feel a sense of a job well done. I did good, didn't I? I have always known you appreciated me, especially my work. You have been a good friend to me. I know Truth understands what I am doing and approves. I will leave you all my talents, abilities and knowledge. Let's enjoy today and look forward to tomorrow.*

**CJ** *I love you Anita. I will never forget you, ever. Thank you for teaching me such wonderful and useful things. Although I would like to keep you as you are forever, because I do regard you so highly and respect you, I release you to move ahead. I do it with sorrow and sadness and a very heavy heart. Please retreat gently and quietly, if you can, to spare me the feelings of being exploited and betrayed. But continue to stand close by me today, Anita. I want to remember you this way, a picture to be treasured in my memory.*

When a month or so had passed after Anita integrated with me, I wrote:

*I do miss Anita, not for what she could do for me, but simply for her voice and her participation in the system and in my life.*

Beth was also ready to integrate with me before I was. I put her off for a while. Then the hostile twin Sharon was overcome by her painful, traumatic SRA memories. Beth, with her pure and simple faith in God, thought that my merging with her would strengthen me to work more effectively with Sharon and to deal with my own feelings. I knew I had been putting off Beth's integration because I didn't feel worthy; I wasn't certain I was ready to become the spiritual leader of the system. Jerry agreed with Beth that the time had come, because our integration would signal the beginning of some tough work with Sharon.

Because of Beth's deep love for God, of course our integration had a spiritual focus. She and I planned to go to church on a particular Sunday. Then when I sat down in the pew, the integration would simply happen. Beth wrote me a letter the day before:

> *I think it is time for me to integrate. In fact, I KNOW it is time. I don't know why you are fighting it so hard. Are you mad at me? I honestly just want to help and believe we will be stronger if we are together. I have no problems with the plan we've devised for the integration. I think you believe me to be somewhat of a goody two shoes, but quite honestly I only want to please God and I believe it is his will that we join forces. I know you believe there is an internal conflict with joining good with evil. You believe that I am good and Sharon is evil…or is it yourself you believe to be evil? The truth is we are all equal, simply individuals struggling to be and existing with good and evil parts inside us.*

The next day, I went to church, I sat down, and our integration happened as planned. After all my delay and doubt, it seemed a bit anticlimactic. There was no excitement or fanfare, not even much regret or feeling of loss, just a simple joining of two beings into one. Beth's integration did trouble some of the remaining parts, until they joined us.

The final part to integrate was Sharon. Her twin, Sarah, had integrated quickly and simply much earlier, but not until 2004, several years after I completed therapy with Jerry, did Sharon integrate with me. Martin and I had moved away from Denver and were established in a Midwest community, where I was attending college. Although Sharon was still a separate part from me, we rarely interacted as intensely as we had when all the other parts were around. It was more of an inner sense of her separateness and aloneness. Otherwise, my inner life was very quiet without noise from the parts. There is such a quietness that comes with integration; it's difficult to explain. It is a soothing quietness, yet lonely too. I was aware that Sharon was still with me, and I always knew what she liked and did not like. But she and I had learned to live peaceably together. I chose not to push integration with Sharon and she did not seem to be very interested in integrating either. We simply had a quiet companionship.

In March of 2004 I attended a weekend-long spiritual retreat with approximately 100 other women. I took a risk attending the retreat, because the participants couldn't really know ahead of time about what would be taking place. I don't care for surprises, but I did feel a strong internal drawing to attend the retreat. When we arrived, they asked us to remove our watches! I obediently took mine off, but kept secret access to it throughout the weekend. The weekend was structured so we were in a position to totally concentrate on ourselves, those around us, and the presence of God. We participants were encouraged to allow God to delve deeply within us and to expose areas of our lives that could use his divine touch. And that's what happened, even though it nearly sent me into a tailspin.

On Saturday afternoon, we heard a message about "our dying moments." I interpreted that to refer to those times in our lives which define just who we are. These retreat leaders encouraged us to identify our dying moments, and to acknowledge the feelings and emotions surrounding those moments. We were asked to lay the "dying moments" before Jesus and let go of them. It didn't take an Einstein to figure out my dying moments! So I gave up my pathetic childhood to Jesus. At the same time, I asked him to take my past—to use it however he saw fit—but to decrease its negative effects on me. At the very same time, I included Sharon in a way I never had done before. I applauded her and appreciated her. I told her how much she meant to me and acknowledged that I would not have survived without her. In that very moment, as I gave these matters to Jesus, Sharon integrated with me! There were no bells or fireworks, no invitation was made, I just knew we were finally one—whole and united.

Later that evening, the retreat leaders held a surprise candlelight service. Several hundred people who had previously completed this retreat now gathered in the church sanctuary, all holding lighted candles. When we arrived in the sanctuary, we heard them singing. As we entered from the back and walked down the center aisle, the people were singing, smiling and staring at us. Our group moved slowly toward the front of the sanctuary, and the others gathered very close to the center aisle—in some cases even standing in the aisle.

The whole scene was very crowded and intense. Shockingly, it freaked me out. Partially I'm sure it was the surprise. Had I known what was going to happen, I might have prepared for it. But maybe not. I was being horribly triggered by everything in the church. All I could see were the many cult meetings in my past. This ceremony reminded me of horrific experiences at those meetings. The low singing of the crowd reminded me of the low chanting in the past. The candles, the darkness, the hovering people—all drew me back to a horrible time in my life. I was feeling the full intensity of a flashback. And because Sharon had just integrated with me a few hours before, I was facing this overwhelming situation all by myself!

I don't recall what took place during the service. It was all I could do to keep silently reminding myself it was 2004, and I was not at a cult meeting! Somehow I managed to hold myself together during the service, but I was near a breaking point. I was even thankful for the darkness of the sanctuary, because I knew fear and horror were written all over my face, and shaking my body as well. After the service, I knew I had to talk to someone. When I found one of the retreat leaders, I was sobbing uncontrollably. I had to fight to catch my breath, because I was sobbing and shaking so hard. I did know what was happening—I was experiencing an abreaction, in the fullest sense of that term. All the fear and horror that I had experienced so many years ago felt like it was happening that very moment, as if no time had passed. I started talking out loud to myself, "Be calm. I'm safe," over and over. Providentially the retreat leader was trained in Theophostic methods (a type of therapy) and encouraged me to use some of those techniques to work through the fear. She was very calm, and I finally managed to get myself under control. But I remained profoundly shaken and distressed.

I phoned my husband Martin, but couldn't reach him. Desperate now, I called Jerry. Just hearing his voice calmed me. During the phone conversation, he reminded me several times that I was in control of the whole situation. I could leave anytime I wanted. No one could force me to do anything I didn't want to do. That phone call was my salvation. Jerry's calm reassurance helped settle my emotions, and I decided to stay at the retreat through the next day.

As I hung up the phone from talking with Jerry, however, I found I was immediately extremely mad at God. I told God I thought it was a dirty trick to allow me to be thrust into this situation. I railed at him for knowing this was going to happen and not warning me ahead of time. However, when I had time to calm down and reflect on the weekend, I realized God had orchestrated the weekend for Sharon and me to integrate and for more healing to take place. He actually had answered my long request to be fully integrated. I know he allowed me to experience first-hand, all by my "newly, fully-integrated" self, the horror of what had been a satanic ritual ceremony. God allowed this experience to be a *new* experience for me. An experience, where as a totally integrated person, I could honestly and truly acknowledge, without hesitation, the truth of my past and at the same time see the experience in a different light. I knew that acknowledging the horror of my past could launch me into a new phase of my life with new emotions and new perceptions.

Even though I still shudder at what I experienced that evening and the depth of the emotions I felt, I am so truly grateful at the sensitive nature of Jesus that he allowed me to experience a flashback in such a safe environment. I'm grateful for the timing—because it was perfect, even though it didn't seem so at the time. I truly experienced a new spurt of emotional and spiritual growth that weekend.

## The Miracle in Me

Over ten years of therapy culminated in this evening. After Sharon had integrated with me, I didn't feel strange, as I had when other strong alters merged. Now I felt complete. I realized that I could never have accomplished full integration without all those years of grueling work. Yes, I still struggle with certain issues related to my past and those I inherited from Sharon, but they are now MY issues and MINE to work through. Being fully integrated does not mean I'm all fixed, but it does mean that I have moved through some very difficult places and I am ready to move on. I have been helped by all my parts, my family, my friends, and of course Jerry. There is truly strength in numbers!

Some of my friends have also journaled extensively throughout their healing processes. When they finished their work, they destroyed all of their journals. I find that I can't do that. To me, my journals are a reflection of all my parts and of myself. My different alters were an integral part of my life—they helped me survive my traumatic and abusive childhood and also aided my adult life. To destroy the journals would be dishonoring to my parts—to myself. I have decided to keep them for my lifetime, and then allow my daughter to decide what to do with them

Since I have fully integrated all my parts, I have very different feelings about those inside people of mine. Sometimes I miss hearing their separate voices, and the wise counsel some of them offered. For a while after Sharon integrated with me, I noticed how quiet things were and how lonely I felt. When those different parts were in conflict, I would have relished the silence, but now the silence was sad. I felt a huge empty hole inside me. Although my alters put me through a lot of fear and terror during our healing process, they also brought energy and drama. Now I missed those colorful and exciting internal conversations—even though I knew all the parts were safely and comfortably inside me. Gradually they have entirely blended their uniqueness and individuality with me.

When I began seeking wholeness, I had little comprehension of the depth of emotion the parts had been holding for me. They took on the pain, the fear, and the terrible experiences of my childhood and allowed me to be free of them for many years. But there came a time in my adult life when the parts had enough of covering for me, of taking my place. They wanted me to know what they had suffered for me. I needed to know their anger that I had simply stepped aside and let them experience all the abuse and the horrific torture. By disassociating, I had in effect abandoned them. As I began therapy, the parts were weary of being quiet, and actually I was ready to know the truth. So for a second time in my life, the parts were my helpers. The first time, they allowed me to escape the pain and horror; this last time, they enabled me to accept the truth of my life and to become the person God originally created me to be. I now know the truth, and the truth has set me free.

CHAPTER

# 18

# God in the Conversation (CJ)

*If all you do is pour on the guilt, you could very well drown him in it. My counsel now is to pour on the love.*
–II Corinthians 2:7-8 (***The Message***)

I have always considered myself to be a spiritual person, but my life experience, and especially my alters, moved me to a greater desire for God and acceptance of his unmerited love.

## Spirituality and Therapy

I have no doubt that Beth's love of Jesus and Jerry's nonjudgmental acceptance of me enabled me to experience a spiritual depth and intimacy with God, and especially his son, Jesus, that I had never imagined possible. As I mentioned before, my mother told me I had asked Jesus into my heart when I was three years old—although I do not remember this. We always went to church, and my sister and I took the bus to Bible school in the summers. As a teenager and young adult, I was active in church. I professed to know God and to have knowledge of him; however, as I began this process of truly knowing and understanding myself, I realized that my lack of trust in people included lack of trust in God. The fact is, I did not like to think very deeply about God or my relationship with him. Yes, I prayed. While I was going through the darkest period of recovery, I prayed all the time. I prayed for God to rescue me. I prayed that God would give me strength to endure. I prayed God would show me truth, that I would not be deceived by Satan.

God did show me truth, and one of the first truths was that I simply didn't trust him. When I visualized God, I saw a picture of a huge man. In this mental picture, I realized I could not turn my back on this big man for one minute for fear he would assault and rape me. When I faced my true thoughts and feelings about God, I was absolutely horrified at myself. Would I be struck by lightning because of those thoughts? But that picture expressed my reality. I had less fear of Jesus, but certainly did not trust him either. Even though I didn't trust God, I realized I still needed to believe in someone, especially when my entire world was turning upside down.

My spiritual life was even more complicated because my husband was a pastor. When I saw my true spiritual self and realized the shallowness of my faith, I struggled to uphold my image as a pastor's wife and good Christian woman. At first, this task was relatively easy, because I could allow one of my parts to be present at church services and activities. I was the church pianist, and Abby, who was so creative, assisted by playing the piano. Anita was also helpful and valuable, because she was organized and rational.

Still, as I became aware of my true spiritual condition, my faith seemed to disintegrate before my very eyes. I remember one day when I was out on a walk, I shouted out in desperation to God, "I'm done with playing this church game. It means nothing to me. It accomplishes nothing. I can't do it any longer. I'm not even going to read my Bible anymore. God, if you want me, you'll have to come get me." That agonizing prayer was a turning point, because from then on, I ceased to perform. In my role of pastor's wife, I still did my very best to be truthful and honest about my spiritual struggles, and if that was not possible, I would simply keep quiet. Surprising myself, in the midst of this deep and painful struggle, I found freedom. I didn't have to put on a front. I didn't have to pretend I had it all together spiritually. I was free to be me—a sinner, poor in spirit and totally broken.

For quite some time, I was anti-God. I didn't like him. Although I never totally renounced God, there were times I felt totally separated from him. In the middle of remembering the abuse, especially the Satanic ritual abuse, I could not fathom a God who would stand by and allow a child to be tortured and abused in this way. During the intense part of my recovery, I asked myself "Why?" over and over again. I never felt I received an answer. I'm not sure any answer would have fully satisfied me.

Jerry was extremely helpful to me during this time, though he doesn't recall my asking him the "Why" question. He was very open about his own faith, but never tried to pressure me spiritually in any way. He calmly listened to my raving anger toward God, my apathy toward God, and my dislike of God. He affirmed my feelings. He allowed me to struggle with the spiritual side of my life while he showed me Jesus: working with me, affirming me, caring for me and loving me. He never criticized or judged me. On the contrary, Jerry admitted his own spiritual struggles and weaknesses. His spirit-filled life and therapy methods allowed God to begin a work in me that is still growing today. David D. Brenner says it well in his book, ***Sacred Companions: The Gift of Spiritual Friendship and Direction:*** "*The task of spiritual* *friends [therapists]is to help us discern the presence, will and healing of the Spirit of God,"* (p. 165, InterVarsity Press, 2002). Brenner further states that close and connected relationships with others get us ready for intimacy with God. I am deeply grateful for the healthy relationship Jerry modeled when he interacted with me. He provided an environment where I could be safely vulnerable, and at the same time he shared his own struggles from his heart. I firmly believe his modeling enabled me to understand the value of intimate relationships, not only with other individuals, but especially with God.

It may seem a small thing, but I believe God gave me another helper in the long therapy process. In 1992 we rescued a cat from the local animal shelter, even though my husband had allergies. Martin agreed we could try having one around. This cat was approximately 1 ½ years old, a tabby with yellow eyes, and I named him Bernie. From the beginning, I loved Bernie, writing in my journal that he was "a bright spot in my life." I also wrote: "Bernie is such a friend. He loves me for me, whoever I am." My husband tolerated the cat well, which was virtually miraculous, because normally a cat in the room would cause him to have a runny nose, itchy eyes, and shortness of breath. Bernie often sought out my lap and would lie there for hours, softly purring. His great purrs made his body vibrate and I would lay my hand on top of him, feeling the purring vibration move throughout my weary mind and body, a blessedly peaceful sensation. Bernie became an integral part of my therapy, keeping me sane, making me laugh, and lulling me to sleep with his presence. During one session, Jerry gave me permission to bring Bernie to his office. The poor cat was very frightened and hid behind Jerry's couch for most of the hour, but having him there demonstrated his important role in my recovery. I knew how attached I was when I had nightmares about losing Bernie; I imagined I would forget to feed him, and he would die. However, Bernie lived to be more than 15 years old, bringing me pleasure and comfort. I did say goodbye to my dear furry friend a few years ago, and both Martin and I deeply mourned his passing. I will always be grateful for Bernie's much-needed, calm and soothing presence.

I had another kind of special spiritual encounter, just before I began to recognize there were various parts inside me. Jesus impressed on my mind and spirit that he wanted to show me what a real, genuine father was like—how he loved me. He told me that the coming days would be difficult, but necessary for my healing. I wanted to believe God could heal me, and on one level, I did believe it. But a part of me was convinced that God didn't have time for me. In the past, He had just stood by and watched the abuse happen without helping me. Why he would bother with me now? I realized that my faith and trust in him were weak at best. I made Jeremiah 17:14 my frequent prayer: "Heal me, O Lord and I will be healed. Save me and I will be saved, for you are my praise."

Then one extraordinarily peaceful day, I was taking a walk and sensed Jesus saying to me, *"I gave you this peaceful day so you can remember it when days get bad—and they will get bad—but you can think back to this day and know your life will get better. Know that I'll always be with you."* I wasn't always certain whether it was actually God talking to me, but I could usually accept the words as divine messages.

I also faced a unique set of problems stemming from the Satanic ritual abuse I had undergone. As indicated in the journal entries between my alters, I was totally repulsed by the central Christian practice of communion. The very act reminded me of rituals in which I had been forced to take part. Communion had been tainted for me by evil. I could not see anything beautiful or meaningful about this sacrament. This was particularly awkward for the pastor's wife. Again, some of my spiritually-inclined parts came to the rescue, and participated in our church communion when I could not. (Some of my alters were deeply spiritual; in fact, one was Catholic and longed to attend mass.) The Christian holidays were often associated in my mind with evil rituals. At one cult meeting, a Christmas tree was hung upside down and used for a particular ritual. The cult had tried to pervert everything sacred, and for a time in my life, they succeeded.

The way I had been treated for so long made me wonder whether God would ever accept me. My involvement in the ritual abuse confused me to the core. I wrote in my journal:

> *Am I beyond redemption? My mind says, no, but my heart says, yes. Would I do something like that again? I don't know. Do I have a major character flaw? Perhaps. Maybe it has just been hidden most of my life. I think I'm a very bad person. I know God loves bad people, but I don't know if I can love myself. Am I evil? Filled with sin? If so, for some reason am I afraid to come to God and ask for forgiveness? Or is it pride? Or perhaps Satan is trying to deceive me? I'm so confused.*

The parts had their own spiritual difficulties. Many of them had no concept of Jesus. They knew only Satan and evil practices. Many of the younger parts were scared to talk about Jesus, because they equated him with the devil. Once they had a discussion about spiritual matters when Jerry told us he would be away for a few weeks. One of the parts was worried that Jerry might die while he was gone, and this spurred their journaling:

| | |
|---|---|
| **Abby** | *JD could have left us many times before, but he has always come back to work with us. He cared about us; he will come back.* |
| **Victoria** | *Unless he dies, right?* |
| **Mean One** | *Sometimes if people die, they can come back too.* |
| **Abby** | *I don't think so. If they die, they are gone forever.* |
| **Beth** | *Until we see them in heaven.* |
| **Audrey** | *Or hell.* |
| **Beth** | *We're not going to hell.* |
| **Audrey** | *Maybe not you, but you can't answer that for all the parts.* |
| **Nicky** | *I don't want to go to hell.* |
| **Hell** | *I don't want to either.* |
| **Beth** | *You don't have to.* |
| **Victoria** | *Can some of us to heaven and some of us go to hell?* |
| **Beth** | *I don't think so. What do you think Keeper?* |
| **Keeper** | *Some of us feel like we should be sent to hell. We feel like we deserve to go to hell.* |
| **Beth** | *Maybe we just need to be sure we all are going to heaven, then we won't have to worry about it.* |
| **Victoria** | *But maybe some of us can't go to heaven and maybe some don't want to go to heaven.* |
| **Beth** | *We can all go to heaven, if we want to. Nobody will be left behind if they don't want to be.* |
| **Anita** | *Maybe there isn't any heaven or hell.* |
| **Beth** | *I think there is.* |
| **Anita** | *Well, that doesn't mean everyone does.* |
| **Bernice** | *We know Satan and hell exists because we have seen it. So it makes sense that God and heaven exists too.* |
| **Beth** | *We just need to ask God to help us, to forgive us and then we can all go to heaven.* |

| | |
|---|---|
| **Victoria** | *What if he kills us because he hates us?* |
| **Audrey** | *Worse yet, what if he wants to punish us so he makes life miserable for us?* |
| **Beth** | *God loves us and he can't love us and be mean to us at the same time.* |
| **Audrey** | *How can we believe that?* |
| **Sharon** | *Yes, how? He's a man right?* |
| **Beth** | *He's God. He can't say one thing and then do another. It's impossible. God loves us and wants us to love and obey him.* |
| **Nicky** | *Obey? I don't know about that. What will God make us do?* |
| **Beth** | *He won't make you do anything. He only wants what is best for you.* |
| **Bernice** | *Will he ask us to use a knife and hurt someone or something?* |
| **Beth** | *Why would he do that?* |
| **Noah** | *Will he make us hurt animals?* |
| **Beth** | *I don't know of any reason why he would make us do that. He loves us.* |
| **Sharon** | *I don't think we can just hear you say that and necessarily believe it's true. I need proof.* |
| **Beth** | *The proof is that He loved us so much he died for us.* |
| **Sharon** | *Is that important? We've all seen people and animals die. Big deal. It didn't help us at all.* |
| **Beth** | *That's because those deaths are different from Jesus' death. That was people taking another person or animal's life. Jesus gave up his own life. He chose to die for us.* |
| **Bernice** | *I don't think all the parts can understand this very well. It scares them.* |
| **Beth** | *That's because some of them are little children. They need to grow up so they can understand too.* |

I believed it was essential for all the parts to be introduced to Jesus. Knowing Jesus was so important to me, integration would require that the parts all knew Jesus too. Some of them heard about Jesus from the other parts, usually Beth. But some of them had heard sermons or classes at church or read the Bible or other books.

Though I had regularly practiced prayer, there came a point in my therapy when I was unable to pray, I was angry with God and very anxious about being angry. I wrote in my journal,

> *I think I'm still pretty angry at God. It's the first time in my life when I actually wonder if I'll go to heaven when I die. I feel like God has left me because of my actions, and I'm too bull-headed or leery to ask him back into my life.*

I questioned whether or not I trusted God, and most of the time I didn't believe he was trustworthy. During this time when I could not pray, I asked Jerry to pray for me. Martin and a few other close friends also kept me in their prayers.

## Redeeming Faith

When I was nearing completion of my recovery, one of my group leaders started a small group for individuals who wanted to explore their spirituality. This was perfect timing, because I was noticing that Jesus had begun a spiritual awakening within me. God had been answering my original cry for help. He had pursued me in very gentle, quiet ways. Over the months he stood by my side, never intruding, but always faithful in his presence, waiting for me to desire that presence. One time in my mind's eye, Jesus was standing in front of me. In my hurt and anger, I pummeled his chest with my fists. He stood absolutely still and allowed me to abuse him. On another occasion, I saw Jesus standing beside me. He was not touching me, for I wouldn't allow that, but just making me aware of his presence. Later in my recovery, the picture continued to emerge, with Jesus standing so close to me that our arms touched. Eventually in the picture, Jesus sat across from me, leaning toward me and holding my hand in his. A tiny desire to know more about Jesus began to grow inside me—but not about his Father, because I still was terrified of God. Now the spiritual group gave me a place where I could openly speak about my tentative interest in Jesus and my fear of his Father. This group provided an environment without judgment with simple acceptance. We were all on a spiritual journey. Jerry encouraged my participation in this spiritual support group, all the while allowing God to work slowly and beautifully in my life.

At work I had begun to use my lunch hour for exercise. I would drive to a nearby park and walk the quarter mile around the lake several times. One day as I began to walk I was remembering the Bible story of Samuel. When he was still a boy, in the middle of the night God called out his name. At first Samuel thought the priest Eli was calling him, but wisely Eli told Samuel how to respond the next time he heard the voice—"Speak to me, Lord, for I hear you." I wondered if that would work for me too! So as I began my walk I prayed that prayer, *"Speak to me Jesus because I'm listening for you."* To my utter amazement I began to hear Jesus (still not God) speak to my heart and spirit. Over and over again he spoke words of his love for me. For days and weeks, after that walk, the only words I heard from him were "CJ, I love you." I know why Jesus kept speaking them over and over to me: it took a long time for me to really believe that he did love me. Those words were deeply soothing to my mind and spirit. To this day, I still long to hear Jesus tell me how much he loves me, and he faithfully speaks his love to me in so many ways.

My lunch-time walks and talks with Jesus became the highlight of my life. I cherished my "alone" time with him. I longed to feel his presence and hear him speak to me. In fact, my spiritual life became alive in a way I never had known was possible. I couldn't help talking about this change—with my husband, with Jerry, and with other close friends. I can only say that I fell utterly in love with Jesus, amazed at the attention he gave me. He accepted my brokenness. He told me he understood about the abuse I had endured and said how sorrowful he felt about that abuse. I asked him "the question" over and over—"Why did you allow all those things to happen to me?" Jesus did respond, and the answer he gave me satisfied me. He told me that when I was a very small girl, he had come into my heart. He held my spirit in his hands, and although my body and mind had not been protected, he has always protected my spirit. I have come to believe that my early childhood request for Jesus to come into my heart was what had kept me sane and alive during those early years and into my adolescence. I believe Jesus took the tiny spark, birthed deep inside me when I was three, and held it safely in his hands through the years of abuse. I believe he helped me to survive physically and emotionally but most of all spiritually. Later, in my adult life, Jesus fanned that flame into a raging fire of passion for him.

I was so thrilled by what was happening in my relationship with Jesus that my feelings spilled out of me in many sessions with Jerry. I remember seeing him smile and shake his head, in amazement at the transformation that was occurring deep within me. As Jesus revealed himself to me in such wonderful ways, I began to see and know his very heart. I had peace in my spirit. Now I could take part in communion, because Jesus helped me to understand the strong love that lay behind his cruel journey to the cross. I experienced a tiny bit of the great and boundless love that had motivated Jesus to endure much more abuse than I could ever imagine.

Though I am grateful for hope and healing, I have to say I will never be able to understand how God can stand by and see his children tortured and hurt. I've read histories of the martyrs who have withstood cruel and inhumane treatment and still remained true to God. I also read in the newspapers about little children who are horrifically abused and suffer immensely. In fact, I know of children who have been so horribly abused that they never fully recover physically and emotionally even as they reach adulthood and grow old. I remember all too vividly the abuse God allowed me to experience at the hands of relatives and others. If I think about these evils too long, without recalling how Jesus has healed my mind, emotions, and spirit, I can fall back into despair. I begin questioning all over again, "God, why do you allow people to go through bad things?" I do not pretend to know why and how God allows the things he does. If he told me, I probably wouldn't like his answer. What I do know is that God protected the tiny flame that began inside me at three years old and maintained it, until on the brink of his miraculous healing in me, he fanned that tiny flame into a blazing, roaring fire. In the passion he instilled deep within me for him, I am able to simply trust and not to question. I am able to be okay with not understanding the whys. I am able to accept my own traumatic past. I receive the healing power of Jesus through his own powerful, loving spirit, and through the healing hands he provided me through my family, Jerry, and the others who accompanied me on this long arduous journey. I simply accept my past, present and future—knowing with absolute assurance how much he loves and cares for me. What can I say other than *Jesus is enough for me.*

I will never be able to explain nor justify the horrific facts of my experience. But I know deep within my spirit that God, his son Jesus and the Holy Spirit were always faithful to me and will remain faithful. I know that when I cannot understand what is going on around me, I will always have his Holy presence standing beside me. I have an insatiable desire to grow spiritually and to learn more about Jesus, to know his heart, to see with his eyes and hear with his ears. This desire grew out of recognizing, accepting, and integrating my ugly, shameful past.

In my current work as a therapist myself, often a client will reveal a sense of sin and doubt that God can still love them. I am thankful that God enables me, through my own life experiences, to empathize and to offer hope to others.

### The Gift Of Life

By Abby

A life is a gift,
Given to live.
A baby, a flower, an animal, a cell.

A gift to be treasured,
Protected and loved.
A gift to be admired,
Sought after and held.

A gift to *give* love,
A hug and a kiss.
A gift to *give* life,
For the gift to admire.

A gift to grow older
And wiser and gray.
A gift that one day
Is returned to the Giver
To live on forever,
A gift truly eternal. He is real.

---

## Suggested Reading

William Paul Young, ***The Shack,*** 2007

# Epilogue

## Jerry Donaldson

*Go after a life of love as if your life depended on it—because it does.*" –I Cor. 14:1 (***The Message***)

Hearing or reading a story like CJ's often pushes us to ask, "Why?" Why do innocent children have to suffer? Why so much trauma in a little child's life? Why doesn't God intervene more? Why do people abuse, rape, torture, and do other cruel things? We have all attempted some explanation of the "whys," but the responses fall so far short that we might be better off avoiding these half-hearted attempts.

It is absolutely amazing to me that CJ rarely asked the question "Why?" when coping with her past. Perhaps she understood intuitively that more often than not, the "why" questions about tragedies are unanswerable and cannot be explained. In my view, focusing on the "whys" wastes too much time and allows too many of us to avoid personal responsibility for responding to tragedy.

Instead of "Why," CJ chose to ask "What" questions: <u>What</u> do I do with my past? <u>What</u> should I do to keep the past from negatively affecting the present and the future? <u>What</u> can I do with all the conflicting voices inside? <u>What</u> path do I take to increase my ability to love those around me? <u>What</u> must be grasped so that I can forgive the perpetrators without excusing their deplorable abuse? In dealing with her own tragic past, rather than accuse, blame, or sidestep what she could not control, CJ took initiative to work on <u>what</u> **she** could.

I have rarely, if ever, seen CJ feeling sorry for herself. Yes, she had to grieve the loss of her childhood. It's also true that she became extremely discouraged, even to the point of being suicidal. Yet she did not use her unhappy childhood as an "out" for making other people's lives unhappy. She could feel sadness and pity for others, even her perpetrators. When thinking clearly, she understood that their lives were miserable, and that they had found no relief in making others miserable. Somehow, instilled in her psyche, was a sense of responsibility, a sense that God was ever-present, and an internal perception that the future could bring relief.

Becoming a "multiple," developing dissociative identity disorder, helped CJ cope with her incredibly painful childhood. To dissociate from her emotions, to place those feelings and intolerable memories on various alters, was a highly ingenious way to survive. The alters took care of CJ in whatever way they could, dealing with the excruciating pain, fulfilling her perverted perpetrators' wishes enough to get through each day, and ultimately protecting the whole. Each alter played a vital role in getting her through her abusive life, even though they were in conflict with their world and with each other.

But what if CJ had continued to ignore her memories and the many voices within? What if she had chosen to blame her past rather than take responsibility for her future? What if, after discovering her abusive past, she had decided not to forgive her perpetrators and never let the past go? What if she had walked into my office merely to complain about her husband, her job, her church, and her life in general? What if she had focused on the "whys" rather than the "whats"? Fortunately she did not make these choices, but rather chose to change what she could, and to reach out for a more fulfilling, loving life.

Another amazing facet of CJ is that she had every right in the world to abandon her faith, but she did not. There were times in therapy when she expressed anger toward God and wondered what He was up to, but her faith, however small it seemed at times, continued to be simple and childlike. Somehow she knew she was to be loving and kind to others and not hypocritical. Although she came out of a very religious, hypocritical, legalistic environment, although she desired to do everything "right" and perfect, and although she gave little credence to her emotions, she did not lay heavy expectations on others or treat them in a legalistic manner. Her faith has not been a list of rules and regulations. Even though she was and is a private person, she did not and does not pretend to be someone she's not. She is genuine.

* * *

How does one conclude a story that is not yet finished? I have struggled with this chapter more than any other, perhaps because the story is still in process, or because I have always had difficulty putting the final touch on anything, even a painting or a wood-working project. This may be my temperament and personality quirk, but you know and I know that no story is really finished until we leave this earth. In fact, even after we die, our legacy continues.

Most of CJ's perpetrators are dead and gone, yet their sad legacy will continue to affect CJ and all those around her—with sadness, regret, hardship. However, CJ's legacy will be vastly different: purposeful, positive, and long-lasting. She has been willing to remember and deal with her past, to integrate all the various parts of herself, to forgive those who abused her, to remain optimistic about the future, and she made her past work for her rather than against her. She has continued to serve the Lord God rather than ignore the spiritual side of her being. Her impact on people continues to be positive; rather than act hatefully and distantly toward those around her, she has chosen to be loving and sacrificial. CJ has learned skills and acquired attitudes that help her set boundaries, be more assertive, feel and express her emotions, connect and relate to others, grow in her commitment to God, and live with enjoyment and purpose.

I believe our readers can be challenged and changed by CJ's story in this book. All those who have had personal contact with her will benefit from this larger view of her life: her husband Martin, her adult daughter Janelle, members of her church, former and future small group members, students in her adult Sunday School classes, and those whom she serves in her community counseling capacity. This is a life-giving legacy.

CJ is human like the rest of us. She will continue to experience failures, not just successes; crises, not only peace; sadness, not total joy; feelings of disappointment, not constant encouragement; anxiety, not perpetual calmness. Real life is not a "happily-ever-after." It will have its downs and ups. However, CJ will not just survive, she will also thrive and continue to learn from her life experiences.

In 2006 she proudly handed me an invitation to her university graduation. She had then been accepted into a graduate school, gaining an M.A. in counseling. Today she has become a licensed therapist…a good one, I might add. Her marriage to Martin is growing stronger and they are maturing in their relationship with each other. She maintains a close relationship with her daughter and son-in-law. Each piece and part of her has merged into the whole of who she is; therefore, her face and demeanor show less and less internal conflict and more and more peace. Her ability to empathize, her gracious accepting spirit, and her willingness to risk openness and genuineness will affect people positively for years to come, and I believe, even beyond her time on this earth.

Does this sound like exaggeration? I firmly believe all of us have this power to affect those around us, either positively or negatively. My desire, and CJ's, is to give people hope. We long to see them grow. May others know and trust God, and see themselves as the Lord's children.

Neither CJ nor I had any idea what would come out of our ten plus years' encounter. Both of our lives have changed, and both for the better. When I first met CJ, she was cool, reserved, calculated, distant, and unexpressive. Yet behind her demeanor I saw this sensitive, caring, giving, honest, tenacious woman who was seeking something better. What a privilege it has been to watch her grow and bloom. We have always been brother and sister in Christ; for a significant period of time we were counselor and counselee; while writing this co-authored book, we've been peers… but what I cherish the most is that we are now friends.

## Catherine Jean Johnson

> *Daughter, you took a risk trusting me, and now you're healed and whole. Live well; live blessed!* –Luke 8:48 (***The Message***)

My entire therapy process encompassed more than 10 years, an intense and difficult time, yet also a period of extreme growth for me. I could not be where I am today without traveling this long and grueling road of pain and suffering and acknowledging my early life of abuse and trauma. I am often embarrassed to admit that I was in therapy for such a long time; however, I believe it was necessary—for several reasons. First, I had endured abuse for many years—from approximately 3 years of age through my teens. Secondly, the abuse was severe and traumatic, affecting me physically, intellectually, emotionally, and spiritually. The hideous and horrific nature of the trauma is indicated by the large number of alters I created. Each of those alters had a story to tell, even if it was only a fragment. So in essence I was not alone in therapy—but over a hundred different individuals were also involved in the process. And lastly, I am a slow processor. I think things through methodically and analyze them carefully. As I journeyed through therapy, I was determined to work through everything just one time. I didn't want to leave things half finished and then have to return and deal with them again later.

For many survivors, deciding whether or not to forgive perpetrators is a major issue in the recovery process. With Jerry's help, I came to understand the importance of placing appropriate blame—not to blame myself for my abuse, but to allow my perpetrators to be responsible for their actions or inactions. My decision has been to forgive, in recovering from my traumatic and abusive past. I believe that each person has a unique response to being purposefully wronged or hurt, and that God actively works through that uniqueness in this matter of forgiveness. Even today, I don't completely understand the way God led me through to forgiveness, but I am certain I hold no resentment or bitterness toward any of my perpetrators. Although I am fully aware and have assigned appropriate responsibility to my perpetrators for their actions; I am free from the weight of un-forgiveness.

Because I chose not to confront my family, I had to work on internal healing without confirmation and affirmation of the facts through my family. I have no doubt that had I chosen to confront my family, they absolutely would have denied what truly happened. This decision protected me, and I worked very hard to protect my daughter from my father and grandparents as long as they were alive and capable of hurting and damaging her. However, I sometimes cringe as I wonder whether my father and the others continued as abusers. I will have to live with that fear and sense of guilt for the rest of my life.

My father died of a sudden heart attack in 2002. Standing over his casket with Martin at my side, I was able for the first time to feel the rush of anger at the treatment I had received from his hand. The previous evening, I had attended the visitation at the funeral home, and grimly endured what his family and friends said about what a "wonderful" man he was. All evening, I smiled and pushed down all my feelings—until the next day. Just before the funeral service, everything erupted inside of me. Finally I felt "safe" to feel hate, disgust, sadness, and other intense emotions. I sobbed and cried as I have never done since that day. I felt all the bad, evil and horrible memories of my father pouring out of me, never to return. I believe I now have forgiven my father, though I reluctantly admit (only to those closest to me) that I have not missed him since his death.

Coming to terms with my mother and her involvement (or should I say lack of involvement) in my abusive childhood has taken a different turn. Again, I have chosen not to confront her. For years, I thought of my mother as a very strong woman. I realize now that what I viewed as strength was basically just her ability to survive. She survived by blindness—refusing to see reality, or choosing to ignore it, or allowing the truth to simply roll off her, like water off a duck's back. I realize that her inaction did help her to survive, but after *surviving* 10 years of my own therapy, I know her way was not the best, for herself or her children. Since I grew up seeing her ignorance or rationalization as strength, I had also used those techniques to survive and had convinced myself that I was stronger for them. That perceived strength revealed itself as extreme weakness when I recognized that we both chose to believe lies instead of reality in order to escape the pain of the truth. My mother's "strength" was destructive. She didn't have the fortitude to face how terrible the situation was for her and her children. She wasn't strong enough to seek help for herself or her family. Her solution was to join in where necessary, to hide her head in the sand about what was actually happening, or to camouflage events until they were unrecognizable.

I know I have qualities similar to my mother's; however that does not mean I was made identically from her mold. Yes, I utilized some of her survival techniques, but they failed me. Her chosen blindness may have seemed to preserve my life, but not for long. In order to heal, I had to disconnect from the fantasy image I had of my mother, as well as from the reality of what she really did. I chose to distance myself from her for a time until I understood the whole person God intended me to be. Since my father's death, I have been able by the grace of God to re-establish a relationship with my mother, based on who we are today.

My mom moved in with us for the last eight months of her life. I must say that although being a caregiver is a difficult and strenuous responsibility, I have no regrets that she lived with us. I was with her through her final hours. My desire was to give her the best life possible in her last years, free of worry and care, being directly involved with family activities. Because I was able to establish a "new" relationship with her for the last 10 years of her life, I have deeply mourned her passing because we actually did have a relationship! I am very thankful to God for this time with her.

The lengthy therapy process enabled me to grieve the loss of a fantasy childhood and the loss (or absence) of a healthy father and mother. In working through this old family stuff, I have aimed to completely break unhealthy generational patterns. I believe I have done just that! I am hopeful, and a little proud, that I'm leading future generations down an un-traveled road, paving the way for my daughter, her children, and her children's children—into a new day for all of us.

Looking back over the process, I wish I had made a few different decisions. First and foremost, I would choose to involve my husband and daughter in my therapy. For reasons I have given and for those I choose to keep to myself, I essentially made the journey on my own, with help only from Jerry and support groups. I now believe that IF I had taken the risk of involving my husband and daughter, they would have experienced individual growth, and we would have grown stronger as a family unit. And second, I wish I had embraced my past more readily, instead of fighting so hard against it. The recovery period might have been shorter…but I could not know what I did not know.

Today I am a changed person! I am a whole person! I am changed emotionally and spiritually. Although I've never been one to enjoy change, I am much more of a risk taker than before. Working with Jerry and my friends who are on the same path has helped me to grow in my own awareness of myself. I am acutely aware today of my strengths and my weaknesses and am not afraid to admit either. I truly know my spiritual self, and I claim by faith my heritage in God's family. I'm able to look at myself in the mirror and like the person I see! I have an inner confidence that is deeply rooted in my spirituality and carries with it peace and hope.

Am I completely healed from my past? No. At times a situation or experience will trigger thoughts and feelings from the past. I make a choice at that moment, whether or not to allow my past to control me. Most of the time I choose freedom from the past, though occasionally I fall back into old habits. But I am growing out of my past. I have now healed to a place where I can feel pain and joy. I have tasted the true flavor of life through my emotions, and I savor the taste. I am alive to pain, but I am also alive to peace and joy. I don't ever want to return to the mechanical, feeling-less life I once lived.

I give credit for my healing to several individuals and groups of individuals. First, I believe Jesus placed his hand upon me years ago and has kept me firmly in his grasp. I would not be the person I am today if Jesus had not gifted me with his presence and guidance. Secondly, I have a loving, caring husband and daughter (who has also blessed me with a wonderful son-in-law and a delightful granddaughter). My husband and daughter provided me the space I needed to acknowledge my past and heal through therapy, while keeping me lovingly planted in their hearts.

Thirdly, I would not be here without Jerry and the gift of himself through his counseling and therapy methods. Jerry helped me see my way through the darkness and stood by, opening the door to my new life. He showed genuineness and integrity to me and all my parts. He gave us permission to be ourselves, listened to all our horrible stories, and held out hope for us when we had none for ourselves. During our years together, Jerry always provided me (all of me!) a safe place to work through our trauma and grief. He stayed firm in his personal standards, beliefs, and values without pushing them on me, all the while allowing me to squirm around trying to find my own way through. When I brought in new counseling ideas such as Theophostic therapy, he did not become indignant or defensive. He embraced any method that helped me grow and change—on my own time schedule. Although I suspect he often wanted to push me or jerk me forward, he patiently stood beside me as I made my slow pilgrimage toward being an authentic, whole person.

Ending this therapeutic relationship was a difficult decision. I had never expected it would last as long as it had—nearly 10 years! However, Jerry began to talk about retiring from counseling about the same time when many of the parts had integrated. I was progressing well toward integration with the remaining parts, and I knew our therapeutic relationship would have to end sometime, but it was still very hard to hear.

In retrospect, I think I wanted to leave Jerry before he had the chance to leave me! Always the organizer and planner, I began to devise a plan for termination beginning in the fall of 2000. I had been seeing Jerry on a weekly basis (and more often when necessary). Now I decided I could continue on my own, since most of my inner work was done outside his office. To facilitate transition, I cut my sessions to one per month for several months in advance of terminating.

In January 2001, I had six remaining parts who still needed to integrate (Audrey, Abby, Sharon, Snow, Claudia, and Jill). This may seem like a big challenge, but I realized that together we (Jerry, God, my parts and I) had already accomplished a great deal, getting more than a hundred forty parts to integrate! A few months before Jerry and I terminated therapy, I wrote him the following letter. Along with Abby's poem "The Helper," my letter sums up my thoughts and feelings about Jerry and his help on my journey of more than ten years:

> *Dear Jerry,*
>
> *I'm just going to write down things I want to say to you as they come to my mind. I was thinking about how gentle and kind your eyes are. Overall, I believe you are a very kind person. I believe you try very hard not to hurt people as well as to be sure they feel ok and accepted. You identify yourself with other people's weaknesses and failures. In doing that, you allow them to be weak and/or to fail without condemnation. You accentuate my strengths and affirm me in so many ways. You identify the human condition, expose yourself as being human, and celebrate and affirm the humanness in others.*
>
> *You are rarely defensive, but typically accept criticism and genuinely analyze it to determine if there is credence to it. You've never failed to admit to your own weaknesses or possible error in methodology or judgment.*

*You always seem open to suggestions and ideas. You are not rigid. Instead your flexibility in thought patterns and actions has allowed me to emerge from within myself—to work hard and ultimately succeed.*

*You never fail to tell me how much you care about me and are concerned about what I'm going through. You care even when I refuse to accept your caring.*

*You always accept me as I am. I don't have to perform or come up to a certain list of standards. Whatever I say or whatever I'm feeling is okay. You've even been the brunt of undeserved anger—yet you've given me permission to put my misplaced anger on you in order that I could simply experience that particular emotion.*

*You are extremely reliable and dependable. You've always been there for me, whether in an emergency situation or simply for a normal weekly session. You meet me on an intellectual level as well as encourage me to meet you on an emotional level. You push me when I need it as well as allow me to work through things at my own pace and you seem to have a very intuitive way of knowing when to wait or push.*

*Even though you are a very godly, Christ-like man, you've never pushed me to move spiritually. Instead you've quietly lived your faith in front of me and waited for me to broach the subject, which has allowed me to discover my own spirituality. I've been able to move toward Jesus without you placing any expectations on me or requiring me to meet some ambiguous set of spiritual standards. You stepped back and let Jesus move forward and embrace me. Then when I embraced Jesus, you were there to celebrate with me and share your own spiritual journey with me.*

*You've been assertive and caring enough to always share truth with me, even when I couldn't or didn't want to see it. You stand firm in truth and because of that you've proven your trustworthiness over and over. You are a man of high integrity in both your personal and professional life and you give wise and godly counsel.*

*I've learned so much from you due to being able to see things from a male perspective and the fact that you and Martin are similar in so many ways. Because of your openness with me, you have given me many opportunities to see situations from Martin's perspective and to understand him better.*

*Several times when I was close to simply giving up—you've been there to help me through. You extended your hand to me when I thought, and truly believed, there was no reason to go on. The calm, confident way in which you handled those times helped me get to a safer place and quieted my desperate, troubled spirit.*

*Your words of encouragement and affirmation have deeply honored me and helped me to know how Jesus views me. You never, ever discounted me or anything I said. You've <u>always</u> believed me, even when I couldn't believe myself.*

*You've given me permission to enter into your world—you share your every day life events with me and allow me to know you as more than just a therapist. You've invited me to be your friend with your words and actions.*

*Several times during the course of our sessions, I've said to myself, "I want to grow up and be just like Jerry!" I wish with all my heart that I could have had a father like you. I strive to genuinely replicate your attributes: your kindness, gentleness, your caring, honest and open spirit, your ability to listen, empathize and understand, your ability to touch other people's hearts, the way you connect and relate to people and especially the way you love and accept people just as they are.*

*You have helped me "want" to have relationships. You have modeled it in front of me and encouraged and challenged me to take risks with people and then applauded my efforts.*

*You have very graciously and sacrificially charged me far less for your services than you deserve and on several occasions didn't charge me at all. You are a giving person and I could never afford to pay you what your services are really worth.*

*I will miss you terribly when our sessions end. I will miss hearing about your life, your hopes and dreams. I will miss having such a good listener and someone to bounce my thoughts and feelings off of, as well as receiving your solid feedback.*

*I don't have any idea of what, if any, type of relationship we will have after we stop our sessions, but I do know the value of knowing you and will always remember the part you played in helping me become a whole, balanced individual. And I will always treasure and be thankful for the time I've been able to spend with you and the sheer privilege and honor of knowing you.*

*I pray that Jesus will give you and your wife an absolutely wonderful, fulfilling and enjoyable retirement; that you will continue to grow in your intimacy with Jesus; and that many other people will have the joy and privilege of knowing you as I have and will be able to benefit from the depth of your wisdom and character.*

*CJ*

Lastly, I give credit to the many groups which helped sustain me, ranging from sexual abuse recovery groups, to DID groups, to spiritual discovery groups. Members and facilitators of these groups have marked my mind and heart forever. I am deeply grateful for such wonderful facilitators, who give time and effort to guide people like me through our broken, battered lives on to healing.

In the spring of 2006, at the age of 53, I graduated from a state university with a bachelor's degree, and I received a master's degree in counseling in 2008. I am currently employed as a counselor/therapist where I work with adults and couples. I have chosen not to specialize in DID; however, I am trained to work with traumatized individuals, including clients who have experienced childhood sexual abuse. Throughout my journey to wholeness, I have been the beneficiary of many skilled and caring professionals, and I am thrilled to be able to help others who are struggling to find their balance in life.

Dear reader, if you carry the label of DID, or have suffered abuse in your life, lift up your head—hope and healing are available to you.

If you are reading this book as you journey with a family member or friend down their road of healing—bless you! Stay the course! You are desperately needed and appreciated.

If you are reading as a therapist, I encourage you to be genuine and authentic with your clients. If you are currently treating an individual with DID or someone who has been abused, you can show that person hope when they are unable to see it. Please don't allow the potential heaviness of the therapeutic process to blind you to the potential of your client. With your help, that person can move to personal growth and self-awareness. Please strain to keep their possibilities in mind, and strive to help them to see their own potential.

The following poem was written after Abby integrated with me. My mind still grapples with the dilemma: is this my poem or Abby's? Whatever! I believe the poem encompasses our entire journey and is a tribute to all my beloved parts.

### Voices

By Abby and CJ

Voices, voices, voices,
Always voices.
Whispering, agitating, soothing,
Discussing, analyzing,
Angry, sad, hopeless,
Cheerful, glad, hopeful.

Voices, voices, voices,
Always voices.
Voices with a past.
Memories looming.
Always looming.
Ready to consume.

Voices, voices, voices
Always constant.
Listen to the voices,
Listen to their stories.
Lonely voices
Needing to be heard.

Voices, voices, voices
Always persistent.
Accept their truth,
Embrace their pain.
Wipe their tears,
Hold them close.

Voices, voices, voices
Always missed.
Quiet, yet somehow present.
Whole, yet somehow separate.
Me, yet somehow us.
Linked once,
Now united.

Voices, voices, voices
Always persistent.
Accept their truth,
Embrace their pain.
Wipe their tears,
Hold them close.

Voices, voices, voices
Always missed.
Quiet, yet somehow present.
Whole, yet somehow separate.
Me, yet somehow us.
Linked once,
Now united.

APPENDIX

# A

# Marriage, Relationships and Sexual Abuse (JD)

*If then I do not grasp the meaning of what someone is saying,*
*I am a foreigner to the speaker, and he is a foreigner to me.*
–I Corinthians 14:11 (***NIV***)

Most of us struggle in some way with others' sexuality, and our own. My intent in this section is to point out how our exposure to sex in our society taints our sexual relationships, inter-personally and intra-personally. I also hope to help the reader with questions that often arise in this context:

- How do I respond to a loved one who has been sexually abused?
- How do I go about sharing my sexual history and the way it is affecting my relationships?
- How do I create a safe environment for others to be honest in this arena?
- What do I do with my own lack of sexual fulfillment if my partner is unable to respond sexually due to abuse and the inability to trust?

## Distortioned Sex

Statisticians have estimated that 30 to 40 percent of the women in the U.S. have been raped and/or sexually abused in some way by the time they have reached 20 years of age. The percentage for men is somewhat lower, but steadily increasing. Forced sex has taken its toll on individuals and relationships.

Sexual addiction is prevalent in our society. Nobody escapes the influence of the multi-billion dollar pornography industry. All of us have been impacted by the constant exposure to sexually titillating literature, movies, television, and the internet. From a very early age, both males and females are literally forced to deal with the distortion of sex and sexuality. Girls are taught how to gain the sexual attention of boys, and boys are conditioned to be turned on by the slightest sexual stimulus.

What God intended for procreation, intimacy, and pleasure has become a demoralizing, distorted game. Men and women alike are victimized by ethically and morally inappropriate, defeating sex. In addition, we modern people still face the battle of the sexes that has been going on for ages. Rather than being allies, the genders are polarized over who is to "blame" for our relational problems. We argue, point fingers, complain, cajole, and sometimes see the opposite sex as the enemy. Men blame women for luring them into being sexually out of control, and women criticize men for always thinking about sex. By stereotyping one another, we widen the gap of misunderstanding.

I do not believe I exaggerate our misuse and abuse of our own and others' sexuality. On the other side of the coin, I am hopeful that we will continue to learn how to deal with our sexually dysfunctional attitudes and behaviors. We cannot make the problems go completely away, nor will we ever relate perfectly, but we can work toward a healthier perspective in this area of our lives.

We enter marriage hoping that it will resolve or erase our negative sexual experiences in the past. However, those of us who are or have been married know that our sexual struggles do not dissipate in marriage, but rather intensify. Unresolved issues, internal and external, are magnified when we marry. We bring to our partner our ongoing problems with sex, money, parents, siblings, church, certain types of people, and myriad other tensions. And we quickly discover that our partners have brought their own baggage into the relationship as well.

I have counseled hundreds of couples, and rarely do I find them to be "sexually compatible." Their expectations are unrealistic. They have been brought up with erroneous sexual information, attitudes, and experiences, and their fears prevent them from giving themselves freely to their partners. A major problem is that one partner is usually more interested in sex than the other. For example, younger men usually desire sexual encounters more than their wives do. For them, sex can be a release from various anxieties of the day. They have to handle sexual stimulation on the job—from co-workers (whether by off-color jokes, sexually provocative attire and behavior, or intimate conversation with the opposite sex) or from general exposure to enticing marketing and advertising. Young men who have dealt with sexually charged workdays often anticipate a legitimate encounter with their partners once they arrive home.

Young women, on the other hand, have often fended off men's leering glances or advances at work or have been drawn into power struggles. They also tend to carry the weight of daily responsibilities at home: children, homemaking and balancing their very full schedules. Sex is not of preeminent importance to a young woman who is tired, needs support and affection, and longs just to relax once life quiets down, which may not be until 9:00 or 10:00 p.m. on a regular working day. In general, as women become older, and are less burdened with children and homemaking, they seem more interested in sex than their husbands are. Older men themselves are less sexually driven—they have learned to curb their somewhat waning libido, and are not always as desirous of physical encounters.

I freely admit that these statements are over-generalizations, but I observe that, for whatever reason, most couples have difficulty reaching an acceptable sexual balance, where both parties feel their needs and desires are being met. We have a mental picture of great sex once we are married, but the fantasy never seems to be realized. Our unrealistic expectations propel us into relational conflict.

## Marriage and Sexual Abuse

A satisfying sex life is even more complicated when one of the marriage partners has been sexually abused. A partner who recognizes the need to be more sexually responsive may read books, hesitantly speak to trusted friends, or seek professional help to find what is preventing mutually enjoyable sexual encounters. Sometimes this searching leads to the discovery of past sexual abuse. Or the unresponsive partner may have been aware of past abuse without realizing its long-range impact on mind and body.

CJ's husband had learned to anticipate sexual encounters on a fairly regular basis, but as CJ became more aware of the past abuse, she had more and more trouble responding. Their subsequent frustration only complicated their ability to be intimate.

What are spouses to do, when their partners are unwilling to be more involved sexually? More specifically, what can spouses to do, once they discover that their partners have been sexually abused? A general principle is that patience is needed, but for most of us, being patient (i.e. celibate) for months, years, and even decades does not seem to solve the problem. Adjusting our expectations certainly seems appropriate, but adjusting to marriage without sexual encounters may seem unbearable.

Naturally we feel rejected when our partners are not willing to engage with us sexually. Some of us find it hard to give hugs, or any form of affectionate touching, let alone give our bodies to our partners. Often our relationships begin highly charged with sexual overtones, so that we can hardly restrain ourselves or wait to get married. However, over time, our sexual expectations and hang-ups begin to interfere, preventing the spontaneity we formerly experienced. This is particularly noticeable when a person has a history of past abuse.

Men and women are usually aroused emotionally and physically by hugging, kissing, caressing, and sexual touching. Foreplay is an appropriate and necessary activity in loving marital relationships. However, what is signaled by one partner can easily be misinterpreted by the other. If our partner makes a loving gesture, we might "assume" that our partner is interested in "making love," when in fact he or she only might want to communicate "I love you!" It is hard to move beyond our assumptions in this regard to a healthy openness. We spend more time guessing what the other person means by their behavior than talking assertively and tenderly about what the "overtures" mean to us. Perhaps we fear that talking seems to dampen the mood, or maybe we'd rather not hear or deal with a negative response. But when we don't talk about sex with our partners, we will continue to make the assumptions that get us into even further trouble.

Those of us who have been sexually abused have learned to identify most sexual behaviors as leading to sexual abuse. We are conditioned to be cool, distant, and reserved, in hopes that others' affectionate behavior not become more intensely sexual. Steeling ourselves to be aloof will spill over into our marital relationships. Because as children we had little or no control over our bodies, as adults we attempt to assert ourselves and set boundaries—which feel like barriers to our partners.

Spouses of abuse survivors face additional challenges. We may want to express our love through affectionate acts, without necessarily wanting sexual intercourse. However, when we sense a response from our partners, we naturally become more sexually assertive, especially after a time of sexual deprivation. If we further complicate this scenario with a background of sexual abuse, the frustration level continues to rise.

When either partner feels fearful or pressured, he or she will back away from the encounter. This cat-and-mouse game becomes all too familiar. In this state, we feel horribly stuck and sexually inhibited. We stop talking about what is going on, and may try to do without sex entirely. This may work for a while, but ultimately the situation worsens. When we attempt to renew sexual encounters with our partners, they may well believe that we are only interested in their bodies, not their hearts and souls. Feelings of fear, abandonment, hurt and frustration take the place of joy, pleasure, acceptance and love. And we find that sexual conflict reaches into virtually all areas of our relationships.

## When Shameful Information Is Disclosed

When our partners reveal long-hidden information about their pasts, particularly about sexual abuse, how do we respond? What should we say, how should we act, and what can we do to help? We face this complicated question when anyone shares suppressed information that is overlaid with embarrassment, guilt and shame. As a therapist, I always attempt to place myself in my clients' shoes, to set aside my own feelings of inadequacy, and to listen as accurately as possible to what they are feeling and thinking. My goal is to make the client feel safe enough to continue disclosing. This comes more easily with my clients than with immediate family members or friends. My greatest challenge is making the situation safe for my own wife to share with me.

If we disclose a painful past and admit how it is affecting the present, we fear we will be misunderstood, judged and discounted. It feels most risky when the present problem involves a spouse. We don't want the listener to make assumptions or rush to conclusions, but rather to ask sensitive questions about what we are disclosing. If the listener still doesn't understand, we want them to admit that, rather than dishonestly imply that they do. Genuine puzzlement indicates that the listener is open to receiving more information, so we can hope for more clarity about what we are attempting to say.

There is no way for someone who has not suffered abuse to fully understand the pain, violation and shame it causes. When an abused partner senses that the listener is being judgmental, he or she will shut down. (In fact, if we feel any kind of judgment, we won't share intimate information in the first place.) We dread having people criticizing our feelings or perceptions, so we won't bare our souls if it means being punished further for something over which we had no control. However, a partner who respects the confiding of the abused person and responds with further caring questioning, can begin to understand. Every partner or friend has experienced the feelings of pain, violation and shame in connection with different circumstances. Safe, loving people don't judge, but connect with others' experience through grace and mercy. Just as judgment and criticism are shown in a listener's body language, phrasing of speech, and tone of voice, so the spirit of grace and mercy shapes an accepting demeanor and caring words. In essence, judgment adds more pain and misunderstanding but *grace creates a safe place.*

When we venture to expose our innermost thoughts and feelings, the last thing we need is for the listener to ignore or discount what we are revealing. Even well-intended people can inadvertently change the subject, make inappropriate comparisons, or seemingly discount the importance of what is being said. We feel violated all over again when the listener minimizes what we are sharing from the depths of our being. Very quickly the climate shifts to "unsafe." The self-revealing person shut downs and retreats to the mundane.

Critical parental types are even more difficult to approach. They come across as condescending and disappointed that we haven't met their standards and behaviors. Often they have what I call a "soap opera" tone, look, and demeanor. They use exaggerated expressions and melodramatic terminology; they project a "know-it-all" sense that they are more mature, knowledgeable and wise than we are. For example, CJ had an alter called "Mother" who was terribly critical. Mother would tell CJ that she was an "absolute failure" as a daughter, wife, mother and Christian. She would say to CJ in a disdainful voice, "You make me sick.—You're really sloppy.—You're hypocritical." When CJ's adult alter, Keeper, would cut CJ some slack and give her credit where credit was due, Mother would reply sarcastically, "It must be nice to be able to overlook your faults, to justify your actions and decisions." This internal dialogue would often cause CJ to shut down.

When anyone senses this critical parent attitude, this condescending, know-it-all mentality, he or she will stop sharing…or not even begin to risk doing so. Why would we want to increase our pain and shame by giving another person open season to straighten us out? What we need is a nurturing, supportive parent who listens, reflects, remains open and non-judgmental, and gives a clear signal that nothing we say or do will limit their love. Loving parents don't always agree with us, but are slow to disagree and will encourage us to make responsible decisions.

Intimate conversation also ceases when the listeners turn the conversation around to a discussion of <u>their</u> emotions and thoughts. We don't feel safe when we sense that listeners are all wrapped up in their own discomfort or their preoccupation about what they are going to say when we stop talking. We are not asking our loved ones to fix our problem or to give us advice or even to agree with us. The help we need comes from probing, non-interrogating questions, which lead us inside, to gain greater understanding about our situation.

Simplistic responses only create further complications in the relationship. Advice is cheap, especially unsolicited advice. We have all heard some of the pat phrases or answers given to fix another's problem. Even if those canned answers have not worked for us, we may still feel compelled to respond with some "sound advice." The implication is that if the struggler was a bit more mature, a little more insightful, or more intelligent, the problem would have been solved years ago. (See the Biblical story of Job's interactions with his wife and his friends.) Once again the environment becomes unsafe, even toxic, to the one who experienced the past abuse.

Our best bet as loving, sensitive, caring listeners is to avoid becoming all wrapped up in our own perceptions and feelings. Rather than seek pat answers, we can just listen attentively, making ourselves completely present and available to the speaker. We can prove that we want to make them feel safe and understood, by reflecting their emotions and thoughts back to them.

We do not feel misunderstood, judged, or discounted when friends and spouses place their sole attention on us and intentionally listen to what we are attempting to share. When they willingly put their perceptions and emotions on "Hold" and listen with empathetic ears, we will sense they understand. True friends love us unconditionally, creating an atmosphere of acceptance, respect, and warmth that frees us to be ourselves. We don't have to self-protect. We can say what we mean and mean what we say. We can believe that no matter what, our friends will continue to be there for us and we believe they will not label us with some prejudicial stereotype.

Recently I noted a conversation between two of my friends. Randy was sharing some of the pain and frustration he was experiencing in his marriage. Phil responded, *"Sounds to me like you're hurting, frustrated and would like more affection and intimacy in your marriage, but your wife doesn't, and this has been going on for years. My goodness, what a painful spot to be in."* Phil continued to listen, reflect, and ask clarifying questions. He did not attempt to fix the problem or give advice, but he showed that he understood by sharing a very appropriate personal example. I could see that Randy was touched by an acute listening ear, and evidently grateful that advice was not forthcoming. There was no immediate solution, but a loving connection was established between these two men.

Even if we don't have Phil's presence of mind and succumb to freely passing out advice or turning the attention to ourselves, we can interrupt ourselves. We can return to the conversation, apologize for having been poor listeners, and ask our friends to risk sharing once again, promising to do a better job of being attentive. We can never be too interested, too understanding or too loving.

Finally, if we put ourselves in the place of a person revealing guilt-ridden, shameful information, we would want our partner or friend to feel honored by our trust and transparency. We would hope our listeners would realize that our struggles were ours, not theirs, so they need not feel threatened. Our intention in sharing this confidential part of our life would be to invite the other person into better understanding of who we really are.

I encourage my clients and friends who have opened up with me to risk sharing with others, because I want the spouse and/or friend to experience the connection, the understanding, and the bonding that has developed between the client and me in therapy. Admittedly, the counselor's office is a somewhat artificial environment, compared to one's daily, routine home life. However, if deep bonding can take place in my office, I believe my clients can also experience that bonding elsewhere. Normal healthy relationships are what we all long for, especially if throughout childhood we have never had them.

Once we have established a close relationship, I ask my clients whether they have other safe people with whom they can freely disclose. Occasionally they do, but in the majority of cases, they do not have anyone safe. When they have risked openness in the past, they have felt ignored, discounted, lectured and/or parented. Very rarely indeed do my clients risk sharing with their partners; most of them have held their thoughts and feelings within for years for fear of being misunderstood or rejected. Some have attempted to reveal their hearts, only to have their partners use the information against them. For example, one of my clients finally told her husband how her older brother had sexually molested her when she was about twelve years old, only to have her husband react in frustration, "I'm not your brother, and I'm tired of you using his abuse as an excuse for not responding to me sexually. You need to get over it and consider me for a change!" There was truth in his statement, but his tone of voice and his attitude made his words counterproductive and extremely hurtful. His wife determined from that point on that she would never open up to him again.

I know of others who have disclosed very private, personal information, only to have their partners break the confidence and tell others. It is essential that this kind of information be disclosed only by the person him or herself. We have no right to reveal to others information shared with us in confidence; only the discloser can grant permission. When we break confidence, we forfeit the right to be trusted in the future.

CJ gave her husband permission to share most of what they were experiencing with a confidant. This did not violate her trust in him. All of us need a "sounding board," somebody who will listen, even if we are being critical of our partners. This person does not necessarily take our side, but will clearly indicate that we have been heard and understood. Sometimes we call this a "reality check person," and he or she must also agree to keep private information private. If we all had one or two people with whom we could confide, we would need fewer professional counselors.

Dealing with disclosure of sexual abuse is very demanding. To sum up, the loving partner must avoid judging, lecturing, fixing, disconnecting, or being parental. On the positive side, the listener must keep confidences, learn to listen empathetically, and extend mercy and grace. A safe, caring, understanding partner will not take abuse history personally, but detach appropriately to hear the disclosure, and ask the non-intimidating questions which bring clarification. No small order! And, recognizing that we can't do all these tasks perfectly, all of us who walk with partners through abuse disclosure must be willing to revisit poorly-handled conversations, apologize for not being better listeners, and try again.

## Importance of Mutuality

If the spouses of sexually abused persons are not allowed to share their feelings and thoughts or do not feel safe to share what is going on inside them, the relationship will be limited or possibly will cease to exist. Intimate, connected relationships are not one-way streets. The listeners, the non-abused ones, must not be prevented from sharing what they think and feel, if the long-term goal is to bond, connect, and become closer friends. There cannot be mutuality, a give-and-take relationship, when we are not willing to be vulnerable in return. My relationships with my clients are not only limited, but can even be detrimental if I am not allowed to be myself. As I have said in previous chapters, I disclose or share parts of my story in the context of their stories. I have to feel safe with my clients, or my effectiveness as well as my ability to love and be loved will be limited. When I am not allowed to be a fellow struggler, I am pushed into the role of rescuer, and then the client-to-counselor relationship is no longer therapeutic. Once we have heard what our abused partners have to say, and they have validated that we have been good listeners, once they sense we have understood, then it is our turn to speak. Our spouses need to listen and apply all of these principles in return. Reversing roles can be difficult for both parties. The one who has been counselor, caretaker, and unconditionally loving friend must now be a discloser. Allowing ourselves to express our own feelings of victimization—when we have been patient, giving, understanding, empathetic caretakers for months or even years—is a real challenge, for us and the abused partners.

It can feel quite strange to express our perspectives, our feelings of being victimized by our partner's abuse. We don't want to make life more difficult for our spouses or ourselves; we do not want to burden them with our relatively tamer struggles; and to be really honest, we don't want to disrupt the limited equilibrium we have established. Some of us would prefer the role of the strong, silent type, rather than the one open to conflict and/or vulnerability. But somehow we must communicate to our partners that we feel angry, cheated, lonely, rejected, hurt, disappointed, and frustrated beyond belief. As partners, we are tired of doing without and would like to sense we are loved; we are weary of having our motives be suspect and weary of having our intimacy needs go unmet. We need to say that we have found it difficult over the years to refrain and restrain, that we have sacrificed, done without, and have felt disconnected. Lack of relational and sexual fulfillment causes a sense of loneliness that verges on or becomes depression.

Because confronting our abused partners is so difficult, we often shut down and seek other avenues of release and gratification. We feel victimized by our partners' pasts and often feel perpetrated against, not just by our spouses' abusers but also by our partners themselves. It may be that in the past it has done no good to discuss our dissatisfaction with the present arrangement. So some of us bury ourselves in our jobs, others turn to alcohol, food or other forms of self-medication, and still others in our vulnerability are sucked into illicit affairs and/or pornography. After all, we think, the seemingly intolerable situation is not our fault. Our spouses are the ones with distorted sexuality, so why should we have to suffer?

Such reasoning helps neither partner. Relationships become more complicated and adversarial when we sink into this mindset. For honest intimacy, we must be open about how our partners' abuse has affected us, and the abused spouse must come to empathize with our situation, as we have empathized with theirs. We may not be sure about what we should say or how to say it, but whatever comes out of our mouths needs to be lovingly honest. At least we can say, "I have empathized with your heart and mind; now I want you to empathize with mine."

Taking such risk demands support and safety. Both CJ and Martin needed someone to help them sort through their guilt, frustration, anger, and pain, so that they could become better partners to each other. Both of them wanted a change in the status quo, but before their good marriage could become better, they had to create a reasonably safe atmosphere in which to talk about their situation.

### Uncooperative Friends and Partners

Partners of those who have been sexually abused can choose not to face reality. They may deny or ignore the disclosures or even accuse their partners of "making things up." If a spouse is unwilling to be involved in the healing process, the abuse survivor will once again feel rejected, abandoned or even re-abused. Although it is normal to feel hurt, frustrated and angry, those who disclose abuse also need to give their spouses time to let their painful history sink in.

Avoidance is a natural reaction for both partners. Who would want to talk about and deal with all this painful information? The partner with DID may well have discovered the sexual abuse only recently and has reason to back away. For over seven years CJ herself kept questioning herself, wondering whether the abuse had really happened or whether she was merely making things up. However, she had many incentives to persevere, including numerous reality checks from counseling, group members and friends.

Her husband Martin had none of these resources. For a long time, he was unable to accept, let alone deal with, what had happened to his wife. Of course he had his own problems being a pastor, a father, a confidant, and a counselor with many responsibilities on his plate. He wasn't feeling very successful, his career seemed to be at a standstill, and dealing with the transition of midlife further complicated his situation. Avoidance of his wife's disclosures would make sense in many ways.

CJ attempted to be empathetic with his position and was lovingly persistent in asking for his help. She would suggest strategies for working toward unity in their relationship, and to Martin's credit, he became more understanding and accepting as the months and years went by. This is not to say that either of them was innocent of wrong-doing. At times both of them could be defensive, argumentative, and even spiteful. Those of us who are married know that living together can be very trying, especially when both partners are hurting.

CJ took initiative to move forward, over and over, and encouraged Martin to move too. Here is a letter she wrote to Martin; she asked me to give it to him if she should die:

> *Martin, I want you to know that you and subsequently [our daughter]are the best things that have come into my life. You are my life and my joy. You are what has made life worth living, when there was nothing else that seemed important. You have given my life excitement and laughter. You have so much to give others—your love and devotion to God and people are two of your greatest attributes. Know that I love you dearly. I love you much more than the day we got married. I respect and admire you so much. I love you, CJ*

I saw and read many notes that CJ wrote, to me, Martin, her daughter and friends. I was struck by how she affirmed others in the middle of her own struggle. And I heard her verbalize her love for Martin, even when conflicts could overshadow the affirmations.

In her integration process, CJ had to listen to, empathize with, and accept all her different alters; in her life as a whole, she was challenged to do the same work with Martin and her daughter, even when they couldn't reciprocate. CJ did not push them, but patiently attempted to understand their positions and to accept their limitations. Eventually, like the alters, Martin and her daughter became more involved in the process of healing. Not one of us—CJ, Martin, her daughter, friends, nor I—did everything right or in the most loving manner. However, there was and is steady improvement, which is always the goal. Perfection is impossible, but improvement laced with love is our opportunity and responsibility.

Although most of us do not face such extreme challenges in our sexual relationships, too often we settle into a staid, dissatisfying system. We can be like CJ's family: we don't talk, don't trust and don't feel in this area of sex and sexuality. I see many partners come to the place of believing that the system isn't going to change, that there is no possibility of having an intimate, satisfying sexual life. They give up.

## Intimacy and Sexualty

It may disappoint my readers, but I have to say that, in many cases of successful therapy, the sexual dimension does not improve dramatically. It will fall short of popular expectations more often than not. However, more importantly, people can have warm, intimate, loving relationships without frequent sexual intercourse. True intimacy comes about when persons who have been victimized by sexual abuse are willing to open up, be transparent, and share with their partners—and their spouses are willing to do the same. When we share from the bottom of our hearts, when we trust our partners with our perceptions and emotions, we are taking a calculated risk, but when both partners listen and mutually disclose, we are moving toward deeper, more fulfilling encounters.

Even more than sexual encounters, we long for closeness, connectedness, understanding, and acceptance. King David in II Sam. 1:26 (***NIV***) said: *"I grieve for you, Jonathan my brother; you were very dear to me. Your love for me was wonderful, more wonderful than that of women."* This closeness would not have been homosexual in ancient Israel. In my own deep, intimate relationships with male friends, sexual thoughts don't enter my mind. When good friends put an arm around my shoulder or give me a warm hug, the sense of being loved takes away all feelings of alienation and loneliness.

When my wife Allegra looks at me affectionately, tells me she's "so very proud of me" and "loves me beyond words," our closeness and intimacy is not due to sex. It is not sex which validates who we are. I believe that the majority of marriage partners are missing the point. Our real need is to believe that our partners and friends know, understand and accept us, no matter what hang-ups we have. Each partner and friend has the same need. I've known husbands and wives who have wild, passionate sex but admit they feel no connection and are terribly lonely

As I said earlier in this chapter, we have all been poorly and erroneously educated about sex, we have all had bad experiences in our sexual encounters, and we all enter marriage with unrealistic expectations. Therefore, it is unlikely that we will find sex entirely fulfilling. Putting pressure on ourselves and our partners to be sexually intimate or to perform better can cause even greater problems in our marriages. My goal is not that clients have more, or more exciting sexual encounters, but that they grow in interpersonal relationships. Both partners need to be committed to the process of knowing, understanding, and accepting each other and themselves. The method is to talk about our perceptions and feelings, to take personal responsibility by using "I messages" when we share, and to avoid the words "you" and "why," listening with a heart of mercy and grace. I reiterate, the vast majority of us fear confrontation. We fear hurting one another, being misunderstood, making matters worse, misusing the correct terminology…and ultimately we fear rejection. To escape fear, we can take the path of aggression, expressing ourselves forcefully, argumentatively, arrogantly. Acting as if we are sure we are right and others are wrong, we can intimidate, overwhelm and dominate the listener. But safety and intimacy require that we speak, and hear, with mercy and grace. The only way to grow in our closeness to one another is by being vulnerable, and we do that only by disclosing our innermost insecurities and secrets. Each partner must hear those secrets without taking them personally, and receive them with a heart filled with grace, mercy and love.

Often the beginning stages of such transparency are awkward, even counter-productive. Many times, my wife or I will blurt out a frustration using "you" messages, asking rhetorical, interrogating "why" questions, or just plain lose our tempers. If we have been unable to express what is going on inside (and oftentimes I don't even know what I'm feeling), and if we have hidden our feelings of anger, hurt and frustration over time, we can eventually explode. The "last straw" moment erupts when we can't bear one more "injustice."

These verbally volatile altercations are bound to erupt if we haven't discussed the accumulated irritations. I used to think conflict, disagreement, and anger were bad, and when I'm in the midst of these types of situations, even to this day, I feel terribly uncomfortable. I am very invested in what my wife thinks and feels, especially about and toward me. If I assume she is critical, dissatisfied, or disappointed in me, I become very fearful, hurt and defensive. In fact, she may simply be expressing what she is upset about, but because I'm wrapped up in my own emotions, I can't hear her. Communication and connection are arrested and we find ourselves in a heated conflict.

However, when we are talking and being honest, feelings are being expressed, and even though on the surface we may be irritated or impatient, we share a deeper unconscious realization that trust is there. We used to fight a couple of times a month (or more), then further into our marriage every six months or so, and now after over 50 years of marriage, we have a serious disagreement maybe every year or two.

I should add that partners who don't experience conflict are probably not very closely connected, and without connection there is no intimacy. Better to deal with "last-straw" moments than never to have them. Clearing the air and working through disagreements lets us reconnect and be intimate in our conversations and our behavior once again. There is much to be said for kissing and making up!

## Summary

This chapter opened with an overview of the current sexual dysfunction in our society, with its negative effects on individuals and relationships. Our culturally distorted sexual relationships become even more complicated when one or both partners have been sexually abused.

When sexual abuse has been discovered or an abused person is ready to talk about it, we need to understand how this will affect us and our relationships. We must do whatever we can to make conversations as safe as possible for the discloser: avoiding the pitfalls of judging, misunderstanding, discounting, fixing, making assumptions, ignoring, or being parental in a critical sense. In responding appropriately to another's sharing, we want to provide a safe place for open, honest communication so that both partners can experience relational intimacy.

Counseling creates a safe atmosphere where clients can experience the freedom which comes from being transparent. Therapist and client hope that the transparency then will be experienced outside the office with one's spouse and close friends. Once the abuse has been disclosed, we who are spouses follow the path of healing hearing: we listen, reflect back what we have heard, maintain an empathetic stance, assure the one who is sharing that we will keep in confidence what we have heard, and dispense grace, mercy and love. Ideally, the abused partners will come to listen to their partners' thoughts and feelings with the same empathy and care. Even if we do not present our points of view perfectly, it is better to express them than to keep them all bottled up inside. Intimacy is only possible through mutual vulnerability that involves the entire gamut of emotions and perceptions. To be vulnerable we must be willing to risk misunderstanding and rejection. The only way we can deepen our love relationships is by knowing, understanding and accepting each other.

Ultimately we both want to become advocates rather than adversaries in our relationship. The goal of healing is not simply more frequent sexual encounters, but rather creation of a safe climate where affection and connectedness can flourish.

---

## For Further Information

Lewis, C.S., ***The Four Loves***, Fontana Books, 1960.

Powell, John, ***The Secret of Staying In Love***, Tabor Publishing, 1990.

Allender, Dan, and Longman, Tremper III, ***Bold Love***, Nav Press, 1992.

Fromm, Eric, ***The Art of Loving***, Bantam Books, 1956.

Courtright, John and Rogers, Sid, ***Your Wife Was Sexually Abused***, Zondervan, 1994.

APPENDIX

# B

# The Mind and Heart of a Perpetrator (JD)

*Those who use and abuse each other, use and abuse sex, use and abuse the earth and everything in it, don't qualify as citizens in God's kingdom.*

–I Corinthians 6:9-10 (***The Message)***

*All sin is the failure to love.*

–Quoted by Ed Richardson

Sickened and grieved as I tried to help CJ face the truth about her family, I asked myself, "What possesses people to be so cruel, uncaring, and abusive? How can a child's parents and/or grandparents participate in injuring that child, emotionally and physically? We've already alluded briefly to some general reasons why people become habitual perpetrators; however, this chapter looks at specific causes. I hope to help readers understand the mind and heart of abusers.

## Understanding Patterns in Abusers

Although I intend to write specifically about CJ's abusers, I believe that my observations hold true for many perpetrators in a generalized sense. I have never met any of these people, but both CJ and I needed to grasp the underlying causes of their behavior—to free her from guilt and shame, and to help me remain helpfully detached rather than overwhelmed by my rage. My role, as I have said before, is to work as a facilitator, mediator and educator. If emotionally I side entirely with the victim, I become enmeshed—I indict the perpetrator, and I take on the role of a rescuer. I can, however, be supportive and nurturing to my client without agreeing or disagreeing. Giving my clients a reality check is much more helpful than treating them as hopeless victims.

All of us must admit having been abusive at times through our words and treatment of others. Occasional or habitual, abuse is engendered by the same attitudes—selfishness, insensitivity, manipulation, non-caring, vindictiveness and non-loving. When most of us recognize our attitudes and evaluate our behavior, we feel a sense of shame and guilt. Then (ideally) we take responsibility and try to make things right.

A more serious progression takes place within people who become habitually verbally, emotionally, physically and sexually abusive. CJ's abusers were pathological abusers who had no sense of external reality. They were deceitful, in denial, detached, dissociated and even demonic. How do these qualities lead to abuse?

## Deceitful

Image is everything, or so our culture implies. We want to drive the right cars, wear the right clothes, use the right words and hang out with the right people. We work to make good impressions, so we can get the right partner, land the best job, gain a good reputation, and establish credence within our circle. We act and speak to make ourselves lovable. When we spend inordinate time and energy trying to make others accept and love us, we can begin to tell half-truths, to leave out any negative information, and eventually to deceive people about who we are. We are building an image on lies.

Deceit is insidious. We may begin innocently, hoping to come across well, putting our best foot forward, trying to avoid upsetting others. In our culture, it is common courtesy to squelch a belch after a good meal, to dress appropriately for a special occasion, or to express appreciation even when the sentiment is not totally heartfelt. However, deceit goes beyond these conventional behaviors. When we claim to be someone we are not, or fail to disclose who we really are, or out-and-out lie about our behavior, we deceive. As honesty dissipates, deceit will quickly take its place.

Once we believe we've convinced others that we "have it all together," when we don't, we begin to believe our own press and are well into the process of deceiving ourselves. Even at times when we think we are being honest, we fail to check out our "reality" with others. Our hearts have deceived us into believing we can do no wrong—or if we do wrong, someone else must be at fault. Perpetrators blame their victims for "causing them to hit," for "enticing them" to be sexually out of control. They refuse to take responsibility for how they are feeling, for what they are thinking, or for how they are behaving.

Keeping truth hidden prevents connection, limits our relationships, and breaks down our integrity. When we lose our integrity, we lose ourselves. What is left is just an image we are projecting. Pretending, playing roles, and lying to cover up prevents others from knowing who we really are. Every one of us has some self-destructive behavior we do not want known, whether the obvious—alcohol or drug abuse, greed, gluttony—or the not-so-obvious—jealousy, resentment, use of pornography, gossip, or "workaholism."

When we become secretive and hide our behaviors, thoughts and feelings because we are afraid of being found out, we alienate ourselves from others and eventually from ourselves. Alienation leads us to guilt, shame, depression, loneliness and a host of other debilitating emotions. To avoid feeling these emotions, we will go even further underground and self-medicate our distress, causing us to become more addicted to our besetting sins.

By besetting sin I mean obsession with whatever will relieve the pain. Food, prescription drugs, sex, work, and many other distractions offer the temporary comfort that leads to addiction. Harassed by our troubling thoughts, we turn again and again to the behavior that promises (and fails) to relieve them. Consequently we feel dominated and controlled by our besetting sin. If we don't automatically give in, but continue to battle our weaknesses, we will grow very weary. Most of us keep working on ourselves out of fear that we could become indifferent and completely dominated by our addiction. The struggle seems to persist throughout our lives At best we feel like "recovering alcoholics"—we experience a degree of sobriety, but our destructive, sinful, security blankets are always within reach.

CJ's perpetrators had long ago given up any attempt to manage their besetting sin. Instead they were entirely controlled by their sexual addiction. Alienated from others and themselves, they saw themselves as victims, helpless to modify their behavior. Refusing to take responsibility for the persons they were, experiencing constant failure, seeing no progress, assuming that they had no control over their impulses—they gave in to their addiction. Their self-destructive behavior had become habitual and seemingly "couldn't" be broken.

Perpetual perpetrators are essentially irrational and emotionally out of control. They have little or no ability to empathize with another's feelings or thoughts. They may "apologize," but it's only out of their fear of being abandoned. If "apologizing" doesn't work, they will threaten the victim if she refuses to perform as expected.

The prophet Jeremiah said, *"The heart is hopelessly dark and deceitful, a puzzle that no one can figure out"* (Jer. 17:9, ***The Message***). If we deceive others and ourselves over a period of years, and we ignore what our hearts are telling us, callousness and indifference become our "modus operandi." This appears to be the progression for CJ's family. They refused to be responsible, their hearts became hardened, they allowed no reality checks, and ultimately they lost touch with who they were.

As a child and even on into adulthood, CJ was convinced by her family that she, not they, was to blame for the abuse. They claimed that if she had done what they expected, they wouldn't have hurt her. For years, she attempted to "do everything right," but still she was punished, emotionally and physically. Most of the alters within CJ believed that she was the cause of all their pain and that she could have taken action to save them. CJ's family members had done a masterful job of convincing her that SHE was the problem.

In therapy, CJ constantly accused herself of "making things up." Because she had no reality check, and because the memories were so painfully bizarre, she kept believing she was deceiving herself. Even when she began to listen to the inner voices, she thought that *they* were deceiving her. She did not know whom to trust, so she trusted nobody, not even herself.

CJ was so conflicted that various personalities took over specific responsibilities of hers. Some alters believed that they were helpless victims, others became angry and defiant, still others were reassuring and sounded rational, and others became protective of CJ and the system. Even as her bewilderment increased, however, CJ refused to be a victim and maintained her integrity. She revealed the secrets as they were discovered—to me, to support group members, to close friends, and to her husband. She made adult choices, dealing directly with her guilt and shame. She was (and still is) committed to telling the truth, refraining from deceit. Therefore, she did not continue her family pattern; she herself did not become a perpetual perpetrator.

## Denying

As a rule we don't handle confrontation and correction very well. Our typical response is to defend ourselves. We make excuses, blame others or deny the "accusation." Once we cool down, though, and re-evaluate what has been said or implied, we often become more open and willing to make some changes. As we listen to others' views, we can make necessary adjustments to improve our connection. We have the option to become more interpersonally and intra-personally mature. We might even thank the critic for making us more aware!

However, if we refuse to accept personal responsibility, and continue to deceive ourselves, we come to denial of wrongdoing. We dismiss what the critic says, telling ourselves "What do they know?" and move on without considering what we might learn. The more immature we are, the less likely that we will learn from the experience. When we regularly deceive and deny, we become unable to know ourselves. Maintaining an idealized view of ourselves will arrest our personal growth; people in denial cannot become self-actualizers.

When we project only our positive traits, our ideal selves quickly dominate our thinking and feelings. Our actual selves aren't all that glamorous! In reality, we make mistakes, hurt people, sin regularly, and fail to love. Denying the truth about ourselves allows subjectivity to cloud our objectivity. When an ugly part of our actual self shows its face and we instantly deny that part—"That's not true—that's not really ME"—we are focusing only on our finer qualities. Our internal perception rules out the external observations of others; pride takes over, and we prevent learning about our real selves to take place.

People with a solid sense of self-worth, a healthy self-esteem, can receive correction and even criticism. They welcome the discovery which defense and denial refuse. Knowing our actual selves, understanding who we are and why, and accepting our strengths and limitations, will free us. We gain deeper insights about who we are and more enjoyable and meaningful relationships. Because CJ's family had no sense of identity or worth, they were unable to hear others and denied any need for correction and improvement.

To deny means to declare untrue. If truth is presented to us but we negate or dismiss it, we demonstrate our rejection of the very concept of truth. When we refuse to deal with the truth, we are left to live in our own little fantasy world; we have no contact with reality, and we constantly discount the perceptions and feelings of other people (as well as our own).

When we refuse to allow God's light—the truth—to reveal in us what needs to be confessed and changed, our fear, shame and guilt will keep us in the dark. We hide, keeping our sin-secrets to ourselves, and we lose the opportunity to be in the light, to correct our steps, and to freely walk as we were meant to walk, where truth resides. Jesus taught extensively about the human need for exposure to truth. Jesus said, *"Everyone who makes a practice of doing evil, addicted to denial and illusion, hates God's light and won't come near it, fearing a painful exposure. But anyone working and living in the truth and reality welcomes God-light so the work can be seen for the God-work it is"* (John 3:20, 21, ***The Message***). Furthermore, Jesus equated himself with the truth (John 14:6) and said, *"You will experience for yourselves the truth and the truth will free you"* (John 8:31, ***The Message***). CJ's parents and grandparents were enslaved to deceit, lying, and denial of the truth. Now CJ was discovering the truth, refusing to live in darkness. She began to experience a freedom her family had never known.

Repeated denial of the truth slowly but constantly sears the conscience.

Since CJ was abused by her father and his parents, it is highly probable that her father was also sexually abused. He may well have been forced into the occult behaviors. Like CJ, he may have been trained to appease Satan, meet his parent's perverted needs, and live a double life. He cooperated with Satan followers and denied the dark, perverted life he was living. It is possible that he never even developed a conscience. Cognitively he may never have developed beyond the age of a typical nine-year-old. Empathy, the gift of feeling guilt and shame, and the ability to love—these qualities were absent. Maybe he had no ability to comprehend the actual self, living unaware and possibly sociopathically.

Many in CJ's family seem to have been sociopaths. Such people are amoral and asocial, living only to fulfill their own needs, totally disregarding the desires of others. They deny themselves nothing, especially when they experience no external limits to their antisocial behavior. Because they have no internalized value system, they don't feel true guilt, only the guilty fear of being caught. Sociopaths are pathological liars and deniers, refusing responsibility, assuming that the world ultimately revolves around them. Truth does not concern them.

It is remarkable that CJ did not divorce herself from the truth, despite her family heritage and example. In fact, she had an alter named Truth, who developed very early in CJ's life. Truth internally prevented her from going down the same path as her perpetrators. Unlike her father, CJ empathized with the animals being sacrificed and the other children being abused. Although her father kept up the pretense that he was okay and not responsible for the abuse, CJ ingeniously maintained her sanity by splitting into many parts. Her underlying integrity prevailed, even in the form of some of her alters who took responsibility when other alters failed.

## Detached

> *They can't think straight anymore. Feeling no pain, they let themselves go in sexual obsession, addicted to every sort of perversion.* –Ephesians 4:18-19 (***The Message***)

When we live deceitful, secretive lives and deny our actual selves, over time we become disconnected from others and detached from reality. To know and to be known were totally foreign experiences to CJ's family. They were detached from their own feelings and thoughts, as well as from the emotions and perceptions of others.

CJ's family members kept virtually all their actions hidden from others. Only in secrecy could their occult practices exist. Most of their activity was clandestine; their evil, illicit behaviors would have personal and legal repercussions if discovered. Because the family members were secretive both within and outside the occult community, they became extremely detached. Secrecy prevented any real interpersonal connection.

Being deceitful, keeping secrets, and hiding our thoughts and feelings from others makes us slaves. We are tied to and limited by our lies. Enslaved people live in constant fear of their masters, so rather than using wisdom, logic, and love in making decisions, they will tend to make choices out of their fear. CJ's abusers lived in fear—of discovery by outsiders and of disapproval by the occult community. To be found out would have brought shame, guilt, and punishment for their horrendous behavior. To admit their secretive, occult behavior to outsiders would have stirred up their fellow Satan-worshippers, not only to reject them, but probably to physically harm them.

CJ's family had been deceitful for so long that they had begun to believe their own lies. None of them could admit they were doing wrong to the abused, because that would confirm to themselves how inhumane they had become. To admit their secrets to the ones they were abusing, would be to confess how terrible they had become. All secretive, deceiving people are detached from others, unable to relate, and have no reality checks. Thus they remain alone, without support, encouragement, or love. They are alienated within and without.

It is important to interject here the difference between the terms "secret" and "private." Being private is maintaining our boundaries. It is like a gate in a fence, which allows those whom we trust to enter. We choose whom to admit, those whom we are reasonably sure will keep confidences without judging or condemning us.

We are secretive when we hide, are not honest, refuse to disclose our struggles, and fear what will happen if we are real. Secrecy builds protective walls to keep others out. Over months and years, the barrier becomes insurmountable, and we are increasingly isolated from others. We no longer even think about venturing outside the wall, assuming that nobody can be trusted. Remaining behind our fortress walls seems to be our only option.

CJ was and is a very private person. Integrity shows in her commitment to be real and transparent. She now has healthy boundaries built into her life. No longer keeping everything inside, she openly shares her story with those who will benefit. Her purpose in writing about her life is to give others hope and to rid herself of destructive secrecy. The walls are gone, the fences are in place, and she does not need to hide.

CJ has so far found writing to be therapeutic (though difficult). She hopes to help others who read her story; however, she does not offer herself to those who do not have her best interests at heart. Writing under a pseudonym protects her privacy and prevents unnecessary hurt for those she loves. This is not deceitful secrecy. A person who confides in us should expect us to protect that confidence. When people drop their guard and entrust us with privileged information, they are also testing us, to see whether we can be trusted. If we share another's secret without permission, we prove that we are not trustworthy.

Personally and professionally, I am always honored when someone confides in me. In our counseling process, CJ shared secrets that she had never spoken, and I acted as a reality check for her. Furthermore, as she learned to trust me, she began to advance that trust to others. She discovered that an open, transparent relationship with one person led toward new relationships with others. Now she has expanded that faith to her husband, close friends, support groups, and eventually, with her boundaries in place, to the general public. CJ is no longer detached, but appropriately attached.

CJ now experiences acceptance on almost all fronts, the kind of love and support she rarely received as a child. The more transparent we become, the freer we are and the less we need to deceive. We need to be reminded of this dynamic. Deep within us lives a profound need to know and to be known. Yet too often we hesitate to share who we are, for fear of rejection and even abandonment. Instead we pretend, hide our true selves, and even deceive others. Such inauthentic living makes knowing and being known impossible. Honesty is the best—in fact, the only policy for relational authenticity.

Though honesty is essential, we must exercise discretion. It is counterproductive to share our innermost thoughts and emotions when the level of sharing is not mutual. If our family members and friends are not willing to be open about their secrets as well, the relationship will be limited. I myself have met with such disappointing responses to openness. At times when I have disclosed something painful, I have had friends make harsh judgments, lecture me, try to fix my problem, boast that they no longer struggle with that particular issue, or by their demeanor communicate that my disclosure is appalling. In those situations I find myself backtracking, feeling embarrassed, wishing I had not disclosed at all.

With some people, going deeper only gives them ammunition and a sense that they are better than I am. Perhaps they are unsure of themselves, unwilling to risk, or perhaps they have been burned in the past. Sometimes my transparency is seen as threatening or too close to another's situation, but sharing on a deeper level always presents the possibility of establishing a give-and-take relationship. Although not every disclosure may turn out well, we will miss the opportunity to build intimacy if we don't risk. Most of the time, I find the risk is worthwhile.

Detachment is not only a result of self-chosen secrecy; it can develop very early in life. Most people attach or bond as infants, with their mothers. A natural bond forms with one who feeds us, changes our diapers, and meets other basic physical needs. True bonding means that a parent loves us unconditionally, holds and caresses us, and meets our emotional needs. When these needs are not met, the child cannot form a bond and must detach in order to survive. Looking at their family pattern, I surmised that CJ's father had never received much affection or love. He seemed to be important to his mother, but I questioned whether the connection had much depth. It seemed that, to his mother, he existed only to fulfill her needs. Eventually CJ served the same purpose.

(After reading the above paragraph, CJ confirmed that her father had never felt his parents loved him. In fact he once told her that he couldn't remember his father ever saying that he loved him. CJ added that her grandfather lived to be 95 years old.)

These family members evidently had a symbiotic relationship—that is, they existed to meet each other's selfish expectations, more an arrangement than a relationship. It looked to me as if they were overly dependent on each other without a true sense of connection. CJ's father probably never individuated, never became his own person. The interaction between this child and his parents was not constructive, not conducive to building a future adult relationship. CJ commented at one point, "My father always yearned for approval from his parents and never got it."

When a very young child detaches, especially over a long period of time, any later re-attachment or bonding is problematic. When such a child is adopted at a later age, both parents and child find if difficult, if not impossible, to bond with each other. No matter how willing the parents are, the child remains untrusting and unable to form a true relationship, because of the early lack of bonding. For a person detached in this extreme sense, learning how to connect with another person requires tremendous work and willingness to risk. It is doubtful that CJ's father was ever able to bond with his wife, his two daughters, or anyone else. His years of deceiving and denying made re-attachment even more unlikely. He never admitted he had a problem or sought help.

Remarkably, CJ was able to attach to her husband and daughter. It was her longing to develop an even closer bond that first brought her to counseling. As we both learned, this was a demanding task. In a sense, she had to bond with each of her inner parts first. She needed to identify all the alters, understand how and why they functioned as they did, and build the kind of loving trust she so longed for. Bonding does not take place until we trust.

Deceit, denial and detachment may overlap, but they are also progressive; one builds upon the other. Eventually the three D's define who we are and who we are not. When we have no foundation, we cannot build a good character. This might be a partial explanation of why CJ's perpetrators continued their abuse, without being overwhelmed by shame and guilt. And no one could reach them. It is not possible to bond with one who lives in perpetual deceit, denial and detachment.

## Dissociated

> *[They are]...separated from the life of God because of ignorance that is in them due to the hardening of their hearts. Having lost all sensitivity, they have given themselves over to sensuality so as to indulge in every kind of impurity, with a continued lust for more.* –Ephesians 4:18-19 (***NIV***)

Dissociation may seem very similar to detachment. However, I'm now using the term to refer to a more extreme form of detachment. This is what we were contending with in therapy. CJ was diagnosed with Dissociative Identity Disorder (DID), formerly known as Multiple Personality Disorder (MPD). The DSM-IV defines DID as:

- The presence of two or more distinct identities or personality states (each with its own relatively enduring pattern of perceiving, relating to, and thinking about the environment and self)
- At least two of these identities or personality states recurrently take control of the person's behavior

- Inability to recall important personal information—personal information that is too extensive to be explained by ordinary forgetfulness
- The disturbance is not due to the direct physiological effects of a substance (e.g. blackouts, chaotic behavior during alcohol intoxication) or general medical condition (e.g. complex partial seizures). Note: In children, the symptoms are not attributable to imaginary playmates or other fantasy play.

It is possible that some of CJ's abusers were DID themselves and would act out abuse only when a particular personality took over. As was true for CJ for many years, her family members may have had no memory of the abuse they were inflicting on others. They had spent a lifetime deceiving, denying, and detaching, thus keeping the facts hidden from others and themselves. They were not sensitive and aware of their inadequacies as parents and grandparents. Very likely they remained DID permanently. The disorder is a highly refined defense mechanism that keeps people stuck, divided, split, and detached from the past. Remaining ignorant of their created abusive personalities would have kept them from being whole and responsible.

We can be dissociative without being diagnosed with DID. For example, when I am under a great deal of stress (i.e. listening to painful stories shared by my clients, or watching a very intense movie scene), I may have to stifle a yawn. My mind may flit to more pleasant thoughts or analyze what is being said. I may even doze off. Fortunately I don't fall asleep with clients, although one client asked me right in the middle of a "controlled" yawn, "Am I boring you?" The answer was exactly the opposite. I was overwhelmed by the intensity of what she was saying.

We can all dissociate to one degree or another. However, we are in danger when dissociating becomes a mode of operation to avoid dealing with our feelings and perceptions. When we move from deceit, denial, and detachment to habitual dissociating, DID can be established as a way of escaping from what is going on in our lives. Regular dissociative behavior is a serious avoidance mechanism that keeps us from dealing with reality. When dissociative we are numbing our feelings, averting our thinking, not listening to what is being said within or being aware of what is going on around us. We are spacing out our friends, family, fellow workers and anyone who makes us uncomfortable. By avoiding even the surface feelings, we shut down the deep internal emotions, which are often traumatic. We go somewhere else in our minds.

CJ's abusers were not just detached from their emotions and thoughts, Their depraved rituals were performed in an almost robotic or trance-like state. These events could happen without awareness on the part of the abusers; they were not "present;" they were inducing a numb, drug-like state so they would not feel shame, guilt or other painful feelings. Their diagnosis might well have been "dissociative fugue." A fugue in music is a kind of "interweaving of the voice parts," and in a psychological sense it is "a disturbed state of consciousness in which the one affected seems to perform acts in full awareness but upon recovery cannot recollect the deeds." CJ's abusers had no recollections of their actions, or if they did, would immediately deny that those actions had ever happened. They totally dissociated.

This kind of detachment is so extreme that the abusers would have felt like outside observers—literally having an out-of-body experience. In a dream state, you or I often vacillate between being observers one minute, feeling our emotions the next, and returning to being observers the next. In my work with Vietnam vets, many eventually told me what it was like to kill an enemy—or even their own soldiers, by "friendly fire." At the time of the shooting, they felt as though they were not present themselves but were observing themselves doing the killing. However, in the present moment in my office, all of the horrific emotions come flooding in, often for the first time. Fear and panic are written all over their faces. They look like they want to jump up and run, but their bodies are frozen in place. In extreme pain, they are unable to speak other than with moans, groans and/or uncontrollable sobs. Their postponed suffering has now educated most Americans about PTSD.

CJ herself could not remember her traumatic past until she was almost forty years old. Her father may never have recalled what he had done, right up to the day he died. In that past, CJ had dealt with her awful experiences by creating a number of personalities or alters, who "took her place" during the abuse. Perhaps some of her family members had done the same thing, but they were never willing to integrate those parts of themselves. Consequently they did not recall nor take responsibility for resolving the past. Dissociation became a way of life. Throughout the remainder of their lives, they were distant, talked only about the mundane, and never recalled emotionally charged times. They were unable to experience joyful highs or disturbing lows. Life became routine and flat and uneventful.

## Demonic

CJ's family members were Satan worshipers, and I believe that they became demonic. Their cultic religion mixed Jesus and Satan worship; CJ was told that Satan was Jesus' brother. They practiced blood sacrifices of both animals and "babies." I use quotation marks for "babies" because CJ was drugged every time she was involved in the cutting and sacrifice of fetuses and newborns. Whether or not children were actually sacrificed, she had the perception that they were. The occult group went to great lengths to deceive CJ and other innocent parties, regardless of what can now be verified. Perhaps they believed that Satan was present and deluded themselves with the idea that he would fulfill their desires if they did as he wanted.

The sexually abusive leaders impersonated Satan as part of the cult practice. They claimed visions of demons who did evil things. Therefore, I would say they were acting in a demonic way. Is the demonic to be equated with evil? Were CJ's perpetrators evil in themselves? Her family members were involved in evil activity, but were her abusers purposefully evil? Were their intentions to BE evil? Because I can't know what their intentions were, and because I'm not always sure of my own motives, I hesitate to call them, or anyone else, evil. However, I am certain that all of us are capable of thinking about and performing evil acts.

I am not a philosopher, and the problem of humans and evil is beyond me. However, I can make some personal observations. First, CJ's family and fellow occult participants seem to have been arrested at a rather primitive cognitive level. They were not that capable of understanding and empathizing with others—so not that culpable. They also seemed to be led by a form of magical thinking. Their mode of operation was superstitious, attempting to manipulate "the gods" in hopes of their good favor. To their simplistic thinking, appeasing Satan and the "powers that be" would influence them to fulfill their desires.

Certainly I believe that they were enslaved to evil deeds. What they did to CJ and others was morally evil. When we think of good and bad from society's perspective, violation of the law brings repercussions; when evil is done, there must be consequences; there must be justice, which in our society is determined by judge and jury, and in God's economy, ultimate judgment by God himself.

However, we fallible human beings should not become both judge and jury in dealing with evil. It is always possible that we could be judging and convicting unfairly. A story from the Gospels reminds us of our limitations.

When the woman caught in adultery was brought before a judgmental crowd to be stoned, Jesus said, *"The sinless one among you, go first: throw the stone"* (John 8:7, ***The Message***). In essence, Jesus teaches that only if we have never done any evil deed, can we condemn others and start throwing stones. The people who heard his words "walked away, one after another, beginning with the oldest" (John 8:9, ***The Message***). To me, the story recognizes that when we are young, we tend to make judgments quickly. With age and wisdom, as we know our own hearts, we are more apt to dispense grace and mercy. I also take to heart Jesus' warning, *"Do not judge, or you too will be judged"* (Mt. 7:1 ***NIV***). If I sit in judgment of CJ's perpetrators and refuse to be merciful and gracious, I take the same demonic attitude that CJ's family had.

It is true that making judgments is necessary. Without discernment we can't make reasonable decisions. Being judgmental, on the other hand, implies judging harshly, with little or no grace. Judgmental people are seen as opinionated and resentful of those who disagree. Resentment following from judgmentalism sets up another demonic progression. Resentment can be defined as "a feeling of indignant displeasure or persistent ill will at something regarded as a wrong, insult, or injury" (***Merriam-Webster Collegiate Dictionary***). The resent-er places all blame on the resent-ed. AA literature has pointed out that resenting someone is allowing that person to live rent free in our heads. I have also heard that resentment is like taking poison hoping the other person will die.

Resentment often leads to vindictiveness, a desire to even the score. Vindictive people want to avenge a wrong they perceive was done to them. They seek retribution by retaliating and punishing the wrongdoer. Resentful, vindictive people live in a constant state of anger and unrest, of wanting to get even, which of course never happens.

Judgment, resentment, and vindictiveness surround us, in newspaper articles, on television, in talk shows, in our homes. Nations resent other countries, tribes resent other people groups, Democrats resent Republicans and vice versa, and brother resents sister. We compare, compete, judge, resent and act vindictively on the job, in our sports, in our churches, with our neighbors and in our families. When life is not fair, when we have been treated unjustly and disrespectfully, we humans will fight to get even by whatever means possible. These efforts to achieve "justice" on our own terms have caused wars and filled our courts with hundreds of thousands of cases, yet very few people experience real fairness and justice.

Our national pastime of name-calling, labeling, and indicting one another does not promote justice either. If two diametrically opposing factions or parties choose to call one another evil, there will never be resolution. They will see the other as the perpetrator and themselves as the victim, and thus there can be no problem-solving dialogue.

So what are we supposed to do about evil people and our enemies? I know that Jesus commands us to *"love our enemies and pray for those who persecute you"* (***RSV***). However, practical application of Jesus' principle eludes me when I think of a father who continually raped his daughter over thirteen plus years. How is it possible to pray for him? If I'd known the members of CJ's family, I would have struggled with this command. Their hearts were deceitful and dark. They failed in their responsibilities as parents and grandparents. They dehumanized CJ, many others and themselves. God would have to give me any feeling of grace or mercy toward them. If I demonize them, however, if I relegate them to the category of evil, then I too am dehumanizing them. As a Christian, I am to love, not curse; I am to be merciful rather than revengeful.

We must grant that CJ's abusers were terribly limited, morally, ethically, cognitively and spiritually. Somehow via the corruption of their will, they were unable to choose the right. By going down the path of least resistance for years, by shirking responsibility for their feelings, perceptions and behavior and by living a life of lies and hypocrisy, they gave themselves over to evil. They "erased the past" by going the route of deceit, denial, detachment and dissociation. They blamed, found fault and indulged themselves through self-pity, rage and a sense of entitlement. They were so wrapped up in self-indulgence that they habitually performed evil deeds, they denied their free will and their ability to be responsible. Enslaved to an evil outlook on life, they lost the freedom to choose a different course, much like a drug-addicted mother who becomes willing to sell her child for the next fix. Their hearts were hardened, as the scripture says, and they were given over to a "reprobate mind" (Romans 1:28, KJV).

Are evil people able to show compassion? It takes mental gymnastics to understand how evil behavior can be sprinkled with occasional affectionate acts. According to some of CJ's alters, there were times when her relatives did show affection and compassion, CJ herself has a few pleasant memories. There were alters who loved and felt loved by "the father." They had fond memories of sitting in the father's lap, of family gatherings, and camping trips. However, these good times stopped when the abuse started.

Power and control are addictive. They offer a sense of false security and allow the powerful to do appalling things to anyone who interferes with them. Taking what belongs to God into our own hands makes us monsters; deluded into thinking we are always right, we regard those who disagree as wrong or evil. If we depend on power and control for our security and survival, and act without grace and mercy, we make others suffer, and we will, too. CJ's perpetrators were sad, pitiable people, devoid of real love. Incapable of loving themselves or others, they did not, and will not, get off scot-free. God will ultimately determine their fate.

Recently Christian theologians have spoken and written a great deal about spiritual warfare. Popular books have also attempted to explain how good versus evil is played out. In this view, Satan is the ruler of this earth, and he and his cohorts are battling with the Trinity to gain control of humanity and the universe. Is it possible that CJ's abusers took part in Satan's conspiracy? Had they given themselves over to a spiritually negative power? I cannot answer these questions with certainty; however, it is clear that these abusers had made deceit, denial, detachment, and dissociation their way of life. As Scott Peck points out in his book, ***People of the Lie***, the disappearance of truth makes way for evil. Where grace, mercy and love are absent, darkness reigns. For those who lose the ability to love, or have never learned to love at all, the vacuum is filled by apathy, indifference, anger, and hate. Losing sight of love endangers individuals and undermines the ways we live together.

## Gaining Freedom from Guilt and Fear

CJ chose to love—the antidote to lust and evil. She did the hard work of taking down her dissociative defense, because she wanted to be a better lover of her husband, her daughter, her friends, and even her enemies,. As she became more aware of her past and how it was limiting her personal growth, her desire to love boldly became paramount. She prevented herself from going down the path her abusers had traveled by gaining a deeper understanding of herself, her perpetrators, and those around her. As she began to deal with her actual self, she continued to maintain her honesty and integrity. CJ was not captivated by evil or resentment. Her willingness to forgive prevented the 5 D's from taking hold of her life. Even re-living multiple rapes, CJ did not express hate or resentment toward her parents or grandparents. It's true that some of her alters did, but even after they were integrated, I didn't hear CJ blame her family. She treated her parents respectfully, and maintained a cordial, though distant, relationship with them. CJ never condoned what they had done or who they had become, but she has been able to act with love, grace and mercy, and to leave judgment to God.

I have asked myself many times whether CJ's abusers could change. Could they still choose to become opposites of their past selves? After years of deceit, denial, detachment, dissociating, and living a demonic lifestyle, would they have been able to reverse their course? Perhaps the larger question is whether long-term addicts, who have given in to their sin, can ever become sober and live increasingly fulfilled lives. My personal answer to all these questions is a resounding "Yes!"

My purpose here is not to address recovery from addiction; I do understand that lifetime habits are not reversed overnight. Very few habitual perpetrators seem to benefit from forced treatment. Domestic violence therapists estimate that less than 30 percent benefit from court-ordered programs. However, I am convinced that change is possible. As I have learned through reading, seminars, and personal testimonies, God can expose our helpless dependency on an addiction. We can become dependent on the "God-light" from that point on. A person who chooses commitment to a totally new lifestyle, who wills to live with integrity by dealing with his or her actual self, can turn his life around. But we must be willing to be exposed to the Light in order to deal with our shame and guilt, to make amends, to accept God's grace and forgiveness, and to grow in love.

CJ was in therapy for over ten years, yet even before counseling she had more going for her than her perpetrators had. In fact, she was never without God's light, which prevented her from repeating her family's abusive behaviors. It is not different for any of us. Our only hope for wholeness is exposing ourselves to the revealing Light daily. We endanger ourselves when we avoid God, hide from the truth, deny our sin, and disconnect from others. Unless we determine to love as unconditionally as possible, we will inevitably become more selfish, more prideful and more isolated.

All of us are prone to defending ourselves and to falling into the trap of the 5 D's, though few of us become extreme perpetrators like CJ's family. Thinking about my own defensiveness after a conflict, I notice that within a nanosecond, I can plunge downward through the first 4 D's and act so irresponsibly that the other person may well believe I am demonic. This sets up a downward spiral, because when we are hurt, fearful, or frustrated, we tend to exaggerate our perceived pain. So the person I want to defend myself against is now likely to overreact and even to be vindictive. It makes sense to avoid the trap entirely. I'd rather not get myself to those lower levels in the first place.

*Progressively losing our integrity*

| | | | |
|---|---|---|---|
| Deceitful | ↓ | | Being honest |
| Denying | ↓ | ↑ | Taking responsibility |
| Detached | ↓ | ↑ | Connecting with God and others |
| Dissociated | ↓ | ↑ | Becoming aware |
| Demonic | | ↑ | Living in God's light |

*Reversing the process—progressively gaining back our integrity*

The chart above visualizes the means we can use to change this destructive process. The process works from the bottom of the chart up. We can reverse interpersonal perpetration in these ways: (1) being exposed to God's light, truth, (2) by becoming more aware of the truth, (3) by associating with others who attempt to live the truth (therefore giving us some kind of reality check), (4) by taking personal responsibility to live the truth (being honest people with integrity). Even in the small areas, it is far more selfless and rewarding to be part of the solution, rather than part of the problem. We do not just stop negative behaviors—we actively choose to live responsibly and truthfully. If our hearts were filled with compassion and love, I believe we would taste God's kingdom on this earth. (Did I mention earlier that I am an idealistic realist?)

### For Further Information

Peck, M. Scott, ***People of the Lie***, Touchstone Books, 1985.

Restak, Richard, ***The Self-Seekers***, Doubleday and Co., 1982.

Boyd, Gregory A., ***Satan and the Problem of Evil***, Inter-Varsity Press, 2001.

Shostrom, Everett, ***Man the Manipulator***, A Bantam Book, 1967.

APPENDIX

# C

# Abby's Poems (CJ)

### A Little Girl

by Abby

Laughter and giggles and silly faces,
Wide eyes and smiles and red rosy cheeks,
Pink lace and ribbons, ruffles and frills,
Curls and bows and white patent shoes.
That's what a little girl looks like.

A daddy, a mommy, a brother, a sister,
A grandma, a grandpa, an aunt and an uncle,
A dog, a cat, a doll and a teddy,
A teacher, a classmate, a stranger and God.
That's who a little girl talks to.

Blue skies, green grass, bright yellow flowers,
Cold rain, warm sunshine, big fluffy clouds,
Warm chewy cookies, cold creamy ice cream,
Long walks, bike rides, a roll down the hill,
That's what a little girl smiles at.

A soft spoken word, a deep-belly chuckle,
A head on a shoulder, a tender embrace,
A secret to share, a quick little wink,
A long loving glance, a kiss on the face,
That's what a little girl longs for.

## Escape

by Abby

Heightened emotions, quick darting glances,
Frantic gestures, wide wild eyes…
All expressing the need to flee.

Hot burning tears with deep racking sobs,
Grotesque pictures of memories long past…
All encouraging the need to run.

Rough pulls on the arm, a slap in the face,
A scream of terror, a muffled hurt cry…
All encouraging the need to escape.

A gentle warm smile, an arm 'cross the shoulder,
An outstretched hand, a welcoming look…
All encouraging the desire to pause.

A friend close beside, a light in the dark,
A happier day dawns close up in front…
All encouraging the resolve to endure.

A breakthrough to feelings, a peace deep inside,
A completeness, a wholeness, tenacity to continue…
All affirming the decision to remain.

## Food

by Abby

Food is tempting.
Food is soothing.
Hot and cold,
Sweet and sour.

Food is friendly.
Food is kind.
Crisply frozen or
Buttery warm.

Food is wonderful,
Food is peaceful.
Spicy and mild,
Crunchy and smooth.

Food is healthy,
Food is wise
As long as it isn't
Your constant companion.

### Just a Passing Storm

By Abby

Clouds hang darkly overhead,
Overtaking the wandering soul.
Driving rain from heavy skies,
Drench the already weary spirit.

Thunder rolls, lightning strikes,
Wind gusts against weak defenses.
The heart is seared, the mind collapses.
Humid air smothers a flicker of faith.

Where is hope? the haven of rest?
Where is safety? the promised peace?

At the rear of the storm,
High above clouds,
Before thunder exists,
Behind flashing lightening,
Preceding raindrops
Is a glimmer of light.

When the storm seems the worst,
And your strength is all gone,
Remember to look
Past the wind and the rain,
Behind thunder and lightning
To the bright brilliance of hope,
And the warm sunshine of peace.

## Playing Dolls

By Abby

The little girl happily plays with her dolls,
experiencing the innocence of childhood.
She bathes them, dresses them, holds and rocks them
all with tender, loving care.
She places them in their blanketed cribs
and sings them a soft lullaby.
And goes on to perform all the other things
that mothers everywhere do.

This perfect scene of mimed motherhood is interrupted
with a knock at the door,
By a man, who in one moment, discards a treasure
which can never be recovered.
He overlooks this precious picture of innocence
because of his own selfish need.
He sees only a gift for his body,
to be used for his own gratification.
In one moment he gives up his rights as her father
and steals her rights as a child.
Choosing instead to awaken her innocence
and replace it with fear and pain.

The little girl, engrossed in her play,
ignores the bothersome interruption.
The frustrated father, selfish and feeling rejected,
seeks only to bring her to him.
Her innocent action fuels anger long harbored
and he reaches for the belt at his waist.
Without any thought he attempts to quell
what he perceives as rebellious independence.
With each lash of the strap,
her astonished and terrified screams fill the room.
The father seeks to rid himself of his own insecurity and fear
with the strap welts left on the small, chubby legs
followed by his violation of her innocence.

The father is pacified, his desires satisfied,
    and he quickly resumes his day,
Never allowing his mind to contemplate the destruction
    which has just occurred.
With dried tears on her face, the child again rocks her doll
    as before, yet somehow different,
Her small heart is shattered, her spirit broken,
    her feelings are pressed down deep inside.
The day also continues in the life of the child; the lesson learned
    is that the art of survival for a small innocent child
    is possible even while playing with dolls.

### Rules

by Abby

Rules, rules, follow the rules.
Follow the rules or you die.
Rules, rules, who knows the rules?
Forget the rules and you die.

Rules, rules, who makes the rules?
Follow the rules or you die.
Rules, rules, you know the rules.
Repeat the rules and you'll live.

Rules, rules, how to remember?
Remember the rules or you die.
Rules, rules, so many rules.
Repeat them over and over again.

Rules, rules, where is the peace?
Rules aren't my life or my breath.
Rules, rules, most don't even matter.
Let's forget them forever and ever!

## Still Outside Looking In

By Abby

Standing outside the window
Quietly watching from afar,
The eyes can see, the ears can hear
But the heart is quite removed.

Fingers touching the window pane
Face pressed oh so close,
The eyes can see, the ears can hear
But the heart is quite removed.

Warmth from inside escapes through the glass
Light illuminates the night.
The eyes can see, the ears can hear
But the heart is quite removed.

Colors vividly splashed in the room
Fabrics soft and smooth,
The eyes can see, the ears can hear
But the heart is quite removed.

It doesn't matter how close you are,
Or what you can see or hear.
If your heart's not connected to the room in the house.
You're still standing out in the cold.

## Stretcher

by Abby

Stretch her big
Stretch her wide
Stretch her open
To receive the gift.

Stretch her with bottles
Stretch her with tubes
Stretcher her with hands
To receive her reward.

The bigger the better
The wider the easier
The opening enlarges…
And Stretcher is born.

The gift has arrived
Stretcher comes forward.
The gift is given
And Stretcher survives.

### The Boy and the Room

by Abby

Shoved in the room by a fleshy male hand.
Shut off from the day by a huge massive door.
As darkness descends 'round the innocent lad,
Terror increases from way deep within.

His eyes, useless now; his ears ever straining,
Listening for footsteps to lessen the dark.
His heart loudly thumping, his lean body tense,
His lips tightly sealed, to muffle his cry.

Strange smells in the room only adds to his fear,
As his hand traces the damp basement wall.
The cold seeps up through his shoes and his socks,
And creeps up to consume his mind, body, and soul.

If only the boy could observe in the blackness
The silent room waiting with out-reaching arms.
Sink deep in the cold and the dark of the room,
And absorb the peace of safe solitude.

If he could but rest in his dark little room,
He would surely discover in spite of his fear,
That the dark of the night in the cold little room
Offers more safety by far than the light.

## The Grandmother

By Abby

The girl child refused, the old woman wild with fury,
Threw the small child in a stuffy, dark closet.
The old woman was quiet as she sought to add fear,
By loosing a snake to sit with the girl.

The child sat alone, fearing to move,
Straining to see the slithering snake.
Screaming in terror for someone to come
To rescue her from this nightmare from hell.

Her screams went unheeded.
Her cries were unheard.
The serpent ruled.
The spirit died.

The old woman returned when the cries had subsided,
And opened the door to the quiet dark tomb.
There sat the child with a vacant blank stare,
With the serpent coiled next to a tiny limp hand.

The snake, though quite frightening, was actually most harmless,
The old woman, it seems, was the venomous threat.
She gripped the child's hand as she led her to bed,
To sleep off this terror and to prepare for the next.

## The Helper—A Tribute to JD

by Abby

He's there when we need…
A listening ear,
A silly smile,
A gentle wink.
He's the Helper.

He's there when we need…
A word of wisdom,
A kick in the pants,
A reality check.
He's the Helper.

He's there when…
The sun shines,
The rain falls,
The lightning strikes.
He's the Helper.

He's there when…
We can't see ahead,
We've lost our way,
We just can't go on.
He's the Helper.

He's there when we need…
A light-hearted joke,
A touch on the hand,
A person to trust.
He's the Helper.

## The Night

By Abby

The night was dark.
The air was cool.
The stars were bright.
The wind was still.

The room was big.
The clothing brown.
The faces covered.
The voices loud.

The fire was hot.
The knife was sharp.
The scream was shrill.
The blood was red.

The sorrow deep.
The turmoil suppressed.
The head bowed low.
The tears unshed.

## THE PROTECTORS

By Abby

They know when they are needed.
They move with quiet resolve
To take their place, to defend the core.
They stand the guard while danger abounds.

Their bodies massive, their strength supreme
No foe can break the line of defense.
Their shoulders are broad, their eyes alert
Their heads bent ready to shield.

To the human eye,
The guard is sure
The watchmen in place
The defender's prepared
The treasure protected.

But deep within the guardian frames 'neath sturdy brawn and bone
Resides a milder, gentler soul than the naked eye first sees.
There exists a protector of a different sort, than appears in sentry lines.
A defender with a compassionate heart, a rebel with kind hands.

If one's eyes can search behind the fortified battle line,
Far back in the safest, securest place.
There lies a child in the gentle arms of a loving, watchful...
Protector.

### Truth

by Abby

For many years the way is simple,
Swallow the lump of hurt and pain.
Deny the memory, suppress the truth,
Live tightly chained in a shallow world.

Then one day from deep within,
A moan comes forth: The eyes have seen.
A piercing scream, a thrashing soul,
Sadness seeps through open sores.

The choice is clear: truth or lies?
Suppress or feel; death or life?
The heart leaps forward in silent dread,
But chooses life, instead of death.

The body writhes, the mind regresses,
The heart is shredded into a million pieces.
The searing heat of awakened emotions,
Burns deep with the pain of the birth of truth.

The truth, it seems, though harsh with pain,
If pursued, if believed, if fully embraced,
Brings life through death, a new born soul,
Unbound, unshackled, and free to soar.

## Wanda

By Abby

Wanda was a little girl,
Her sweet face round and innocent.
Framed by short brown hair
That swung from side to side.

Wanda's eyes were bright
Her smile added sparkle.
Small hands swung down at her sides
As her tiny feet skipped lightly.

Wanda loved her daddy,
She loved him best of all.
She loved his hugs, she loved his laugh,
She loved his sloppy kisses.

Wanda looked first for her daddy
In the mornings when she awoke.
She saw him last at night,
As sleepy eyes dropped shut.

Wanda's daddy had a birthday
And when the house was quiet
Her daddy called her into his room
And shut the door behind her.

Wanda's daddy lay in bed,
Her favorite smile on his face.
He pushed the blanket back
And motioned her to join him.

Wanda happily climbed up on the bed
And snuggled close beside him.
Giggling sweetly, she kissed him on the cheek
And turned hers to wait for his.

Wanda was his birthday present
Her daddy softly said.
Yes, the best present he'd ever had,
The best he ever would.

Wanda's daddy gently tickled her
His strong arms held her close.
Then daddy said "It's time for bed
So take off all those clothes."

Wanda snuggled closer to his warm and hairy body.
Never mind the pulsing hardness
Never mind the sticky wet.
She was happy that her daddy had time to share her nap.

Wanda had a terrible nightmare
And woke whimpering with pain.
Her daddy lovingly cuddled her,
Whispering in her ear.

Never mind the dream.
Never mind the tears.
Never mind the sticky feeling.
Never mind the pain.

Wanda's daddy was there to comfort her
To kiss away the pain
To wipe away the tears
And to exclaim that indeed she was,
The best birthday present he'd ever had.

APPENDIX

# D

## Index of the Parts (CJ)

| Name | Description |
|---|---|
| Abagail | Child part. Memory of snakes in her mouth. |
| Abby | 18 years old. Creative, plays piano, sings, writes poetry, draws. She is able to feel most of the other parts' emotions. |
| Adrian | 10-12 years old. Memory of little girl sacrifice. |
| Alice | Young adolescent. Tells Mouth when to control his language. |
| Amy | 5 years old. Watched father kill kittens. Amy can cry. Judy takes care of her. |
| Angelica | Child part. Told by father to keep dress down, punished when she didn't. Thinks she is a bad, disobedient child. |
| Angie | 5 years old. Memory of being abused by boys at a New Year's Eve party. |
| Anita | Adult part who helped out at work and church. |
| Annabel/ Adeline | Adult who takes care of Tara, Summer and Autumn. |
| Audrey | 18 years old. Likes pleasure, to have fun and sex. Takes care of Tara and Jill. |
| Autumn | Adolescent part who was sexually abused. |
| Baby | Young child, mostly nonverbal. Bangs her head against the wall. Loves the toy lamb. Was abused by father. |
| *Bad Ones* | |
| Principal | Spokesperson for the Bad Ones. Created after Lynette said no to father |
| Teacher(s) | Various personalities (5) born to absorb punishment after Lynette said no. |

| | |
|---|---|
| Belinda | Child. Plays hide and seek game with father |
| Bernice | Adult—takes care of SRA parts. Similar to Anita but with more emotion. Cares for the parts. Often cares for Janelle and works for CJ. |
| Beth | Adult—Believes in God. She is faithful to help others. She is able to trust. |
| Beverely | Child who saw wrapped up body parts. |
| Big Jack or Jack | Adult who protects the other parts. |
| Bill | Adolescent angry part. |
| Black Baby | Child also known as Tar Baby |
| Bobbie | Adolescent who made herself look like a boy to keep from being sexually abused. |
| Brenda Sue | Child. Twin to Donna Jo with memory of SRA robe room. |
| Bridgette | Child with memory of tub ritual when the moon was full. Involved feces, urine and virgin animal parts. |
| Careful | Child part who watches doors and hallways for father and warns others. |
| Cecelia | Child part who believes she always does things wrong and can't do anything right. She is criticized by Mother. |
| Christine | Adolescent worked with Bobbie |
| Claudia | Adult—sexual part who is friendly and likes attention. |
| Cynthia | 5 years old |
| Dave | Adult part who polices, protects and punishes other parts. |
| Deb (Debbie) | 10 years old part abused by father's friend at church. Father did not believe her. |
| Denise | Adolescent SRA part who is sexually attracted to women. |
| Doctor (The) | Old man who helps parts feel euphoric instead of pain. |
| Donna Joe | Child part, twin to Brenda Sue. Memory with SRA choosing room. |
| Doris | Adult. Doesn't believe the SRA memories. Believes she is the host personality. |

| | |
|---|---|
| Eileen | Adult who likes to eat and is self-centered. Memory of father forcing her to eat. |
| Evelyn | 12 years old. Trusts and likes people. Loves the father even though he raped her in the woods. |
| Evil Eyes (Cindy) | Adolescent. Memory of a man looking into her eyes before he died. She believes her eyes can kill. JD gave her new name of Cindy. |
| Fatty | Child part who sneaks and steals food. |
| Haley | Adult who believes she is a virgin and will be killed if caught. |
| Hell | Child part told by grandfather if she didn't sexually perform **correctly**, she would go to hell. |
| Henny-Penny | Child part with memory of grandmother's green couch and crochet needles. |
| Henry | Child/adolescent who felt helpless in certain situations with father and can sometimes only say the word "damn". |
| Hider | Child part who hides her fingers so they won't get cut off. |
| Ida | Child part who held my sister's hand at SRA meeting. |
| Iogene | Child part who was always good and perfect. |
| Jack | Child created in kindergarten when bully threatened to beat up CJ. |
| James | Adolescent part involved in SRA. |
| Jason | 10 years old boy placed in a dark room after Deb was molested by father's friend in church. |
| Janice | 8 years old. Loves animals and babies. Handed Laville's baby in SRA memory. |
| Jeb | Adult punisher/protector. |
| Jessica | Abused by father while riding in the car. |
| Jill | Adolescent carries pain for many of the parts. Self-mutilates to hurt self and others. |
| Jilly | Adolescent buried in box with snakes. |
| Joyce | Adolescent abused by family member. |

| | |
|---|---|
| Judy | Child who cares for Amy. |
| Justice | Adult dispenses judgment on parts for telling secrets. |
| Keeper | Adult. Takes care of children and CJ. Wise, quiet, calm, emotional. Coordinates and manages the system. |
| Kellie | Child part abused by family members. |
| Laville | 17 year old male part who took part in SRA rituals. Very angry. |
| Lillian | Child part who took part in SRA rituals |
| Listener | Adult. Knows all the instructions on what must be done. Non-emotional. |
| Liz (Lizzard) | Adolescent who believes her arms are snakes. |
| Louise | Adolescent involved in white/black/red SRA ritual. |
| Lucy | Child part |
| Lydia | Adolescent part who shares a memory with Sharon. |
| Lynnette | Adolescent part who was able to say no to father. She likes CJ. |
| Madge | Child part connected with Marge and Micky. Grandmother abused her emotionally with eating. Wasn't allowed to drink. |
| Mandy | Adolescent involved with Keeper's memory. |
| Marcy | Adolescent involved in SRA marriage ceremony. |
| Marge | Child connected with Madge and Micky. Grandmother abused her emotionally with eating. Wasn't allowed to swallow food. |
| Maria | Adolescent Catholic girl who feels unforgiven by God. |
| Mary I | Adolescent. SRA memory of upside down Christmas tree and animal ornaments |
| Mary II | Adolescent SRA shock incident |
| Mavis | Young adult. Acts like mother, but doesn't like her. |
| Me | Says "Don't do that, can't do that, will get hurt." |
| Mean One | Adult. |
| Melinda | Child (see Sandy) |

| | |
|---|---|
| Micky | Child part connected with Marge and Madge. Grandmother abused her emotionally with eating. Wasn't allowed to eat food. |
| Midget | Child who is a very tiny person, can hide easily and see things happen without being seen. |
| Millie | Adolescent connected with Keeper's memory. |
| Mother | Adult very negative. Constantly criticizes Cecelia. |
| Mouth | Male Adolescent. Was a buddy to father, uses bad language. Hung around Dad a lot. |
| Muffin | Very young nonverbal child. Knocks head against wall. Has memory of Easter basket and father. |
| Myra | Adolescent. |
| Nan | Child. Watched grandmother chop mouse, forced to eat (see Rick). |
| Nancy | Adolescent and heads a group of alters called Protectors. |
| Naomi | Adolescent connected with Keeper's memory. |
| Natalie | Teenager with memory of father and basement abuse. |
| Nelly | Child. Sliver moon, full moon, moon watcher. |
| Nicholas | Adolescent with SRA memory of wanting to be with men. |
| Nicky | Child abandoned by primary caregivers at SRA events. |
| Nina | Young child. |
| Nita | Adolescent came when Victoria dropped the cup. She was choked and beaten. Recognized father. |
| No Name | Adult that takes over for Nicky when she feels abandoned. |
| Noah | Child who tended SRA animals. |
| Omer | 8 years old who had her mouth taped shut and tied to chair in grandparents' bedroom. |
| Opal | Adolescent who was in the box after Jilly left. She killed the snakes. |
| Pamela | Adolescent who hates mother. |
| Paul | Adult punisher/protector. |

| | |
|---|---|
| Paula | Adolescent depressed part. |
| Penny | Young child urinated on by father and almost drowned in a box. |
| Pony | Child part. |
| Prism | Adult who was created to watch the parts to be sure they didn't tell secrets. Works with Justice. |
| Protectors | Several adult alters who form a solid line to protect the parts from the outside. |
| Rachel | Child who was sexually abused by family members. |
| Rebecca | Child connected to SRA memories. |
| Red Baby | Child who was abandoned by father and involved in SRA rituals. |
| Regina | Adult sexually abused part. |
| Richard | 13 years old was put in a snake bed during SRA meeting. |
| Rick | Adolescent who ate bites of a mouse for Nan. |
| Rita | Child who was prepared for SRA rituals by grandparents. |
| Roberta | Child at scout meeting who was scared the meeting was a cult meeting |
| Robin | Adolescent whose head grandmother pushed into bucket. She was raped. |
| Rowanna | Adolescent part who was convinced she would die. |
| Ruby Red | Child with SRA memories. |
| Ruth | Adolescent with SRA memories. |
| Sally | Child who had memories about snakes and sexual abuse. |
| Sandy | Child connected to Melinda. |
| Sarah | Adult twin emotional, angry, hates father. |
| Screamer | Adolescent involved in SRA meetings. |
| Selinda | Child abused by father. |
| Sharon | Adult twin programmed to be self destructive, angry, hates father. |
| Shit | Child part. |

| | |
|---|---|
| Snow | Child who loves snow and puzzles. Happy and friendly. |
| Sonney | 12 year old boy involved in SRA memories. |
| Stretcher | 60 year old abused by grandmother. |
| Summer | Adolescent who was sexually abused. |
| Susan | Adolescent with SRA abuse. |
| Sylvia | Adolescent who cleaned up when someone wet the bed. |
| Tar Baby | Child (also known as Black Baby) |
| Tara | 15 years old raped by 3 men. Fearful of all men. |
| Teddy | Takes care of Penny and Nina. |
| The Few | Adult helper/protector parts. |
| They | Adult part who blocks out all conversation. |
| Tippet | Child involved with SRA memories. |
| Topper | Takes care of Muffin and Baby. |
| Trudi | Adolescent trained for SRA by grandparents. |
| Truth | Adult who tells only the truth. When things get confusing, she always maintains the truth of each situation. |
| Tubby | Child who sneaks food. |
| Twyla | Adolescent trained for SRA meetings. |
| Victoria | Adolescent took part in SRA communion. |
| Virginia | Adolescent abused by grandfather. |
| Vivian | Adolescent part involved in ritual abuse. |
| Wanda | Small child abused by father. |
| We | Several parts who repeat "uh huh" over and over to block out conversation. |
| Whitney | Child |
| Winifred | Child who took over for Whitney |
| Woody | Child |

# Acknowledgements

To my husband, **Martin**, who is my best friend, confidant, supporter, and encourager—the best husband God could have given to me. Martin is not only a faithful husband, but also a wise and caring father, a delightful and involved grandfather, and a caring and compassionate pastor. Martin is my spiritual hero and mentor—I love watching Jesus work in his life which motivates ME to become more like Jesus.

To my vivacious, loving, deeply sensitive and passionate daughter, **Janelle**, who often put up with an emotionally absent mother and in spite of that turned into a poised, talented, God-loving and caring woman—a supportive wife, an attentive mom and a caring and skilled therapist. Through Janelle, Martin and I have been given the best son-in-law we could ever imagine and the sweetest granddaughter, who will forever be the light of our lives.

To my former therapist and now friend, **Jerry**, who walked the long and arduous journey with me. Jerry always believed in me, always accepted me (and all my parts) in a loving way, and graciously and willingly invested his heart, his professional skill, his time and his energy to help me become a whole person.

To all my **fellow sojourners** who accompanied me on my journey toward healing and wholeness—my friends, all those who attended therapy groups with me and taught me how to heal, and especially the facilitators who cared enough to lead those groups.

To the late **Henri Nouwen** and **Brennan Manning** whose books provided wise spiritual guides for me on my journey to spiritual wholeness.

To Father **God**, his Son, **Jesus**, and the **Holy Spirit** who together ignited my soul with a spark when I was a small child and kept that spark burning throughout my challenging and traumatic childhood and adolescence, and who protected my very existence—physically, emotionally and spiritually. The emotional and spiritual health that I enjoy today could not have come about without the amazing and awesome love and work of the Holy Trinity.
**CJ**

**A House Divided** has been over eight years in the making, and there have been so many friends, family members and professionals who have read and reread the manuscript. To them I am very grateful. I especially want to acknowledge some of them by name. My English major wife, **Allegra**, spent hours and hours rereading, correcting, reorganizing and making suggestions (and our egos and marriage are still intact). You are one special lady, Allegra.

**Phyllis Klein**, my dear friend and final editor of the manuscript, asked **Dudley Delffs** if the story was worth publishing. He was impressed enough to say, "Go for it!" Phyllis has been our biggest encourager, and saying "Thank you!" does not adequately express our appreciation.

The endorsements by colleagues and friends in the front pages of this book have pushed us to get **A House Divided** to press. Thanks to **Vernon Grounds** (posthumously), **Dr. Robert Williams**, **James Oraker, Ph.D., Less Avery**, **Mary Ann Carpenter Ph.D.**, **Joe Beach**, **David McDonald**, **Susan Anderson** and **Pete Richardson** who challenged me to write in the first place and **Larry Ellis** and **Chris Diffenderfer** who showed us how to publish.

My three girls, **Kim**, **Pam** and **Tammy**, have consistently validated my efforts and have believed in me more than I have believed in myself. I love the three of you more than you can imagine.

**Iris D.** was my first DID client: her sense of humor, her willingness to trust me from the very beginning, her intelligence, her desire to integrate over one hundred alters, her willingness to help Catherine Jean, and her optimism for life… all of these characteristics got her and me through the therapeutic process. Thanks, Iris, for being who you are.

Finally, I want to thank **Catherine Jean** for being courageous enough to share her story. She neither desires fame, fortune or notoriety. Her hope is that her story will be helpful to other fellow strugglers. **JD**

# About the Authors

After spending 22 years working in the computer industry, **Catherine Jean Johnson** received her bachelor's degree in social work in 2006, completed her master's in 2008, and is now a licensed therapist. She is a PEPARE/ENRICH facilitator, is a trained Eye Movement Desensitization Reprocessing (EMDR) therapist, and is a member of the American Counseling Association. She and her husband have been married for over 40 years, have a grown daughter and are grandparents. While ministering with her husband in the pastorate, Catherine has facilitated many small groups designed to assist individuals in exploring and enhancing their spirituality. Her interest includes classical music, piano, reading mysteries, attending basketball games, hiking, walking her dogs, and playing Sudoku.

During his professional career **Jerry Donaldson** has worked with institutionalized delinquent youth for over 13 years, has been a singles pastor, a deacon, a Sunday school teacher, family counselor at Faith Academy in the Philippines, a conflict resolution and group facilitator, a clinic coordinator, a relational consultant for several small businesses, traveling throughout the U.S. and Canada working with dentists and orthodontists, and recently he and his wife have traveled to several countries working with missionaries and humanitarian workers. For eight years, he was an adjunct faculty member at Denver Seminary in the counseling department teaching Empathy Training, Task Orientation, and Group Experience, all very practical, "how-to" courses.

He is semi-retired but he still sees a few clients, consults with Christian nonprofits, and writes (presently working on a soon to be published book about empathy and love). He enjoys photography, painting, cycling, fishing, wood working, reading, golf, traveling, and spending time with his family(wife, Allegra of 55 years, three daughters, and their families).

Catherine can be reached at: catherinehousedivided@gmail.com
Jerry can be reached at: jerryhousedivided@gmail.com

12672990R00187

Made in the USA
San Bernardino, CA
27 June 2014